Upfront & Personal

COLEEN NOLAN

Upfront & Personal

SIDGWICK & JACKSON

First published 2009 by Sidgwick & Jackson
an imprint of Pan Macmillan Ltd
Pan Macmillan, 20 New Wharf Road, London N1 9RR
Basingstoke and Oxford
Associated companies throughout the world
www.panmacmillan.com

ISBN 978-0-283-07088-4 HB
ISBN 978-0-283-07095-2 TPB

3 5 7 9 8 6 4

A CIP catalogue record for this book is available from
the British Library.

Printed in the UK by CPI Mackays, Chatham ME5 8TD

This book is dedicated to my husband Ray,
for turning my life around and helping me to believe
in myself again – I love you!

And to my beautiful children, Shane Jnr,
Jake and Ciara – you are my life, my love,
my heart, always and forever.

Picture Credits

All photographs are from the author's personal
collection apart from the following:

Mirrorpix: page 3.
Redferns: page 6, top; page 7, top.
Rex Features: page 6, bottom; page 9, bottom; page 13, middle;
page 15, bottom.
PA: page 11, top.
Getty: page 14 top, bottom Nicky Johnston/Universal.
Dan Latchford/Latchfordpaps: page 15, top.
Paul Mitchell/*Woman* magazine/IPC+Syndication: page 16.

Prologue

Sitting in the dressing room I studied my reflection.

Not bad actually. A make-up artist had just done her very best to hide the dark circles under my eyes, carefully cultivated by years of running around after three kids. She'd also painted my lips a bright shade of peachy pink and appeared to have created the illusion that I actually had cheekbones. I was impressed!

Now the resident *Loose Women* hairdresser Lee Din was doing a sterling job on the bird's nest of hair I'd stepped off the train with at the crack of dawn this morning, crafting it into something halfway decent.

'It's good to have you back, Coleen,' he smiled, catching my eye in the mirror.

'It's good to be back,' I replied, trying to channel calm thoughts.

Everything was riding on this moment. Just months earlier I'd felt down and miserable, convinced my TV career was all but over. At thirty-eight I was washed up, unemployable, tarred by the brush of a failed stint presenting on *This Morning* and very worried about the future.

My partner, Ray, was working hard and I was taking every job I could get, but still we were struggling financially. The

1

rainy day we'd saved for was here and now the piggy bank was running dry. I had a family to support and we needed the stability of a regular income. And I needed a chance to prove myself once more. So one night I lay in bed trying to think of all the positive things I could do instead of panicking. I had to think of a plan – an escape route to where I wanted to be. I suddenly remembered that I had a business card for a lady called Dianne Nelmes, a big boss on ITV daytime. I'd met her a couple of times and we'd got on well, so the next morning after I'd seen my sons Shane Jnr and Jake off to school and wiped porridge off my toddler Ciara's chin, I rummaged through a drawer of junk. I sieved through hair bobbles, scrappy bits of paper and Ciara's old dummies until eventually I located Dianne's dog-eared card. Then, managing to fire up the family computer, I typed in Dianne's email address and carefully constructed a light-hearted message.

'Well, I've done the stay at home mum thing,' I wrote. 'But even the kids are begging me to go back to work, so if you hear of anything then please let me know.'

I didn't think she'd reply but she did, promptly, with some great news – that *Loose Women*, a series I'd worked on two years before, was coming back on air. 'I'll let them know you'd be interested in taking part,' she promised.

Now here I was, weeks later, gearing up for my moment, my one big chance to prove myself once more.

'Ten minute call, Coleen,' a runner said, popping her head round the door.

Standing up, I thanked Lee, smoothed down my blouse with my hands and stepped out of the dressing room. Taking a deep breath, I walked down the long corridor of ITV's South Bank studios, to reach the *Loose Women* set.

There were people darting around everywhere, wearing

headsets and jeans, and I could hear the warm-up man inside whipping the crowd into a frenzy. Next to me appeared my old friend and *Loose Women* anchor presenter Kaye Adams. We both rolled our eyes as we were forced to do a kind of ridiculous half hug and air kiss to avoid messing up our hair and make-up. Then coming up the corridor behind us were the other presenters, Carol McGiffin and Jenny Trent Hughes, who were both full of beans and ready to join us on the panel.

'Two minutes!' A producer dashed past indicating with his fingers.

I smiled at Kaye but immediately felt my stomach churn with a mixture of apprehension and adrenalin. I still get nervous to this day!

Then suddenly we were given the green light and I was walking out into the studio with the other girls. There was a sea of smiling faces as the audience cheered, and as I settled into my seat behind the desk I could feel the heat of the bright studio lights on my face. Excitement and exhilaration rushed through me like an electric current.

I was back on the map . . .

One

I made my singing debut when I was two years old, at Christmas 1967 when we did a turn at the ABC theatre in Blackpool in front of about 2,000 old age pensioners.

I can actually remember that very first time when I ventured out on the stage on my own. I had a long nightie on and was clutching my teddy. Everyone looked at me and said, 'Ahh' – as you would to a little kid, wouldn't you! Not realizing how cute I was, I thought, *What are they saying 'Ahh' about?* Then I sang 'Santa Claus is Coming to Town' to rapturous applause.

My family were quite unique in the fact that we all sang together. For years before I came along, my older brothers and sisters had joined my parents in an act called the Singing Nolans. Work could be sporadic in Dublin, so in 1962, three years before my birth, the family crossed the Irish Sea, relocating to Blackpool in search of more regular work. There were many more clubs and hotels to perform at in England, so it turned out to be a canny move.

Mum and Dad were both very talented singers. My mum, Maureen, trained as a soprano at the Royal Irish Academy and had many admirers as much for her bonny looks as for her wonderful operatic voice. She met my dad, Tommy, while they were both performing at Clery's Ballroom in Dublin. They were both twenty. They married a year later and went on to form a two-piece act called Tommy and Maureen: The Sweethearts of Song.

As a couple back then they were both extremely striking. Dad was a dapper, dark-haired man with fine features and a twinkle in his eye. Mum was petite and gorgeous and very Irish-looking, with dark hair and hazel eyes. Until she had me she was really slim, but I guess having eight kids takes its toll! Eventually she ballooned from a size 8 to a size 20. Yet she was always one of these women who knew how to dress, looking elegant no matter what size she was.

As good fortune would have it, each Nolan child proved to have inherited my parents' talent for singing (I'm not sure what would have happened if one of us had proved to be tone deaf. Perhaps we would have been put up for adoption!). So from day one there was music running through my blood and I was pretty much born into the group.

When I arrived in the Nolan household as baby number eight they didn't exactly roll out the red carpet. First, my parents were a tad disappointed – with five girls already they'd hoped for a boy. And second, there was no room at the inn – so my dad emptied out a drawer in the bedroom and that was my cot.

'I hope you put me in the top drawer at least?' I asked Mum years later.

'No, the bottom drawer,' she replied. Well, isn't that the story of my life?

I was born on 12 March 1965 at Glenroyd Maternity Hospital in Blackpool. All my siblings – Tommy, 17, Anne, 15, Denise, 13, Maureen, 11, Brian, 8, Linda, 6, and 5-year-old Bernie – had started life in Dublin in Ireland, so I was the token English one.

The money our family earned was modest, so I'm pretty sure my arrival – five years after my nearest sister Bernie and yet another hungry mouth to feed – was accidental. My mum always insisted I was planned but I didn't believe a word of it! Seven kids and four years down the line another one comes along? I couldn't possibly have been planned!

Back then, before fame and fortune beckoned, there were ten of us crammed into our four-bedroom terraced house in Waterloo Road in Blackpool. Mum and Dad had a room each, as they slept separately, and all my elder sisters were in one room and my brothers were in another. My bed in the drawer set a precedent, as I never really had my own room. Instead I slept with everyone. I would make my mind up each night where I was going to sleep and who I would sleep with, so sometimes it would be with my mum, sometimes in between my brothers, but more often than not, up until we were teenagers, I slept cuddled up to my eldest sister, Anne, in the single bottom bunk in the main girls' bedroom.

As if ten of us packed in like sardines wasn't enough, at one point we even had Nana, Dad's mum, living there, which resulted in Mum giving up her bed in favour of the couch downstairs. In later years I often wondered why my father did not give up his room, as she was his mother. But then that's an Irish woman thing, isn't it? No sacrifice is ever too big in the name of hospitality.

When I was born my eldest siblings, Tommy and Anne, being that much older, were on hand to look after me. All my sisters doted on me – I guess it was like having a real life doll – but Anne particularly was like a second mum to me. She always played with me and when I was older I can remember her spending hours plaiting my pigtails. If there was just one hair out of place she'd have to start again. Anne has always been very organized like that. She likes everything to be perfect. But although my sisters were great with me, I was still my mother's baby. She used to prise me out of their arms, laughing, 'Leave my baby alone!'

I think I was quite fortunate to be by far the youngest, as I never really experienced sibling rivalry with the others and I don't recall fighting with them. Linda and Bernie were really close in age, so they were thick as thieves but also used to fight like cat and dog. And the three eldest – Tommy, Anne and Denise – were always at each other's throats too. Maureen was the little peacemaker, really placid and laid back, and didn't really row.

But I can remember Brian having a fight with Linda when he practically tried to strangle her, and another occasion when she just walked in and whacked a sweeping brush over his head! We still laugh about that now.

The majority of these fights went on when Dad was out of the house. Mum would go mad at us for playing up, but a cross look or holler from her never had the same effect as from my dad. He was the main disciplinarian, and woe betide anyone who dared even snap in front of him!

We lived in that house at Waterloo Road for the first nine years of my life and despite the cabin fever I have absolutely brilliant memories. With ten of us cooped up in there it was always noisy and full of life. It was your typical, small terraced home with a fairly uninspiring back yard. We didn't have many home comforts either. There was no central heating for one thing. Instead the house was heated by coal fires, which were lit by my mum at 6 a.m. every morning. When it was time for us to get up for school we'd all run down to the front room and huddle in front of one of the fires to warm up. Initially there had been two rooms downstairs, but as the family grew bigger my parents had the wall between knocked down and made it into one big room, which contained two fires. Still, with all us kids there was a lot of jostling and elbowing in order to keep warm in front of those two!

When I look back now at how basic we had it, it just amazes me how we got anything done. Mum had eight of us to look after and no washing machine or dryer. She just had a mangle to wring all the stuff out and one tiny little cooker. How did she do that, and more importantly why? My dryer broke recently and it felt like I'd lost my right arm!

There may have been zillions of us but Mum and Dad never stopped us having friends round and the local kids loved our house because they were not the sort of parents who said, 'Don't do this, don't do that.' Mum never complained about us making a mess. There were always loads of girls in one room chatting and laughing, and I have lots of happy memories of tearing up and down the street playing tag, hide and seek or hopscotch. At the weekend I used to be out of that house from 7 a.m. to 7 p.m. – I loved it.

I still drive by our old home when I'm in Blackpool now and feel all nostalgic. I always want to go in. It looks great. It was crap-looking when we were there but now there's a plasma telly on the wall. God, wouldn't we have loved that when we were kids!

Having said that, my parents were incredibly generous. Birthdays were your day and you'd be made to feel really special all day long. They'd throw a big party with all your friends and you'd always get a surprise birthday cake.

Although at times we could be mischievous we never got into trouble. You just didn't back then, because you were really frightened of policemen. And it wasn't just the fear of the police either! If you got into trouble with the law and they took you home then you'd really get it. Without doubt we knew we'd get double from our dad and we were much more frightened of him! So we were respectful kids.

There were still plenty of times I got a good smack off my dad or a good crack off my mum, though. In fact all I needed was a look off my dad and I'd feel the fear. If I had done something wrong I would instantly recognize the look that said, 'You are on your last warning.' I literally used to whimper if he looked at me, so on the whole I knew to be well behaved. He very rarely had to smack me, he would just look at me and I would wet my drawers.

Dad wasn't someone to be messed with. You always knew where the line was. Plus he liked a drink, which could see his temper increased tenfold. And at that point the best thing you could do was keep out of his way.

As well as singing my dad worked in the daytime at the union printers and later Anne was his secretary for a while. While Dad worked Mum would get us ready for school, organize our singing and make our costumes. Yet she still found time to see lots of her friends and had a great social life. She loved her bingo.

As soon as I was old enough to sing I joined my family doing turns at working men's clubs and hotels all over the UK. Because I was so young – starting my career at the age of two – the songs were performed over and over to me by my mum and my sisters until I picked up the lyrics, and I learned them that way.

On nights that we were performing, Dad would hurry home from work and we'd race home from school and there would be a flurry of activity, as we got ready to go out. A lot of our shows were in Blackpool. We'd go to a working men's club and do four turns a night, then we'd all go home and then get up for school. Often we'd get only a few hours' sleep and be late for school the following morning. My parents were always getting letters home complaining about our attendance, but they never seemed that bothered. I guess they assumed that singing would be our vocation so it didn't really matter if we missed a class or two.

When I was very small my mum's youngest sister Aunty Theresa, who never had any children of her own and was very much a part of our family, would sometimes come along to look after me while my parents were singing, and if she wasn't there one of the elder sisters would sit me on her knee until Mum came back.

Locally we were dubbed Blackpool's own Von Trapp family, and we'd do medleys from *The Sound of Music* or *Oliver!* as well as solos. With her trained opera skills, Mum regularly brought tears to people's eyes with her haunting rendition of 'Ave Maria'. It was her favourite song and she'd even sing it around the house – it was like having an opera in the front room. When, years later, Alzheimer's robbed Mum of her ability to sing, it always struck me as the cruellest blow. You could always tell how much she loved to sing.

My father was like Frank Sinatra in his voice and his mannerisms. When Mum and Dad sang together it was magical. They used to do duets like, 'My heart and I', 'My dearest, dear' and 'How wonderful to know'.

From as early as I can remember I saw my sisters and brothers and family go out and perform. It was exciting and at times brilliant fun. In the summer holidays we did lots of cruises. We'd travel Europe, visiting countries like Greece and Italy. Because I was so little I always got a good reception.

I remember one time there were all these Americans on a

cruise ship and when I sang my solo, 'Show me the way to go home', where I donned a flat cap and strutted up and down the stage, they all started throwing money. I continued to sing but almost got lamped in the head by a coin several times. In the end my dad was forced to yell, 'Please can you stop throwing money as you might hurt her!'

Not that I was bothered, I was too busy crying, as I thought the dollars they were throwing at me were toy money. So Mum gave me sixpence to stifle my sobs and she kept seventy-five dollars. I had no idea about the value so clearly I was thrilled!

People occasionally ask me how I feel about having had such an unconventional childhood, and whether it bothered me. But the truth is for me it was just the norm. I never knew any different. It is only now that I look back and feel a little bit sad for my childhood self, because in many ways I did miss out on a normal childhood. Sometimes I wish I'd thought, 'When I grow up I want to be . . .' but my future was always mapped out. I was always going to be a singer. Just like everyone else in my family.

I had friends whose mothers and fathers were obsessed with not missing parents' nights or who stood on the sidelines at freezing football games to faithfully cheer them on. Yet my parents never went to one single parents' night or ever encouraged me to pursue another activity or talent. I guess they didn't feel they needed to – they had decided that singing with my family was my destiny.

As much as I have happy memories I have to admit there was a lot I hated as well. I always felt really miserable leaving my friends playing in the street if there was a gig to go to. Most days I'd be having a whale of a time with my best friend, Alan, who lived on Waterloo Road as well and was a year older than me. We were practically joined at the hip until I moved to

London aged nine. So when I'd see Mum heading down the street with a determined look on her face I'd instantly get that sinking feeling in my tummy. I knew she and Dad were rounding us up ready to pile us into the minibus to go to Scotland or somewhere else equally afar. 'I don't want to go,' I'd whine to myself, but I had no choice. That was just the way it was.

When we were doing our gigs we didn't really have a set running order – sometimes the kids would go on first, sometimes Mum and Dad would.

These days you always hear about artists making ridiculous demands when they play somewhere – asking for dressing rooms to be painted white and furnished with matching virginal white couches, flowers and candles. I mean, Cher is even rumoured to request her own 'wig room', with a bodyguard to protect her beloved hairpieces, but there was none of that in our day. The places we played were definitely no frills and we'd cram into a dingy dressing room, all ten of us. We didn't have any crew or a PA to keep us organized so we'd roll up at a working men's club, pile into a room the size of a closet, and wait, bored, for our turn on stage.

I can remember fights between my older siblings as they battled it out in a confined space not even big enough to swing a dead cat. Tommy and Anne would end up snapping at each other or Bernie and Linda would be squabbling over a drink or a book. Mum or Dad would whack whoever was nearest, there'd be some sniffing, sulking and dirty looks and that was that.

The clubs back then were quite basic: just a big space with table and chairs piled either in rows or groups. The lighting was really bright, and they would generally have a little stage with a tiny dressing room at the back of it and a big bar that ran the length of the room. There would be a separate snooker room, and certainly in one club I remember, and to this day it's still the same, only men were allowed and no women at the bar. Can you believe that in 2009 that rule still stands! Not that I would ever go in one now; I cannot bear them.

The audiences were normally male and female, and particularly in places like the north of England, people gave us an amazing reception. They just loved us. It must have been quite a thing, seeing a mum and dad and eight kids, all of whom could sing, performing. I'd love to see that now. So generally we didn't get any insults about our act, but sometimes while you were singing it was very noisy. People would be talking or shouting up to the bar.

While you were performing you'd be lucky if you had a spotlight. It was normally just the club lights, so as you sang you could see absolutely everyone in the club. The smoke was horrendous, but no one gave it a second thought back then. My dad was an eighty-a-day smoker anyway, so we just grew up around smoke really. It was before all the health warnings, so everyone puffed away.

Although there was lots of beer and spirits around I don't remember any of my siblings ever having a sly swig of booze. I am sure they wouldn't have dared, as their lives would not have been worth living if either Mum or Dad had caught them! But then again, they were kids, so maybe they did?

The other performers would be typical club acts doing the circuit – a comedian or a real club turn singing 'Amarillo' or 'Delilah' and all those other bloody songs that I still can't stand to hear nowadays.

From the age of two to eight this was my life, two to three times a week at least. Sometimes us younger ones would get sent home early on our own. But I hated that as well, as within ten minutes Brian, Linda and Bernie would be fighting. Sometimes it would make me cry but generally I'd just put myself to bed and try to stay out of their way.

To this day when people think of the Nolans they often view us through rose-tinted specs. A good, old-fashioned, all-singing, all-dancing, butter-wouldn't-melt-in-their-mouths clan who were the picture of wholesome family fun. People used to take the piss out of us for being so square! But like all families, things could be very different behind closed doors. Things were actually far from perfect.

It's really difficult for me to say anything bad about my parents. Mum and Dad, they loved us. They adored us. And equally we loved and idolized them. But, as hard as it is for me to admit, I still think they did a lot wrong. They never made bad decisions intentionally, but now I have kids of my own it's made me look back at my own childhood. As a mother myself I've chosen to do things very differently. I think that's the way it goes when you raise your own kids – you're either exactly the same as your parents or the complete opposite.

I'm not sure I could have exposed my children to the environments we experienced as kids. They may have been there with us in all those smoky, run-down clubs but there's no mistaking that it was an adults' world and not a place for small children.

Unfortunately we were singing in places where people would often be drinking heavily and sometimes when we were performing awful fights would break out. Booze-fuelled adults would scream and shout, ready to knock the crap out of each other. It's scary to see a fight like that as an adult, let alone when you're tiny, and I can still recall the fear I experienced back then. I remember once Bernie was belting out 'Where is Love?' from *Oliver!* at a club and there was a horrible fight. I mean we're talking chairs being flung around, glasses smashed, the works. She kept on singing though!

It wasn't nice being exposed to the big bad world of adults from such an early age and I can't imagine putting any of my children through that. No way. I just know that I always felt very anxious and frightened whenever voices were raised. I grew up with a terrible phobia of shouting. If anyone shouts I turn into a three-year-old again. I can feel myself physically shrinking. I want to go into a corner. I grew up with fights and I hate it.

I think that's the reason I'm a bit 'drink police' now. I always get teased by Carol McGiffin, my *Loose Women* co-presenter, because I'm boring and don't like to get drunk. But the truth is I can't be around people who are heavy drinkers and those early memories have a lot to do with it. I've seen the ugly side of alcohol too many times; I've seen how it can distort and change people's personalities and I don't like it.

And it wasn't just strangers that it happened to either. It went on in my own family too. I saw it with my dad. I'm sorry to say that alcohol brought out a very ugly side to his character. It was sad really, as when my dad was sober he could be the nicest man in the world. He was very family-orientated, and although we had such a small crowded house he loved us being kids so we were always allowed to have fun and have our friends round.

You could also talk to him for hours and he just had so much time for us all. Some adults don't really know how to talk to children but he was so interested in everything we had to tell him and really encouraged our thirst for knowledge. 'Dad, where do rainbows come from?' I'd ask, and he'd take so much pleasure from painstakingly explaining. He subscribed to the *Reader's Digest* and was always watching documentaries, so he knew a lot, but if he couldn't answer a question off the top of his head he'd go and find out for me. Dad always helped with our homework too, and if I ever had a maths problem to solve or something I couldn't spell, he'd be on hand to advise me.

He also loved taking us out and showing us things; he'd point out buildings and architecture and tell us about the history of things. When he was sober he was a brilliant dad and in public he was viewed as this amazing man. He was handsome, charismatic, and he just had this talent, this amazing crooner voice. Not to mention the fact that he had eight angelic kids who could sing and a lovely wife to boot. Women adored him!

It's hard to shatter anyone's illusions and talk about his faults – even my friends thought our life was perfect. In fact, in most people's eyes the Nolans were this happy, close family. Don't get me wrong, we were close, God we were close, but we had our problems too and they mainly revolved around our father and his drinking. You see, working the club circuit ultimately gave him the temptation to drink and more often than not he did – and it made him argumentative and selfish.

If we were in Blackpool at a working men's club we could go home while he'd stay behind and drink. But if we'd travelled afar, to Wales or Scotland, we'd have to wait for him to finish and for little children it was just exhausting. Sometimes Dad would be propping up the bar until 4 a.m. and I can remember at times being too tired to even stand, so curling up to sleep on the floor or across two chairs pushed together. Of course that sort of thing just wouldn't happen now. These days you have licences in regard to children and they have to be off the premises by ten, but you just didn't back then.

'Tommy, we need to go, the kids are tired,' Mum would moan.

'Oh, shut up,' he'd snap back. So we'd all sit there resigned to the fact we had to wait.

When Dad had had his fill he'd often drive us home, which just beggars belief really. Because I was so young I never noticed the danger, but for Mum and the older kids it must have been terrifying. How we escaped any sort of accident I'll never know. Dad's best friend, a man called John Quinn, would come to some of the gigs and help with driving and when I was a bit older I can remember worrying that either of them could fall asleep at the wheel.

Dad didn't just drink at our appearances, he also liked to meet his friends down the pub and that was normally when trouble erupted for us. When he'd been sinking the pints he had the shortest fuse in the world and could become aggressive or violent in the blink of an eye. It was my poor mum who got the brunt of it. Whenever he was full of ale he'd want to row with her and he didn't give a stuff about kicking off in front of the kids.

I have an awful memory of being quite small and being tucked up in bed with Mum while Dad was down the pub. That evening I'd decided to sleep with her and was to witness my father at his worst. I don't know if it was the noise of the door banging shut or his heavy steps on the stairs that disturbed me, but suddenly I was wide awake and fear was shooting through my body. Dad was blind drunk and in a murderous mood.

I felt Mum's body tense next to me and I knew she was awake too. We could hear Dad's voice before he even entered the bedroom and it was clear that he was hell bent on goading her.

'Maureen, you bitch,' he spat. 'I know you're awake.'

The aggression in his voice made me tremble but I stayed

deadly still, praying that Mum would do the same. Suddenly the door flew open and he headed towards the bed.

'You think you're better than me,' he hissed at Mum.

The venom in his voice made my heart race and I squeezed my eyes tight shut. *Pretend you're asleep*, I willed Mum silently in my head, but no such luck.

'Oh, be quiet and go to bed,' she snapped.

We both knew what was coming next. As Dad flew at my mother I could hear my heart pounding in my chest, but I lay there too terrified to move, bracing myself in case I got caught up in the crossfire.

'Don't you tell me!' he roared. Then I felt the bed shake and the sound of a sharp slap.

I just knew that although he'd hit her Mum would be staring at him defiantly. *If she just shuts up, he'll get bored and go away*, I'd think desperately. But that wasn't Mum's way. She never did. In fact I think she always spoke up to spite him, despite the beating that followed. There was no way she was just going to be the 'little woman', completely under his control.

There were many other occasions like that and like a masochist Mum always answered back.

It would always end with Dad just walking out of her room back to his and that would be it. I never saw him pass out. He was never a staggering drunk, he always seemed very controlled.

And at those particular moments when my dad was like that I hated him. I hated that he could lash out and shout at Mum, and his behaviour scared me. But sadly it also became kind of a way of life for us. You do kind of get used to it. Most of the time we'd forget about it but every Saturday there was a sense of foreboding in our house as that was the night it usually occurred. Dad would normally go out to the local club in the afternoon because of the football and then come back drunk for his dinner. I hated that feeling of it almost being dinnertime, as I knew he could be home soon smelling of booze and itching for a fight.

Occasionally he'd come home a very pleasant happy drunk and if he did come in and was in a good mood there was this feeling of utter relief that it was going to be all right tonight. But the waiting to see was very stressful – you never knew what kind of mood he'd be in when he walked through the door.

When he was in a poisonous mood and lashed out at Mum, I'm thankful to say he never beat her up badly. It was never a hospital job. He just slapped her around sometimes – a slap to the face or a kick in the shin – but it was still awful. To see your mother being beaten by your father is something you never forget. It's horrific.

I never could understand how he'd treat her like that and she'd still get up and light the fires in the morning. I never could fathom how she could always start afresh, treating the morning after the night before as a brand new day, but she always did. And she'd still go out and buy food for him. He was such a fussy eater and we had no freezer, so every day she'd go and get something special for his dinner. He liked his plain food – meat, veg, potatoes and unsliced bread with real butter – that she'd always get for him. It was more than he deserved.

Years later I can remember saying to her, 'Why did you never leave? At times I prayed to God you would.'

'I did once,' she told me with sadness in her eyes. 'I sat on Blackpool prom with all my cases packed but I couldn't do it, because of you.'

And that was the thing. In those days she couldn't leave my

father and take eight kids with her when she had nothing to her name but housekeeping cash.

'With all you kids and no money where could I have gone?' she explained. 'There aren't many people who could take in a woman and her eight children.'

So Mum's only option was to leave without us but she couldn't do it. Not only would she have been desperately unhappy about leaving us but also her reputation would have been tarnished for ever. The Nolan mother who'd abandoned her kids and split up her family would be condemned all over town. In those days no one wanted to hear the abused wife's tale of woe. Families stuck together for better or for worse. So she wiped her eyes, took a deep breath and headed home to unpack her belongings like nothing ever happened. That's a mother's love for you.

It wasn't just Mum who felt the back of Dad's hand. We all did at one stage or another. I know it sounds awful but in those days your parents did give you a clip around the ear or a smack on the legs with a slipper and you expected it to hurt. Dad would use the flat palm of his hand across our backsides or legs and it killed, but many of my friends in those days got a belt from their mum and dad. However when Dad was drunk he could be incredibly cruel. One incident will always stick in my mind and it sums up Dad at his worst. As I've said, being the youngest of a brood of eight, I'd never really had my own bed, I'd just go from room to room, and on this particular night I was sharing with Bernie and Linda. I must have been about five or six.

There were bunk beds in their room and that night I was on the top fast asleep. It was long past all our bedtimes but my sisters weren't exactly settling down for the night. Instead they were messing around on the bottom bunk, like adolescent girls do, whispering, giggling and laughing. They must have been making loads of noise because suddenly the door creaked open and I woke to see a shadowy figure standing in the doorway. It was Dad and he didn't look happy. I actually remember being fearful for them. *They are so going to get it*, I thought.

'What's going on?' he snarled, his voice thick with alcohol. Not that he was going to wait for my sisters to answer. Instead he just came in, grabbed them and spanked both of them, causing the bunk bed to wobble and my sisters to cry out.

Of course I did my usual trick of pretending to be asleep, wincing with every yelp from my sisters. Then Dad said something that made my stomach lurch.

'You do realize that because of you two I'm going to have to smack her,' he announced coldly.

The next thing I knew, two strong hands had hauled me out of the top bunk and there were blows raining down on my backside. When he'd finished beating the crap out of me he turned on his heels and glared at the three of us.

'Now I don't want to hear another peep from you,' he growled, before slamming the door shut. I can still recall the stinging on the back of my legs but that wasn't the reason I was so distraught. It was the injustice of it all that hurt me the most. It was just so unfair.

As I lay there, tears rolling down my cheeks, I kept thinking over and over, *But why did he smack me? I didn't do anything. They were messing around on the bottom and I was on the top asleep.* But there was no logic to it and certainly no way we'd have ever answered back. So not daring to make any more noise we all huddled together trying to stifle our sobs. We were too scared to get up and go to the loo so we all wet the bed. We lay in it all night, putting our towelling robes on to try and keep us warm in the wet sheets.

That was one of many reminders that life isn't fair – particularly where alcohol is concerned. Dad would never have done that sober, but that night he was half cut and boy did we pay the price.

If there's one good thing that came out of those horrible memories, it's that all these incidents have made me a better parent. When they were younger my sons, Shane Jnr and Jake, fought like cat and dog but I would never hit them. I'm never aggressive and I just won't row in front of children either. No way. No matter how angry I feel I have to wait until they are out of earshot. It's all because of those childhood memories. I remember that fear when it happened to me and I know that it does affect children.

Even when he was sober Dad was fiercely strict. We were never allowed boys in our bedrooms even when we were very small, and he only got worse as my three eldest sisters grew up. Poor Anne, Denise and Maureen got the brunt of Dad's overprotectiveness. He had a real problem with them dating boys and they didn't get to leave home and be independent until they were well into their twenties. I think Anne may not even have left home until she got married to her husband, Brian, when she was about twenty-eight or twenty-nine, and Maureen and Denise were also in their twenties when they left. Even as adults they were still wearing knee-length socks and not a scrap of make-up. They were nicknamed the Three Wise Virgins by the locals at The Oxford, where they used to go drinking.

While Dad did his best to thwart my sisters' chances of talking to boys, Mum did her best to let them have fun. If Dad was going to the pub she'd secretly let them sneak out for a bit, as long as they were back and in bed before him. I can still recall the farcical sight of Mum, knowing Dad would be on his way back from the pub, standing in the doorway hissing at them to hurry up as they legged it down the street! When I tell my husband Ray that story now he always says to me, 'You'd better not do that with Ciara!' But Ray and my father are very different men. My dad was obsessive and possessive.

Even if they were just outside talking to friends who happened to be male, just normal platonic friends, Mum would warn them to hurry up, knowing full well that Dad, a creature of habit, would be home any minute.

'Come on, your dad is coming,' she'd say, and the girls would often run in the back door just as he came in the front. Because it just wasn't worth the hassle of him demanding, 'Who was that?' or declaring, 'None of them are any good for you.' We just knew not to have lads around.

You'd assume that like many fathers Dad had struggled with seeing his daughters grow up and had concerns about them being taken advantage of by unscrupulous boys. But although that was clearly the case with five of us, I did learn to my utter horror many years later that he had altogether different, more sinister motives with Anne, his precious eldest daughter and the first to bloom. But back then, devastatingly, Anne was still suffering in silence and none of us knew.

While Dad was convinced that no man would be good enough for his daughters, on top of that he did not want the family unit to be split up. Singing as a group was our bread and butter and he thought boyfriends might complicate or jeopardize that. On stage he was Mr Charming, at home he was Mr Controlling.

We never really saw any of the money we earned from our shows. Dad didn't split it but at the same time he and Mum had eight kids to bring up, bills to pay, and food to put on the table, so all the money went towards that. They certainly weren't buying luxuries for themselves.

Although living with Dad's moods and drinking meant our family had a dark side, I don't think any of my friends ever thought our family set-up at home was any different from theirs. Alan, my best friend, was the son of our next-door neighbours Mr and Mrs Fleck, who had five kids. Their eldest daughter, Linda, used to hang round with my elder sisters, and Suzanne, next in line, was my sister Linda's best friend – they even share a birthday and are still close now. Alan also had a little brother, Mark, and a baby sister called Joanna. We called her 'the little one'. Funnily enough Alan was the one boy my Dad seemed to accept and he was someone I spent every minute of the day with.

The Flecks were fabulous, like a second family, we were always in and out of each other's houses. As a Scottish family they liked their porridge and I can remember one day Mrs Fleck invited me to have some with her family. I was so excited, until I tasted the first spoonful and realized that Scottish people make it with salt. At which point I gagged and nearly spat it out. If I ever see her to this day she always laughs about giving me porridge with salt in it!

Alan and Suzanne were always in our house and they saw and heard a lot. But I really doubt if anything that happened in our home would have struck them as out of the ordinary and we never talked about any of the fights.

In those days people didn't go on the telly to reveal all on the *Jeremy Kyle Show*. People rowed behind closed doors and that was that. You didn't go gossiping about it. I would never have dreamt of saying to my friends or a teacher, 'Dad hit Mum last night' or 'Dad came home drunk and whacked us.'

In lots of ways we were just a normal family, like all the others on Waterloo Road.

And our big family time, as for most people, was Christmas. We were always offered lots of work over the festive period, but Mum and Dad always declined, as being Catholics they felt Christmas was a time for family. We didn't have much money but Christmas was every bit as important as birthdays to my parents.

Mum and Dad never went to bed on Christmas Eve. Instead they'd wait until the last child had finally passed out and then they set to work! With eight kids and the excitement of Christmas you can imagine how late that was.

Often they'd have a three-hour window between 2 a.m., when the last child went to sleep, and 5 a.m., when the first got up, to prepare everything, so they never got a wink. While we were sound asleep dreaming about Father Christmas they'd be up all night putting presents under the tree.

Our Santa never wrapped presents. All the other presents from Mum and Dad or from one sibling to another would be wrapped, but Santa and the reindeers were too busy delivering goodies to all the kids in the world to bother with gift wrapping. Not that it mattered – in our family every child would receive one special present from Santa (unlike today when Father Christmas leaves 112 presents for each child, individually wrapped) and you knew straight away which one was yours.

You'd come down in the morning and the doll you'd dreamt of would be there sitting under the tree. It was so magical. When I was very young, about three, I got a Tippy Tumbles – a doll that did roly-polys – that I just adored. I'd begged Mum for one all year and there she was! My parents were incredibly thoughtful like that. It was always the present you'd wanted.

Their generosity was selfless too. One Christmas we were so poor that Mum pawned both her wedding and engagement rings to buy presents. She could never afford to get them back.

I used to love playing shop, and the Christmas of 1969, when I was four, Santa did me proud. I came down in the morning and there was a child-size wooden shop all set up in the front room. I literally jumped for joy. Apparently it took Mum and Dad all night to build and they rowed the whole night through over which way to do it. When they finally finished it there was one piece of wood left that neither of them could work out what to do with. Luckily the shop stayed intact! It took up half the lounge and my brothers and sisters had all bought me things to go in it. I had a till and real biscuits and groceries on the shelves.

Every year Mum had to cook for so many people – sometimes twenty-four (you'd have the boys' girlfriends, my Aunty Theresa, random friends and any other relatives) – and inevitably she'd forget one thing or another. So that year in the end, realizing what she'd forgotten, she had to buy extras for the Christmas dinner from me. I'd even nicked things out of the kitchen so she had to buy them back from me from the shop, which was driving her nuts because she was trying to cook dinner. I was an entrepreneur even then!

Looking really stressed, she came into the room asking, 'Where's the beans?'

'Sorry, they're a penny!' I piped up, grinning like a Cheshire cat.

That Christmas was wonderful. I played in my shop all day but once the festivities were over it had to be taken down because there just wasn't room. I only had my shop for one day, but blimey, did I get enjoyment in those hours.

Despite the rule that we never worked Christmas, one year,

when I was eight, my Dad stunned us all by agreeing that we would. He'd been offered a lot of money and we needed it. It caused a bloody uproar. Half the family didn't want to go.

'But Mum, what about the presents?' Bernie whined, stamping her feet.

'You can still have them,' Mum told her. 'But we need to sing too.'

So that morning, Christmas Day 1973, after we'd seen what Santa had brought us and exchanged gifts, we reluctantly changed into our glitzy outfits and headed down the road to the plush Cliffs Hotel in Blackpool. It was a posher venue than we normally played, but our singing seemed to go down well and everyone appeared to be in a festive mood. It was the only Christmas we ever worked, but that day everything changed.

Two

While we were singing at the Cliffs Hotel that Christmas, Dad was approached by a smart-looking man. He had a breath-taking proposal for us. He was called Joe Lewis and ran a company called Hanover Grand, which owned restaurants and function rooms in London. He loved our act and wanted to offer us residency at his prestigious theatre restaurant, the London Rooms.

Dad originally thought he was a chancer. 'It's just big talk,' he scoffed, but then Joe made a firm offer and it was a very good one at that. He would pay a very decent wage for my five older sisters to perform seven nights a week at the restaurant, which was based in Drury Lane, Covent Garden – 240 miles from our home in Blackpool.

Although my dad was sceptical, Mum and the girls were very excited. I suppose my brothers could have been offended that Joe hadn't offered them a deal as well, but to be honest they weren't that bothered. By now Tommy was twenty-four and engaged to a girl called Angela, and Brian was nineteen and also had a fiancée, Lorraine. Neither of them wanted to leave Blackpool.

I wasn't allowed to join my older sisters on stage, as I was too young. Mind you, Linda was fifteen and Bernie only fourteen, so I don't know how they got away with performing – I think this was perhaps just before licensing came in. Being too young to join my sisters singing was brilliant as far as I was concerned. For the first time in my life I actually felt like I had the freedom to be a little girl.

Mum and Dad weren't performing either, which was fine with them, as they were older by that stage, so the group was renamed the Nolan Sisters while the three of us took a back step.

I don't remember the exact circumstances, as I was so young, but after a lot of debate I think it was eventually agreed that Tommy and Brian would stay behind while Mum, Dad, me and my older sisters moved to London. So the next thing I knew I was being taken out of school and we packed up our belongings to move to London. I was quite choked during my last day at primary school, but to be honest I was so used to working and travelling around by then that I adapted pretty easily.

Knowing we were strapped for cash, Joe kindly invited us all to move into the huge mansion he shared with his wife Esther, in Wentworth, Surrey, until we found somewhere more permanent. I'm always amazed that he allowed a family of eight to move into his home, yet he did. He must have rated us very highly.

Joe and Esther's home was a fabulous place – a million pound house then, so probably about £8 million now – and to us it was just like a castle. We still shared rooms, but massive rooms. Joe and Esther had a son called Charlie, a year older than me; he was at boarding school most of the time, but came home for holidays. He took over where Alan left off and became one of my best friends. It was great – we had such a ball.

They had a housekeeper and a gardener, who lived in, and two big dogs, a Pyrenean mountain dog called Dusty and a Great Dane called Dane, which, being animal mad, I loved. They also had a tennis court and a swimming pool. It was just a whole world away from what we were used to. We couldn't believe it.

When term started I was enrolled into a private school called the Park School for Girls, along with Linda and Bernie. It was good to start a new school with them – apart from the fact that on the first day of school they made us sing in front of the other pupils in a classroom, which horrified me.

We actually ended up living with Joe for six months until my parents could afford to buy a house for us all. Mum found a big double-fronted detached house, which had been a doctor's surgery, in Ilford, Essex, and had it converted back into a house for us. Again, it was just fabulous as we had never had a big house. It had six bedrooms, a massive lounge, a conservatory and an enormous dining room, a kitchen, utility room and, best of all, a cellar, which was converted into a playroom especially for moi! As my sisters will probably say, I was a spoilt little cow. I got so much more than them, but they were working all the time and I wasn't. Suddenly I had my evenings free to go to after-school clubs, I'd have friends round to play and host sleepovers. It was wonderful just being a normal kid.

I have some good, happy memories from Ilford, because at that time my father was not working and the drinking had definitely slowed down. Now he was out of the club circuit he only drank on special occasions like Christmas, and birthdays. And although he had his moments it was never as bad as when we were little kids. I felt as though I was having a proper childhood.

At weekends I would accompany the girls to the restaurant,

as I liked to go along to watch and hang out with all the staff, who doted on me. They'd get me Coca-Colas with straws to drink and chat to me while the girls performed. But during the week I was just a normal kid with my little cellar playroom – I was well happy!

Some habits die hard, though, and at this stage I still shared a bed with Anne. My mum and dad had a room each and Maureen and Denise shared a room, as did Linda and Bernie.

There was a time I did perform at the London Rooms and that was in 1974, when I was nine, and a BBC bigwig called Stewart Morris brought Cliff Richard in! He was a producer on the *Cliff Richard Show* and was looking for acts for the new series. He was a very big, obese man, very powerful and straight-talking and he held no punches. We got on well with him and you wouldn't want to cross him. I was actually quite scared of him.

So we all sang for him and Cliff, privately, when the venue was closed. Afterwards Cliff was charming. He seemed to know all our names and said he liked our harmonies.

'I loved it!' he told us, and suddenly we were signed up for our first ever television show. I was nine years old and about to be on telly for the very first time.

The *Cliff Richard Show* was our first real break and it was pretty much a baptism of fire, as millions were viewing it. If the audience liked us it could lead to great fortune, if they didn't we could be packed up and on our way back to Blackpool before the year was through.

Even so, I don't remember being particularly nervous. I think it was because I was so young and I'd never known any different. It was more of a big deal for my sisters, with them being that little bit older and more aware. I can recall them being really excited about going on the telly and they were definitely nervous.

I was just really excited to be singing on his show, particularly as I really liked Cliff's film *Summer Holiday*.

Cliff's show went out on a Saturday but we rehearsed all week for it, which was actually quite gruelling. It meant getting up at 6.30 a.m. in order to travel all the way to the BBC studios in North Acton. After we'd been preened and polished we were bundled out of the house en masse and set off on the ninety-minute journey. We'd get an overground train from Ilford to Stratford and then the Central Line all the way to Acton. It was very boring, as there would be about twenty-odd stops before we all got off.

The TV studio was an interesting place, a real hub of activity, but I remember thinking it was much smaller than I imagined it would be after watching the show on the telly. Cliff was always really nice to us, popping into rehearsals during the week to see how we were getting on. As well as doing our own songs we'd often perform with him too, although it was mainly the older girls.

Our first show was bloody awful; we had no choice what to wear or how to have our hair, and because it was all very new and exciting for us we just did what we were told. We were instructed to wear these awful green matching satin dresses. There was a lot of debate over my dress. I heard Stewart Morris and the stylist whispering, 'It just looks too old on her.'

So someone cut it into a shorter dress and I had long white socks on, little black patent leather shoes and a dodgy haircut my dad had obviously done with a bowl.

But after the first show we were thrilled to hear we'd been well received. From then on we were booked in for a regular slot for the full eight-week series. I believe by then I had licensing to perform about eighty times a year, or something like that, so I think I actually did every second week of Cliff's show.

Travelling to the studio was to become a very familiar and boring journey. We'd always get there for 9 a.m., and often all six of us girls would be asleep on the tube. After hours of rehearsing, Mum and I would travel home to Ilford, but my poor sisters would head straight off to Drury Lane to do their evening turn. I don't know how they managed it.

Despite the workload it was great fun. I was totally in awe of Cliff's resident dancing troupe, Young Generation. They were just brilliant and did routines behind us. We loved watching them. And every week Cliff had some amazing guests. Once, when I was ten, we met Olivia Newton-John and I was transfixed by how beautiful she was. She wasn't wearing a scrap of make-up and her skin was just naturally glowing. And she was so nice with it. It was a few years before she played Sandy in *Grease*, and at this time she was better known for her hit singles 'If Not for You', 'Banks of the Ohio' and 'Long Live Love'.

I also met Roy Kinnear, who was a massive comedy actor. He was this portly, jolly man who'd become a household name on the satire TV series *That Was the Week That Was* in the early sixties and went on to do the cult film *The Four Musketeers*. He'd have us in hysterics. He was just so naturally funny and really sweet to me. He was actually killed some years later during the filming of the second *Musketeers* film. I was really sad when I heard that.

With the prospect of meeting famous people every week, my sisters always seemed excited to be on the show, yet generally if I'd been any more laid back I would have been horizontal. To be honest, once the novelty had worn off it was all a bit of a pain in the arse for a little girl. My daughter Ciara is seven now and I just can't imagine her going on a show with 20 million viewers every week and singing her heart out. But for me that was just the way it was. I never had a choice.

It was around that time that I first remember people changing around us. Folks who had been pals for years were suddenly not friends any more. My older sisters found that friends just stopped calling because they assumed my sisters wouldn't want to know them now they were famous. I found girls at school were suddenly saying, 'You think you're something because you're on the telly,' which so wasn't the case. It was sad because I never went to school boasting, I just didn't do that.

It wasn't until we started having hit records a few years later that I experienced any kind of adulation.

After working with Cliff for one season we were lucky to have other TV opportunities on the horizon. Next in 1974 we did *The Harry Secombe Show*. It was a similar thing – we'd go on and do a little spot or a comedy song with him, like 'Who Will Buy?' from the *Oliver!* musical. He was so friendly, and he and I would often duet together singing songs such as 'The Mouse and the Elephant'. Some weeks I'd even get to do the opening song to the show with Harry.

I guess that as our success grew I was kind of losing my childhood again, but this time I was enjoying it a lot more than when we did the clubs. Yet there were still times when I thought I would just like to go out to play with my mates.

Stewart Morris was producing that show too, and, as much as he'd been a mentor to us, goodness he could be strict. He was the Simon Cowell of his day really, spelling it out in no uncertain terms if he wasn't happy with your performance. Harry and I once did a duet outside in a market and although

35

I can't remember what we were singing, Stewart obviously wasn't very happy and really shouted at me because I couldn't hit a low note during the song. I think I'd also wound him up by fidgeting between takes or something.

Well, Harry was outraged that he'd spoken to a small child like that, so he took him to one side and tore a strip off him. 'You will never speak to her like that again in front of me,' he warned him. I loved him for that!

These days you often see precocious stage school kids on the telly, loving every minute and totally playing up to the camera. I hope to God I was never like that! But I don't think I was – I just didn't know any different, I never have. I don't remember thinking, *Oh my God I can't wait to tell my friends I'm on the telly!* I was more likely to be thinking, *Oh come on, I've sung now, when can we go out and play tag?*

Once we'd finished that series my sisters did another TV show called *Musical Time Machine* with performer Vince Hill. I wasn't involved in that, but I wasn't particularly upset, I was just as happy spending time with my animals.

I'd always had rabbits and cats, including one mad moggy called O'Malley who literally used to climb the walls, and there were constantly scratches all over my hands from where I'd had kittens hanging off them. I also loved horses and was always heading back to Blackpool to stay with my brothers or my Aunty Theresa so that I could go down the local stables. I'd spend hours there grooming and petting the horses.

'You stink,' Tommy would always say, screwing up his nose, when I came back. 'You need a bath.'

We'd always had dogs in our family and for years we'd had a Lion Pekinese called Toby, who sadly died when I was little. On my eleventh birthday, to my great delight, I was able to add two puppies to my menagerie. They were a complete surprise.

Mum handed me a cardboard mug box and immediately this little puppy popped his head out.

I squealed with delight. He was a cute, boisterous little chap, brown with white markings. He was a mongrel but looked like a miniature border collie. I immediately called him Ben, after the Michael Jackson song I loved to sing.

But then Mum and Maureen made the mistake of telling me they'd left another puppy behind at the shop.

'He had a brother who looked so sad,' Maureen said.

'I didn't know which one to pick,' Mum sighed. 'I wanted to get both.'

'Oh please, can we go back and get his brother?' I pleaded. 'Please!'

Well, Mum didn't need much persuading and we quickly raced back to get the other puppy. He was white with brown markings and I called him Bill. After that my dogs went every-where with me.

It was a shame, but poor Ben didn't last that long. One day Maureen and my cousin Angie from Ireland, who was living with us, decided to take the dogs for a walk. While they were out Ben flew off the lead and into the path of a car. Angie came back sobbing and covered in blood. Ben survived that time, but a few weeks later he escaped out of the garden and we never saw him again. It was heartbreaking. But thank God I still had my Bill; he was the nervous one and followed me round every-where.

After the success of *Musical Time Machine*, the older girls got an amazing opportunity. They were invited to support Frank Sinatra on the European leg of his world tour in 1975. This was a very big deal. Our family were all mad Frank Sinatra fans and could hardly believe their luck. That was probably the first time I felt a bit disappointed to be missing out. When I found out I cried.

After my initial disappointment my sisters felt sorry for me, so when they arrived in Paris with the tour they phoned to see if I'd like to fly out to see Frank. To this day it is my biggest regret that I turned them down in favour of going to the stables. Oh my God, I still cannot believe I missed a chance like that. Madness!

That was the highlight of my sisters' career.

For the majority of the tour Mum was out there with the girls, and Dad, who was still working as my sisters' manager, flew out for some of the time while I was with my brothers. I really wish he'd sung while he was there, but he didn't. It's such a shame, as Dad sounded so like Sinatra and had the same laid-back persona on stage. It wasn't contrived, though, it was effortless. He just had the same aura and the same build. Sinatra would have loved him.

For a month while my sisters were away touring Dad and I got really close, as it was just him and me at the house in Ilford. Suddenly we went from a very chaotic life as part of a massive family to a very peaceful one where it was almost like I was an only child. I really liked it. During that time Dad was amazing and it was so nice to spend time with him one-on-one. We'd go to the pictures once a week to see a movie and go for a bite to eat in this little café in Leicester Square. Then we'd walk along the Embankment singing 'A Nightingale Sang in Berkeley Square'. He still wasn't drinking so much, so he was a nice dad at that time. He was also a great listener. At that age the stuff I rambled on about probably seemed quite trivial, but he never made me feel like it was. He'd sit and listen to me waffle on for hours.

Up until that point I suppose I'd been a bit of a Mummy's

girl, but she wasn't a great listener. She didn't have time and could be dismissive. I'd whine, 'But you don't understand!' and she'd flick me away with a tea towel, telling me not to worry. But Dad wasn't like that – he never fobbed you off.

After the Sinatra tour I continued to do my own thing at home while my sisters went off to New York with Engelbert Humperdinck. But by the time I was thirteen my Dad was getting busier and busier managing the girls and Mum often went off with them too, so it was decided that I should move back to Blackpool for a while. I actually didn't mind leaving my school, as I liked doing my riding and hanging out in Blackpool. So I was only too happy to move back into our old house with my two brothers.

Living with Tommy and Brian for that year was such a laugh. Tommy used to call me Bloto and I used to call him Michelin Man. And together the three of us coined the nickname Tufty for Mum because she always wore furry boots. (That pet name actually stayed with her until her dying day.)

I always got on very well with my brothers. Brian was very laid back and bright. He was serious but very dry-humoured, whereas Tommy was wild and should really have been in a rock band. He told the most disgusting jokes, ones that he'd never inflict on my other sisters, whispering them to me at inappropriate moments. Even today, aged almost sixty, Tommy still whispers shocking things in my ear and then says, 'Don't tell your sisters.'

Neither of them were with their fiancées any more and now Tommy had a lovely new girlfriend called Jackie who lived with him. Every evening he playing drums at a club in Blackpool called Flagship and Jackie would get dolled up seven nights a week to go with him. I adored her.

The boys worked during the day and I was home from

school by half two, so they pretty much left me to my own devices a lot of the time, which suited me. I was very independent from an early age and happy to do my own thing, and my brothers are the same. My sisters, on the other hand, very much relied on each other, and still do now. Having said that, in the evenings when Tommy was playing the drums and Brian was going out, it was very strange going to sleep in the house on my own. It was just so far removed from all the hustle and bustle I'd experienced there in years gone by.

During this time I was enrolled in a school that had just four kids. We had this old teacher of about seventy-five called Miss Ainsworth, who used to school us in an old Victorian-style room. She was bloody ancient and reminded me of Miss Havisham from *Great Expectations*. I half expected to walk in one day and see her sitting in an old wedding dress.

I had a friend there called Donna Rutter, who is still my only old school friend and lives in Blackpool to this day. At lunchtime we used to walk to Donna's house then back to school, discussing pop music and boys and thinking we were frightfully grown up and independent.

As my sisters continued to do their thing, my world seemed quite disjointed from theirs. I liked my life in Blackpool, just doing all the normal things teenage girls do – hanging out with friends, going riding, and walking Bill. And I think during those years it was really the first time that I seriously thought about the group and the fact that perhaps I didn't want to follow the same career path. In fact round about then I had my heart set on being a vet or a show-jumper. I was still obsessed with horses, so Dad had got me a little palomino foal that I named Aaron, who we kept in a little field out in the countryside. He was too small to ride, so I'd take him for a walk back and forth.

I also loved hanging out with Donna, going for walks down

the prom or into town. We were joined at the hip. Either she was at my house or I was at hers, doing all those blissful girly teenage things. Why would I swap that for a life in showbiz? I wasn't interested in being a Nolan Sister. But then I got the call to say the girls had been signed up for the *Mike Yarwood Show* in 1978. Mike Yarwood was an impressionist and massive in his day; the show was a Saturday night prime-time slot and they wanted me to join them. I didn't really have much say, it was just assumed I'd do it, so it was arranged that after school every Friday I'd get the train down to London on my own. Someone would meet me at Euston and I'd learn the song and routine on Saturday morning, travel to the studio to perform it and get the train back on Sunday.

Being a parent now, I do think I'd never put my kid on the train on his or her own on a Friday night, but I never felt scared. It was more of a pain in the arse because I just wanted to go out with Donna.

But Mike was actually brilliant. He was just great, so talented. One of the best impressionists of his time. Like all these old-school performers he was quite an affable, avuncular man and really kind to us. I never had a bad word to say about him.

During those summer holidays when I was thirteen and fourteen, my sisters would be performing all over the country on tour and I'd go and join them wherever they were in England. I loved the business then, as I wasn't doing it! I was getting all the rewards without the pressure. I'd be backstage or hanging out with the crew at front of house or chatting to the band. I was quite content to watch them performing from the sidelines. There was never a moment when I looked at them longingly, wishing I could go out there and strut my stuff. I just used to love being backstage.

★

When I was fourteen it was decided that I'd move in with my Aunty Theresa and her husband Jim, as I think my parents had sussed that my brothers weren't around a lot to keep an eye on me. I lived with my aunty for a year and it was actually nice having adults around. She was quite strict with me but in a good way, and for the first time in my life I had a proper routine. She worked in a bakery and I used to leave school and come and meet her there and help behind the counter. I had to wash up if she cooked me dinner, take the dog out every day and hoover the sofa every Sunday, because Bill would moult.

In the front room Aunty Theresa kept this mad budgie called Billy, who'd often fall off the door where he was perched and flutter round the room. Neither Bill nor I liked him flapping round our heads much, so we'd both try and leg it out the room, tripping each other up along the way.

I have really good memories of living there. I loved Aunty Theresa and my Uncle Jim. Sadly he's dead now, but when he was alive the two of us would sit there winding my aunty up and she'd yell, 'I'm going to kill you two!' It was funny.

By now my sisters had released eight singles with Target, which failed to chart. The only one I worked on was 'But I Do' which I sang the lead vocals for. It was produced by Bruce Welsh from the Shadows. I think the deal was that my sisters were contractually obliged to do the London Rooms every week, but Joe would allow them to go off and do other things as long as it didn't interfere and he got a cut.

Although 'But I Do' didn't really do anything, it was certainly another step in the right direction. Bit by bit my sisters and I were getting more well known.

But then Warner, the umbrella label, suggested they do an album called *20 Giant Hits*, which was a compilation of twenty of the best songs of the time. Well, that album was a massive hit and really put them on the map.

They were still signed to Hanover Grand but Dad eventually persuaded Joe to terminate the contract so they could go off and do their own thing. Ending the contract cost my sisters a considerable sum.

It was at this point that Denise decided to leave the group and pursue a solo career. She didn't want to do pop songs or be choreographed and that was the way things were heading.

As the Nolan Sisters became more and more popular, another record label, CBS, made an approach and the four remaining girls eventually signed, agreeing to change their name to the Nolans. It was the start of some very exciting times. First off, the new label were really keen for them to record an album of classic tracks, but it was proving very difficult because the girls were already committed to their three-month summer season in Cleethorpes. With a punishing regime of eight shows a week, they just couldn't get to the London studio.

Ben Findon, the album's main producer, had the bright idea of bringing a mobile recording studio to the house they'd rented for the summer. So we all sang in the very glamorous setting of the garage, which was wired up to a van parked outside.

Although I wasn't performing in the evening with the girls, I did sing on that album and I can remember doing the tracks 'Thank You for the Music' and 'Bright Eyes'. That album was titled very simply *The Nolans*, and it eventually got to number 15.

When I think back now it makes me laugh. These days you hear about groups taking two years to make an album, and how the genius could only unfold in the quiet luxury of a million-pound country retreat complete with intervals for game shooting and food provided by a Michelin star chef. Yet we polished that album off in just a week in a no-frills suburban garage, snacking on crisps and bottles of pop.

That June 1979 I was bridesmaid when Anne married her boyfriend Brian Wilson, a professional footballer with Blackpool. It was clear that she wanted to settle down with him and wasn't so sure about being in the group any more. So seeing as I was now fourteen there was talk of me taking over from her. In truth I wasn't at all sure if it was what I wanted.

Suddenly I was told that CBS were applying pressure. 'If she wants to join, she needs to do it now!' they said.

I was surprised when Dad took me aside with a concerned look on his face. 'Coleen, if you don't want to do it, then don't do it,' he told me. 'I see you married to a farmer out in the country.'

I didn't know what to do. I would have loved to pursue a career with animals but how realistic was it? To be a vet I'd need masses of qualifications and I didn't even go to a proper bleeding school! Plus I could be quite lazy. Would I really knuckle down to prepare for all those exams? So at the very last minute I decided to join. You always think you're going to miss out, don't you? It was the right decision – I would have missed out!

By now CBS were getting Ben, and two other writers, Mike Myers and Bob Puzey, who'd all written for the Dooleys, to pen brand-new songs for us. And the first of this new batch – a romantic ballad called 'Spirit, Body and Soul' – was released in October 1979 and went to number 34. I joined soon after, duly leaving my school in Blackpool and moving back to London, supposedly to be taught by a tutor although that never actually happened. Instead we headed off on a massive tour of

Great Britain. It was the first tour we did when suddenly we weren't supporting, but headlining! Boy, was I nervous then!

It was brilliant, though. We had our own lighting rig, our own crew and we bought a set from the band Queen thanks to Brian, Linda's new boyfriend. He worked for Bronze Records, the label Denise was now signed to. Linda had met him at a family party when he'd come along with his then wife! On the way out he'd told Linda, 'I'm going to marry you one day,' and later he did.

The set had three platforms that the band performed on, with three or four lots of steps leading down which had massive lights on the front of them. At the start of the show the band would come on and then the lights would be switched on to blind the audience. When they went off we'd be standing there, having just sneaked on stage.

Soon after I joined we released a second song called 'I'm in the Mood for Dancing'. It was a much more upbeat track and it immediately sparked a lot of attention and radio play. To our delight it started to soar up the chart, peaking at number 3 in December 1979. Then suddenly in early 1980 things just went crazy. Before I knew it we were on *Top of the Pops*, something that excited me greatly, as it was the biggest pop show in the country. By now we were getting recognized everywhere we went. It was weird but brilliant.

Generally people were lovely, but they could be vile too. I used to think, *But you don't even know me!* I can remember once being in a nightclub with Donna, aged about sixteen or seventeen, when some guy actually spat in my face – a real disgusting footballer's gob. It was foul, but I can also recall thinking, *God, I must be really famous, someone just spat in my face!*

For the first time we had our own band, consisting of two keyboard players, a bass player, a guitarist and a drummer. And like all teenage girls I relished the opportunity to flirt with boys. It was one of the keyboard players who'd caught my eye. He was called Robin Smith and was the band's musical director. At twenty-three he was almost eight years my senior. Not that I cared! He was just divine, tall with dark hair, lovely toned arms from playing the keyboards and a great physique.

I was fifteen, nearly sixteen, and just bowled over by how good-looking he was. When he first joined all the girls were whispering about him, saying, 'He's gorgeous!' But they were all in relationships, which conveniently left him for me.

Up until then I'd never even kissed a boy. Lads had tried to snog me a few times but I'd never really wanted to kiss them. I was a bit scared to be honest, and also I never fancied boys my age.

Robin and I got on really well, and for a while it was quite flirty but innocent. We'd just spend loads of time together – on stage, on the bus, at the hotel – just chatting, laughing and getting to know each other. Gradually it got more touchy-feely and there were definitely lingering looks going on. Then one day we were in the foyer of the Westbury Hotel back in London, chatting and whispering, watching people walking in and out, when a kiss just came from nowhere. It was one of those very romantic moments when you're so close that it just happens. Robin leaned in and instinctively I moved in too so he could kiss me and it was electric. This time I wasn't scared. Suddenly it was like I was in a delicious marathon – making up for fifteen years of never having been kissed. After that we were pretty much inseparable.

At the height of our success we had a big battle with the head of our label, Maurice Oberstein. He was an eccentric American, very tall and thin, with a high, squeaky voice. He had this habit of always wearing outlandish headwear, so he'd have a trilby on one day, then another day it would be a Stetson or a cap with writing on.

The fight we had was kind of my fault. But it was all because CBS wanted us to release 'Attention to Me' as our next single but we wanted to release 'Chemistry'. Although my sisters were all piping up too, I was the one who made the biggest fuss. My boyfriend Robin had written the song along with another writer called Nicky Graham and I was singing the lead. We liked it as it was less poppy. We were trying to change our image. We could all sing harmonies and we wanted to show off our voices. We wanted to progress a bit. Yet Maurice was of the attitude 'If it ain't broke don't fix it', and wanted to go with 'Attention to Me', as it had been penned by our usual writers Findon, Myers and Puzey.

But much as we respected their work, we honestly thought 'Attention to Me' just wasn't as good as 'Chemistry'. There was no doubting that Maurice had a long and respected career, but although I was not even sixteen, I really thought he'd made the wrong decision on this occasion. So the stand-off continued and escalated into a full-on row. I'm normally a very placid person and will avoid arguments at all costs, but at that moment our career was at stake and I just felt he was an old man who didn't have a clue.

'Kids buy records depending on who produces them,' he barked at me.

'No,' I disagreed. 'They buy records because they like the group or the song or both! And "Chemistry" is a better song!'

But it was no good. Maurice was very put out, and it's no wonder really. It must have seemed very precocious of me and I suppose it was the equivalent of some young upstart having a row with Simon Cowell and telling him he knows nothing. But to this day I still think I was right!

However, Maurice refused to budge. After a lot of huffing and puffing he'd made his decision. 'We'll release "Attention to Me" followed by "Chemistry", and that is the end of it,' he snapped.

And that was that!

But CBS didn't exactly play fair. 'Attention to Me' came out with a blaze of publicity and got to number 9 in the charts. Yet when 'Chemistry' was released it was much more of a soft launch. There was no video or promo. As anyone in the music industry will tell you, trying to have a hit record with no promotion is near impossible.

It seemed that after the dispute over the songs, CBS were trying to teach us a lesson by sabotaging our chance of success with 'Chemistry'. But amazingly, despite the hindrance of no publicity campaign, it started to climb the charts anyway and eventually peaked at number 12, completely through word of mouth alone. In those days just getting into the top 20 was a big deal. Once you got there you could usually stay there for weeks. If the song had just been promoted properly it could have been our first number 1. I'd be lying if I didn't admit that the whole 'Chemistry' debacle was bitterly disappointing. But as it happens Maurice eventually apologized.

Meanwhile Robin and me were really falling for each other, so I was very relieved when he came on our 1980 tour to Japan, even though it was tricky for us to have any moments to ourselves. My dad naturally had his eye on us and in Japan I also had a reputation to live up to. Japan is very family-orientated and our fans out there were really young. Because I was the youngest sister there was a lot of focus on me and publicly I couldn't be seen to have a boyfriend. So generally we had to keep it very low-key.

It was crazy over there and we were always getting

mobbed. In England some people hated us with a passion because we weren't trendy – we just couldn't compete when punk groups like the Sex Pistols were all the rage – but in Japan they loved us! I've never known anything like it. It was like Beatlemania, I kid you not. We couldn't leave our hotel room and we had security wherever we went.

While we were out there 'I'm in the Mood for Dancing' was number 1 and we were the first UK band to have a record at number 1 in the Japanese international charts and their domestic charts at the same time. The domestic chart had only ever had Japanese artists in there before, so it was incredible really. That summer we were over there for eight weeks and we were working twenty hours a day every day – that's how it worked in Japan, they didn't believe in days off.

It was a fascinating country to see, but I must admit I wasn't too fussed on the food. Yet nothing amused my sisters and I more than seeing my dad, arguably the world's fussiest eater, politely tucking into the local delicacies he was being offered as our manager. For a man who liked his food plain and simple, seaweed and raw fish was his worst nightmare and he must have had to concentrate very hard not to gag. I think we were all very relieved when my mum flew out towards the end of the tour armed with teabags, butter and biscuits.

I've never worked so hard before or since. We broke many, many records when we were over there, and at the time I was a bit like, 'Oh shut up.' But now being older I look back and think, 'It was fabulous! Didn't we do well!'

I don't know what it was about our image – the British public were great but we never got respect from the industry. It's been almost thirty years since 'I'm in the Mood for Dancing' was released and whether you like it or hate it you have to respect the fact that it was a good pop song.

But while BBC Radio 2's Terry Wogan really got behind us, Radio 1 wouldn't play us! Meanwhile the press constantly printed stories about how sickly sweet and goody-goody we all were.

It was a hard image to live up to. We weren't the Osmonds – they were genuinely nice, didn't drink or have sex , or do anything. Even to this day they are such nice people. Yes, we did sing sweet harmonies and wore matching outfits, but like all teenagers I wanted to rebel. I wanted to drink myself under the table and swear. Having said that now, I'd rather people thought we were nice and liked us, than thought we were horrible.

But in Japan we were never ridiculed for our image, on the contrary we were idolized. It was an incredible time. We went out to Japan about four or five times over a three-year period, doing eight-week stints at a time. Our concerts sold out in fifteen minutes and we just couldn't sign autographs after we'd performed like back in the UK – it was too dangerous! The minute we came off stage we were bustled out of the building and made to run to our car by security. I always thought this was a bit OTT until one day our car was literally surrounded by hysterical fans. They looked so pleading I wound down my window and put my arm out. Well, that was a mistake, my arm nearly got ripped off! It was a good lesson. I never did that again!

A lot of the time we travelled on the bullet train as it was so much quicker, but even then the fans would always be in hot pursuit and when we were at the stations we'd have the army escorting us to a special waiting area. I can remember once sitting in a glass room with hundreds of kids pressed up against the glass staring at us; it was like being in a zoo. Many of them were hysterical and crying. It was scary but then we also knew we were safe, so we'd giggle to each other, saying, 'Oh my God, it's so exciting!' I wouldn't have liked to have that all the time. It's not much fun when you can't just pop out and do normal things like shopping or meeting a friend.

Now I look back on Japan with such fondness. I appreciate it so much now. But at the time, after weeks on the road, I just wanted to go home. I was longing for a slice of proper toast and some baked beans. It was stupid of me really, as I had my boyfriend with me so it wasn't like I was missing him. I also should have been savouring every minute – I knew full well that the minute we stepped off the plane at Heathrow I'd be even more depressed because no one gave a shit when we got back home!

When we did arrive back in the UK Robin and I continued to spend every spare minute together. He was really respectful. When he came to stay at my parents' house in Ilford he'd always sleep in a separate room with no complaints. Funnily enough, by now my dad had mellowed a lot and it was actually as much me and Robin wanting to do the right thing by my parents as them strictly enforcing it.

Around the same time my sister Anne was heavily pregnant and as it turned out she was about to have a terrible experience giving birth. About ten days before my sixteenth birthday, I got a very distressed call from her husband Brian saying that Anne was in intensive care in Torquay, where she lived. Apparently she'd been diagnosed with eclampsia, a very serious toxic condition in pregnant women that can lead to coma, so was being rushed into theatre for an emergency C-section. Mum and Dad immediately rushed down to Torquay to see her, leaving me in the house with Robin.

To be honest when I heard the news I just couldn't get my head round it at first. Then the realization that I could lose my sister and my unborn niece or nephew began to sink in. I was in a terrible state, shaking and crying. Thankfully Robin really looked after me and we sat there in limbo, awaiting news.

Finally the call came through to say that Anne had pulled through but there was only a 50/50 chance she would live. She'd had a baby girl, but she was in a bad way as well. The next twenty-four hours were very emotionally draining. The thought of losing my sister was horrible, but I was also devastated for her little baby. Like all my sisters I'd been really excited about becoming an aunty. All the attention was on Anne, but I was so worried about my niece too. Luckily after four days Anne began to recover, as did her daughter, whom she named Amy.

Now Anne doesn't remember any of it. But for us it was the first time anything traumatic had ever hit us in that way. You just don't think people are going to die in childbirth and we were so relieved that she survived.

With Anne on the mend, we arranged to travel to Torquay to see the baby on the afternoon of my birthday. There were lots of us going down – Mum, Dad, Aunty Theresa, Maureen and Bernie – and we were going to go for a meal to celebrate Amy's arrival and my birthday. Robin and I drove down separately to everyone else, but on the way we got really lost and then were stuck in traffic for about four hours. By the time we arrived at the restaurant it was so late that everyone had left and I'd missed my own birthday meal!

Amy is twenty-eight now, and I still blame her for ruining my sixteenth!

Shortly after my birthday my parents went away for the weekend and left me home alone with Robin. He hadn't put any pressure on me, but I kind of knew that weekend would be the one when I'd end up having sex with him. Unlike with the kissing I wasn't scared, because I felt I was ready for it. It wasn't him forcing me at all. I was madly in love with him. I felt we were both in love. Of course I was nervous, like you are when you're a virgin. I was wondering if it would hurt and initially I was embarrassed about being naked. But it was fine. It didn't hurt at all. In fact it was very nice. Afterwards he was really affectionate towards me and I fell asleep in his arms. The next day I couldn't stop smiling. I think I told Linda first and then Bernie. But then they probably knew from the stupid inane grin on my face anyway.

About a month later, while we were staying in Torquay at Anne's, I woke one morning to a strange feeling of nausea. Running to the loo I only just made it and I was physically sick.

Later I felt better but I had a really bad feeling.

The next morning it happened again, and once more by lunchtime I was fine.

It was odd, as it didn't feel like I had a bug, so at first I convinced myself that it was down to the stress of Anne being ill or that it was psychosomatic. But in the back of my mind there was the niggling reminder that I had lost my virginity to Robin four weeks earlier and that we hadn't actually used anything.

But surely you couldn't get pregnant the first time you slept with someone, could you?

Three

Sitting on the loo, hands shaking, I carefully read the instructions on the pregnancy kit I'd bought from the chemist. 'Oh God,' I thought. 'This can't be happening to me.'

Like the kits of today, you had to wee on the stick and wait for the result to show up. But unfortunately, rather than finding out your fate in minutes, back then you had to wait an agonizing half an hour.

I was carrying out the test secretly in the upstairs bathroom of my parents' house in Ilford. Checking that no one was around, I crept into my bedroom and hid the stick in the drawer, while I lay on the bed waiting for the time to be up. I couldn't help staring at the clock, then at the drawer and back again. So many things rested on what that little test would say.

But in my heart of hearts I already knew what the outcome would be. Intuitively I knew I was pregnant. The way my body felt made it pretty obvious. Half an hour later there was all the proof I needed in black and white.

I didn't cry; the thing I remember the most is how calm I was. Maybe it hadn't sunk in, maybe I was so scared I was numb, but whatever the reason, I knew I had to do something – ignoring things would just make everything worse. When I called Robin to tell him I half expected him to demand instantly that I get rid of the baby. But instead he was kind and caring.

'Whatever you want to do, I'll support you,' he said.

In that respect I was very lucky. If I'd been going out with a boy the same age I probably wouldn't have seen him for dust.

'So what *do* you want to do?' he asked me gently.

'I can't have this baby, Robin,' I told him quietly. 'We've got to do something about it.'

I'd never imagined I'd actually find myself pregnant so young, but now I was, there was only one option – an abortion. There was no way I could go through with the pregnancy. All these thoughts were racing through my head; I was barely sixteen and had just joined my sisters in the group. We were in the public eye and had this goody-goody Von Trapp image. There was no way the youngest Nolan could be caught up in a baby scandal.

'It'll kill Mum and Dad,' I panicked. 'And it'll finish the band and destroy my sisters' careers.'

All the pressures other girls in the same situation would feel seemed to be multiplied for me. I didn't just have to worry about what friends and family would think, I had thousands of young girls looking up to me and my sisters, wanting to be just like us. This would ruin everything, and not only for me but for my whole family. Although I was calm in my demeanour I cannot describe that initial feeling of absolute horror. I didn't dare tell anyone, not even one single sister, even though I'd always confided in them up to that moment.

My biggest fear was how I was going to get rid of the baby without anyone finding out. I wasn't allowed to stay at Robin's house and it wasn't like today, when you can have an abortion and be out in three hours. The procedure was much more risky in those days and you were supposed to be in hospital for twenty-four hours. I could have asked a friend to cover for me but I was too frightened of my dirty little secret getting out. I didn't even want to go and see the family doctor, that's how worried I was.

Luckily Robin took control. He found a doctor in Harley Street, said he'd pay for everything and accompanied me to the appointment. The doctor was very kind and not at all judgemental. In fact he was so sweet to me that I stayed with him for years after that. He kept asking me, 'Why don't you tell your mum or dad or one of your sisters?' But like I told him, I just couldn't. I felt such a bloody let-down to them all.

'Are you sure you don't want to think about keeping the baby?' he also asked.

'No, I can't,' I told him, desperation in my voice. As far as I was concerned I'd made up my mind that I was having an abortion. I couldn't even think about changing my mind; there was no choice for me really, as I was convinced the alternative would be so much worse for everyone.

Would my family have understood? I like to think so now, and I'm sure my sisters would have, but my parents . . . I don't know. Mum's Catholic beliefs would have made it very difficult for her to support my decision, even if she'd known having the baby would ruin everything for our family.

The more I thought about it, the more I knew I couldn't confide in anyone – this had to be my decision alone. I wasn't doing it lightly and I knew it was something I could never go back on, but it was the right thing to do. I might have been still a child to everyone else, but I knew I was grown up enough to do the right thing and make this choice.

Within days I was booked in for the procedure at a private hospital in central London. Robin and I concocted a ruse that we were going for a romantic day out. The night before I tossed and turned in bed for hours, terrified of what the morning would bring, but knowing I had to go through with it. And all too soon the light started to filter through the curtains. So, at the crack of dawn, I showered and dressed quietly, then went downstairs to wait for Robin to pick me up. I was careful not to wake anyone, scared they would see the truth on my face as I stood there, no make-up on and my hair scraped back – not exactly making an effort for our romantic day out.

Robin and I barely spoke in the car; there was nothing left to say. I think we both wanted this to be over.

We arrived at the clinic and I was led into a private room. Robin left after hugging and kissing me goodbye – in those days your boyfriend couldn't stay with you. The next time I'd see him it would all be over and our baby would be gone.

Up until then I'd been holding it together, but as soon as I was in that room on my own I started to feel tearful. It didn't help that the TV was on and suddenly our new video for 'Attention to Me' was blaring out. That was the first time I cried. It was a lovely, happy, family song and here I was sitting in a hospital room, unbeknown to my family, waiting to have an abortion. In those days only bad girls got pregnant and I suddenly felt very ashamed. The floodgates opened and I sobbed my heart out. Shame, fear, disappointment, anger . . . I seemed to have every feeling boiling inside me and they were all finally starting to spill out.

My tears were interrupted as the nurse came in with the doctor. He was like my knight in shining armour and seemed so concerned about my welfare. 'Coleen, you don't have to do this if you don't want to,' he told me kindly.

Grabbing a tissue, I blew my nose and shook my head to let him know he couldn't change my mind. *You have no idea, I can't keep this baby*, I thought to myself.

Realizing that I'd made my decision, the doctor began to explain what the procedure entailed. 'So we'll give you an anaesthetic and take you down for the operation,' he said. 'Then when you wake up we'll monitor you until the morning and then we'll let you go.'

'No, I can't stay the night,' I told him. 'I have to get home by this evening.'

Of course he tried to talk me out of it, as there was a risk I could haemorrhage after the operation, but the fear of my family finding out the truth was worse than the fear for my health.

After they'd left, I took off my clothes and put on the theatre gown they'd given me, and then I got into the bed, shaking with fear. When the porter arrived to take me down to theatre my heart was in my mouth. I was absolutely terrified. The only operation I'd ever had was having my appendix out at the age of fourteen. I was a total coward and it was horrible not to have Mum there supporting me. I was frightened to death.

'Don't worry, Coleen,' the doctor told me kindly. 'It'll all be over soon.'

I bit my lip, trying not to cry again, and then I closed my eyes and waited for the anaesthetic to kick in.

When I woke up I forgot where I was for a minute, but slowly it all came flooding back. I felt groggy and disorientated and there was a dull period-like pain in my abdomen. After a little while Robin was allowed in to see me and sat there holding my hand. For an hour or so I drifted in and out of sleep.

I lay there feeling numb. I'd expected relief, but there was nothing, and I didn't cry. It may sound hard, but I'd prepared myself as much as I could and now I was blocking any emotion out. I just wanted to be at home, to be back in my normal, safe life and to ensure that no one ever got wind of what had just gone on.

Around lunchtime I battled the tiredness to get up out of bed and prepare to leave. But when I went to get dressed I panicked. On the way there I'd worn tight trousers and now I was all padded out after the operation. It was like wearing a nappy and there was no way I could squeeze into my trousers.

'What am I going to do?' I asked Robin, my voice shaking. Bless Robin, he ran out immediately and bought me a dress.

By now it was about 2 p.m. and I told the staff I was discharging myself from hospital. I had to sign a disclaimer because I was leaving so early. Leaning on Robin because I was still woozy, I wobbled to the car. He drove me to his house in Virginia Water, where I slept all afternoon. Later he made me dinner and then, when I was feeling a bit better, he drove me home to Ilford.

I think Mum knew something had happened from the moment I walked in the door. The first thing she said was, 'Where did you get that dress from?' I reeled off a story about how I'd spilt something down my trousers while we'd been out and had needed to buy a new dress. But she didn't look very convinced. She was too busy studying my face.

'What's up with you? You're very pale,' she said.

'I don't feel well,' I told her quite truthfully. 'I'm going straight to bed.'

That evening was awful. The anaesthetic had made me feel emotional, and lying in my bed I felt terribly alone. The events of the day just left me sick to the core. I was scared too. I kept thinking: *What if I haemorrhage?*

All night Mum kept coming upstairs and asking if I was all right. I think she just knew there was something more going on than I'd said, but I never told her the truth.

Aborting that baby was a terrible thing to go through with, and now that I have three children I sometimes think wistfully that I could have had a twenty-eight-year-old child by now. Although I never tortured myself with guilt because I could honestly see no alternative, it did make me realize that there was no way I would ever go through that experience again. I'd made one bad mistake, but to do it two or three times, no, that wasn't for me. After that I went straight on the pill.

'You are very lucky that you've just turned sixteen,' the doctor had told me. 'If you'd been fifteen I would have needed your parents' consent.'

Hmmm, it would have been fun trying to get that! My parents never talked to me about sex at all, and when I tried to ask Mum questions she refused to even discuss periods. So it's no surprise that I was brought up thinking sex was bad, and I didn't even really talk about it with my sisters that much. But being so naive taught me a valuable lesson. When it came to my own kids I made sure I always told them everything and actively encouraged them to ask me anything. And they usually do!

Afterwards, with the relief of my abortion out of the way, things got back to normal fairly quickly. While I didn't obsess over my decision to terminate my pregnancy, after that sometimes I just wanted to be on my own – and that's when my beloved Bill came in. Whenever I needed some space I could take him for a walk and get lost in my own thoughts. He was a constant comfort to me and in many ways became the confidant I needed.

But Bill also got me into trouble more than once! Not long afterwards, I had to take him to the vet's. As he was being examined I found myself leaning on the table, suddenly feeling extremely hot and a bit sick. Then, as I went to reception to pay, I suddenly fell backwards, fainting on the spot. Of course, I was happily unconscious and oblivious, but unfortunately for everyone else I was wearing a mini ra-ra skirt, complete with matching knickers! I'm sure someone would have rushed over to help (as well as to stop me flashing), but the second it happened Bill stood over me, growling protectively at anyone who even dared to approach. Thankfully I came round in a few minutes and called home, red-faced.

'Dad, I've fainted at the vet's,' I told him, and I could almost feel him rolling his eyes, thinking, *Not again.*

'Oh, you'd better get a cab home,' he replied.

Not even a lift, I thought. *Bloody charming!*

Although it rarely happens now, my fainting was becoming a regular occurrence back then and I was always passing out. I found out later it was because my blood pressure was low. When I went out with my friends they always thought I was pissed. But any time I was in hot, enclosed spaces it just happened. Once, a few years later, I was out with Brian and his friends when suddenly I slid down the bar. I must have looked such a sight. Although Brian tried to laugh it off, secretly it bothered him and he was really embarrassed by me!

'Coleen, it's not even funny,' he told me – like I'd done it for a joke!

In the end there was a simple solution. If I didn't miss breakfast I wouldn't pass out. And suddenly my phantom fainting episodes were a thing of the past, much to Brian's relief.

Meanwhile life went on as usual, and in February 1982 we released a song called 'Don't Love Too Hard' which got to number 14. The song featured along with 'Chemistry' on our second album of all our own tracks, which was called *Portrait*.

That year I was able to buy my first home – not bad for a seventeen-year-old! I paid for it with the money I'd earned during another tour to Japan. This time we'd taken part in the Tokyo Music Festival, which was like nothing we'd ever experienced before. It was this massive competition where all these amazing international artists were pitted against each other to find a favourite. It was hosted by Perry Como, a very famous American singer and television personality, and the judges were Elvis's ex-wife Priscilla Presley and Sammy Kahn, who wrote hits for Frank Sinatra and Judy Garland. Beforehand each record company threw a party for the judges, to suck up to them. At ours Dad got up to sing and Priscilla loved it! Everyone did. My dad was in his element!

On the day of the competition there were 15,000 people packed into the concert hall at the Budokan arena in Tokyo. There were absolutely loads of acts performing, some we hadn't heard of, who were nevertheless famous in their own countries, and some massive names like Randy Crawford and Les McKeown from the Bay City Rollers. Randy Crawford was a bit of an eye-opener for us – the first time we'd encountered a star with an entourage around her, keeping her at a distance.

After dozens of fantastic artists had stolen the show time and again, suddenly it was our turn. As we walked on to the stage I can remember seeing a sea of faces and completely bricking it. I was much more nervous than usual, as it was such a massive thing and we'd done days of rehearsals and promo interviews leading up to it. We'd decided to sing 'Sexy Music', which wasn't a song I liked that much, but we gave it our all and afterwards received rapturous applause.

Once the final act had finished there was a break for the scoring and then we all had to stand on the stage together to get the results. It was one of those events where pretty much everybody gets something. It seemed like they were giving prizes out for everything – best shiny shoes award, you name it. But as they were going through everybody, we started to panic, thinking: *Oh my God, we haven't won a thing!* Whispers were going round all the group and family, 'Don't cry if we haven't won anything!'

They announced silver and we didn't win. Then gold and that wasn't us either. All that was left was the grand prize and there was no way we'd get that.

Then suddenly the spotlights were moving over us, and Perry announced, 'And the grand prize goes to . . .' It went on for ages, like on *X Factor*, and then suddenly his voice boomed, 'The Nolans!'

Oh my giddy aunt, it was actually us! Well, we screamed like banshees and started jumping all round the stage. It was just phenomenal, really, really amazing. Then we were whisked off to do interviews. The celebrations went on well into the night, and at the party afterwards Stevie Wonder was even there and sang 'Lately' with Linda and Bernie. The whole thing was incredible.

In this country a lot of people have never heard of the Tokyo Music Festival, but it was a very big thing. For us, to go over and win it and be voted for by people we respected was brilliant.

That was the pinnacle of our fame in Japan, and each of us came back from that tour with a royalty cheque for £50,000 for Japanese sales. It gave me the opportunity to put down a deposit on a lovely little house in Hillingdon in Middlesex, and Robin moved in with me.

At the same time, Maureen, Linda and Bernie were buying their own places too, and over the next few months there was a mass exodus from my parents' place in Ilford. Thinking back, that must have been hard for Mum and Dad. They must have felt a bit redundant, with all their children having suddenly flown the nest. Not long afterwards they decided to sell the Ilford house and move back to Waterloo Road in Blackpool.

Although it was amazing that I was able to get on the property ladder at such a young age, despite our success that was really the only time we walked away with a decent wedge of cash. Throughout our music career with CBS we were all on a basic weekly wage. We sold 9.3 million records worldwide but pocketed just £165 a week each. We weren't writing our own songs, so were clearly never going to be millionaires, but to this day I have no idea who got all the money. I think perhaps in our naivety we didn't realize what was happening to our earnings. In the years when we were churning out the hits there would always be limos to take us from A to B and lavish after-show parties. We used to think: *Aren't the record company great, they do all this stuff for us*. But later it transpired that we'd paid for every limo and every party – so not so great after all!

Still, it wasn't a bad life. I loved my house in Hillingdon. It was a lovely little Georgian three-bedroom detached house. To me it seemed massive, when in actual fact it was quite small. It cost £60,000 in 1982 and I had a £25,000 mortgage on it. Someone told me recently that houses in that street were on sale for £360,000.

It's funny now, as I can hardly even remember being that young, and I can't imagine my son Jake, who is sixteen, living alone in a year's time. It was a lot of responsibility for someone aged just seventeen. In many ways I felt like a baby and I was on the phone to Mum and Dad every day. When I got my first bill I was flummoxed. 'What do I do?' I whined to Mum down the phone. 'How do I write a cheque? How do I use a cooker?'

It was a time before all-night telly, and when it used to go off at night that scared me too, I found the silence really eerie and would jump at any little noise. Luckily Maureen, who was twenty-eight, had bought a house just round the corner and was always a ten-minute walk away if I needed her. I used to phone her all the time and we saw each other nearly every day.

I had Robin as well, and he was a brilliant cook. He prepared the majority of our meals. It was mostly traditional fare. He'd rustle up a homemade steak and kidney pie or a cracking Sunday roast. He could make anything, any kind of meal you wanted. We settled into a routine quickly and strangely easily. He was my first love and I was blissfully happy.

Meanwhile *Portrait* did really well, reaching number 7 in the album charts, and when the record label went on to release it in Japan there was an exciting new twist. We'd always had our albums on vinyl before, but that year it became one of the first fifty pop albums ever to be released on compact disc. Back then a CD seemed out of this world in the technology stakes – I don't know what on earth we would have made of an iPod!

However, all the hype about our first ever CD couldn't prepare us for the disappointment our third single from the album brought. Unfortunately the title 'Crashing Down' turned out to be quite ironic, because that's exactly what it did! To our bewilderment it didn't even make the top 75!

After that, towards the end of 1982, Anne decided she wanted to come back to the group to do our Greatest Hits album, *Altogether*. It meant having little Amy on tour too, which we just loved.

For a while Linda's now husband, Brian, was our tour manager, but then we parted company with him. It was just a bit strained, because he was married to Linda and if we had a problem she would understandably take his side and it caused too much stress.

Then when Brian went Linda decided to leave the group

and go solo. With Brian's help she relaunched herself as a solo artist – to our utter bemusement as a busty blonde bombshell. She even did a naked shoot with just a sheet around her and was soon dubbed 'the naughty Nolan'. Ironically it had always been Linda who'd complained that our skirts were too short or our outfits too tight, but it was a canny marketing ploy on Brian's part.

Around the same time I was asked out by a major heart-throb – David Essex. He came to one of our concerts and after-wards invited me for dinner. He was very insistent and said if I was worried I could bring Linda and her husband too. When I asked Robin he was unsurprisingly having none of it! 'Yeah, go if you like,' he scoffed. 'But I won't be here when you get back!'

To be honest I wasn't that keen anyway. I was seventeen and David was in his thirties. I appreciated he was gorgeous-looking but I wasn't sure I actually fancied him. In truth I was just flattered because it was David Essex but it wasn't worth messing things up with Robin for – now he was someone I did find genuinely gorgeous.

By now Robin had penned us another fantastic song called 'Dressed to Kill', and our record company had allowed us an image overhaul. We looked edgier, more grown-up, and it really was a massive change for us. For the cover we were pic-tured all wearing black, and I had a saloon-girl style dress while Bernie had a man's suit jacket and fishnet tights. We had a very Hot Gossip look, with fingerless gloves and wilder hair. Our choreographer had been in Hot Gossip so he made our rou-tines very raunchy – especially compared to our previous shows. It got a very mixed reaction. Some people loved it (and our diehard fans just loved us whatever we did), but some people didn't like it because they thought it was too big a change from our sweet image.

To mark our new style we produced a free poster to give away with the single, which entered the charts at number 35 and looked set to be our biggest hit yet. But then for some reason the industry watchdog IMRB took exception to the poster, claiming it gave us an unfair advantage, so they removed us from the charts. Our new position was a paltry entry at number 95 and the single never recovered.

By then I think we'd all realized that perhaps we'd come to the end of the road. It was becoming harder and harder to have a hit record. That's the thing with music careers. For the majority of people it's over very quickly. It's very rare to have the kind of longevity the likes of Elton John and Rod Stewart have. For most artists your appeal dwindles away all of a sudden and record companies move on. For my sisters and me the reality was that as we were growing up, so were our fans. Our biggest following was in Japan but it was incredibly short-lived. The average age of the kids buying our records over there was twelve to sixteen.

But the great thing about the Nolans was that we could always go back to our roots. When our pop career began to wind down I don't remember any tears or tantrums or big discussions about what we should do. We just naturally reverted to the traditional Nolans formula doing sell-out tours and summer seasons. When it came to those live shows the age of our fans spanned from eight to eighty. We also got approached to do lots of different projects and I think it suited us all.

One of the things we all ended up doing in 1983 was a song called 'Don't Do That', which was a collaboration with Lemmy from Motorhead and Cozy Powell, the famous Rainbow drummer. Linda's husband Brian worked for their record company and he knew Lemmy very well. They thought it would be fun to have two of the world's most heavy rockers collaborating with the supposedly saccharine Nolan sisters. So as they rocked out we did the backing vocals. We had such a laugh doing that song with them. They were wild.

One morning while we were waiting to do another take for the video, Lemmy said, 'Do you need a drink, girls?' and handed us a bottle of vodka.

The thing about Lemmy is that he looked so scary, completely leather-clad in a black jacket, biker boots and hair down to his waist, but actually he was a lovely, incredible, intelligent man. I could happily sit down and talk to him for hours and he always gave good advice. Lemmy always told me he fancied me but it wasn't really a surprise, as he just loved tits!

At this point I was eighteen and still a bit embarrassed by the size of my boobs. I've always been big-chested and first developed breasts when I was about eleven or twelve. I can remember running downstairs and shouting, 'Look, I've got boobs,' to my dad and my brothers.

Brian was mortified. 'Oh Dad, tell her to stop it,' he cringed.

But after my initial wave of excitement they'd kept on growing, and through a lot of my teenage years I was embarrassed. Particularly as all my friends seemed to be flat-chested. By the time I was thirteen I had a right pair. They had kind of been the bane of my life when we were performing, as some of the outfits we wore made them look huge. On stage I'd take my jacket off to reveal a halterneck catsuit underneath and I'd see a man in the front row's eyes almost pop out of his head. It embarrassed me, but Lemmy said I should be proud. 'You've got great tits, you need to show them off more,' he said.

And then he kept hounding me to go for a drink with him! I was still deliriously in love with Robin though, so I'd say,

'Seriously Lemmy, you're just not someone I could bring home to my mother and I have to judge it on that.'

He just laughed and said, 'Oh that's nice!'

Smiling bashfully, my boyfriend Robin placed a little square jewellery box in my hand. It was Christmas 1983 and when I opened it I got quite a start. There was a ring with a diamond on it.

Is Robin asking me to marry him? I thought. But not wanting to be presumptuous, I went to put it on my right hand.

'No, it's an engagement ring,' Robin smiled, confirming my thoughts. Thrilled, I immediately slipped it on to my left hand and grinned at him like a loon.

But looking back now, I don't think it was actually an 'I want to marry you' proposal, I think it was more of a commitment 'Let's get engaged' thing. He was a shy man, Robin, he was never one to stand up and make a big statement. Which is just as well, as about six months later things went completely downhill!

For the first time in our relationship Robin headed off on a different tour, playing for a male three-piece soul band called Imagination. Their biggest hit, 'Body Talk', had got to number 4 in the charts two years earlier. Although Robin phoned me regularly while he was away, I knew something was up the minute he got back. He'd always been kind and loving but now suddenly he had no patience with me. He'd never been like that before. And a couple of weeks later, when we went on a week-long break to Portugal with Maureen and Bernie and their boyfriends, I knew for certain that Robin had changed towards me.

We stayed in a beautiful villa, the weather was gorgeous, and it should have been a brilliant holiday, but the change I sensed in Robin spoiled it for me. That first day, no matter what I put on he'd frown, so I kept going into the other girls' rooms asking to borrow their clothes instead. It seemed like anything that involved me was wrong.

'That looks awful on you,' he'd say. 'You just look really frumpy.'

Staring at my reflection in the mirror I felt understandably upset. I ran my hands over my hips. I had put on a bit of weight recently and was creeping up to a size 14, but I thought it was mean of him to be so blunt about it.

Then one day when we were wandering round the local town I lost my footing on some steps and fell. I grazed my knees and it really hurt. But, feeling embarrassed, I quickly clambered up, half wincing and trying to laugh. Suddenly I realized Robin was giving me a withering look. 'Oh, for fuck's sake,' he muttered, turning away and not even bothering to check if I was OK. I couldn't believe he was so angry.

'Are you serious?' I asked, hobbling after him.

Everything I did clearly just irritated him and it was a relief to get back home.

After that holiday we carried on living and working to-gether but things came to a head when we arrived in Dublin for a show. He'd been sulky and unresponsive for days, and we were in our hotel room not even speaking to each other. Ever since Robin had got back from the Imagination tour, our sex life had dwindled and we weren't really doing it at all – he seemed thoroughly uninterested in me. I knew something was really wrong. So, as I was putting on my make-up, I said to him, 'I don't think you love me any more.'

When I looked in the mirror I could see the reflection of him behind me sitting on the bed, his eyes intently to the floor. He didn't say a word and my stomach churned; his silence spoke volumes. I turned round and asked, 'Do you love me?' But he didn't look at me. Then slowly, still staring at his shoes, he began to speak.

'No, I don't think I do,' he said.

'Oh,' I said. I'm not sure it really sank in.

Then I went into one of the other bedrooms and told the girls really calmly, 'I think me and Robin have just split up.'

A few days later, back at home, Robin admitted he was seeing someone else. When I asked him he just came clean straight away. 'Yeah, I've met this girl and I really like her,' he told me. She was a backing singer on the Imagination tour.

I told him to move out there and then, which he did, and I was left completely devastated. It was my first real heartbreak and at the time I thought I'd never, ever, get over it. When I was alone I cried my heart out, and then I packed his stuff up and phoned him to come and get it. I even gave him the ironing board and iron, telling him bitterly, 'I don't want anything that reminds me of you.'

At first I was distraught and furious but then fear started to creep in. I was going to be living on my own for the first time. It was scary and I knew it would be the start of a lot of 'firsts' for me. Unfortunately after that I had to keep working with Robin. I was determined never to let him see me upset, but it was really difficult getting through that last tour. We'd all go for drinks afterwards but usually I could only manage one before I headed upstairs to cry. It killed me to have to be around him. Every time I spoke to him I played it cool but then later I'd go to my room and sob.

I felt as if I'd had my heart well and truly stamped on. It wasn't the first time and it certainly wouldn't be the last, but like they say, the first cut is the deepest. And the first time someone cheats on you sends you reeling. With it being my first love I totally took him for granted. I thought it would be forever.

My mum was very matter of fact and told me, 'There are plenty more fish in the sea,' but I just wanted to scream at her.

That experience makes me realize that now I have my own kids I will never say, 'Don't worry about it, you'll go through it so many times.' Because that first time really hurts and you don't believe you'll ever get over it.

When we got back from the tour it took me ages to get to grips with the pain. I'd sit at home sobbing with Bill's head on my lap. The whole Robin experience was a learning curve for me, as I had kind of let myself go. When he came home I'd be in a robe, with no make-up, and I had put on a stone and a half since we'd been dating. When you're young you don't think those things make a difference, but now I know that relationships take effort on both sides.

But there were only so many tears I could cry, and after I'd mourned for Robin, my survival instinct began to kick in. I lost weight and was determined to get over him. And ultimately I was vindicated. Robin went out with my replacement for six months but that all ended in tears. Then one day he turned up at the house and asked if he could get what was left of his stuff. But once he'd gathered it all up, I noticed he was lingering by the door.

'Shall we go for dinner?' he said.

I just thought: *Ha, I'm loving this*. So I accepted.

We'd hardly even tucked into the main course when Robin said, 'I've made a big mistake, Coleen. I love you and didn't know what I had. I've changed and I want to marry you.'

I had to turn away because in truth I was giggling like a six-year-old. *I so can't wait to tell the girls about this when I get home*, I thought. But composing myself, I turned to face him. 'You've said you've changed. I don't think you have,' I told him. 'But *I* have changed. Because of what you've done I've grown up and I can't trust you again.'

He looked gutted and I felt secretly smug. It was great for my self-esteem. It's always nice when the man who broke your heart finally realizes what he's lost, but it's also really sad, because why did he have to go and mess it up in the first place? I knew we couldn't go back to the way things were, and finally I was able to move on. We stayed on friendly terms and although he's a very talented man who went on to have an amazing career, to me he's gorgeous Robin, my first love.

Now I was living on my own I'd often journey up to Blackpool with Bill to stay with my parents in Waterloo Road. I still took my beloved dog everywhere with me, and on one occasion at my parents' he literally saved my life. Before I'd gone to bed I'd had a cigarette in my bedroom. And when I'd finished I'd put the butt into an empty carrier bag with the cotton wool I'd used to remove my make-up and dumped it in the waste paper bin in the corner. But just as I drifted into a nice sound sleep Bill decided to lick my face. I flapped him away but then he let out a bark and grabbed my wrist with his mouth. Every time I pushed him off the bed he jumped back up again.

Drowsily, I opened my eyes. In the corner I saw flames creeping up the wall from the bin. Still half-asleep, I thought to myself, *I don't remember there being a coal fire in this room,* before drifting off again. But Bill was getting more and more worked up and woke me up again a few seconds later.

Finally the penny dropped and I realized my room was on fire. I must have still been a bit dazed, though, because I wandered calmly into my dad's room and said, 'Dad, I think my room's on fire.'

'Coleen, are you dreaming?' he asked me, and I replied: 'Yes, my room's on fire.'

So he screeched, 'Jesus!' and jumped out of bed. He ran to the bathroom, dampened a towel and raced to my room, throwing it on the bin and putting the fire out. Dad then turned round to find I'd already got back into bed and gone back to sleep – well . . . I've always been a good sleeper!

The next morning was a different matter, though. I woke up to see that the fire had damaged the wardrobe and burnt the floorboards. If it hadn't been for Bill I could easily have died that night. Some parents would have been furious, but mine were just glad I was OK; they never shouted at me or demanded I pay for the damage. In fact, I just remember Dad saying over and over, 'I can't believe you got back into bed.' He never forgot it.

Thankfully that was my last brush with death – for a few years at least.

By 1984 our career doing pop records had pretty much ended. We weren't with our record label CBS any more; it had been a mutual decision to part company with them and our hit records had stopped. So over the next couple of years we did the odd album, mainly covers. We released a party album called *Girls Just Want to Have Fun* with Towerbell Records, a Christmas party album and *Tenderly*, which featured all our favourite songs from the 1950s. It was full of Sinatra hits and songs of that ilk. All the really nostalgic stuff that had really been our bread and butter when we'd been growing up in Blackpool. Mum and Dad loved it!

The change of direction in our career meant things weren't so hectic any more. We were still doing album promotion, radio interviews and newspaper pieces as well as the cabaret circuit and summer seasons, but that 24/7 pressure wasn't there. But we certainly weren't rich enough to stop working! Personally I was getting to a point where it was just all too much. I thought we'd done enough. As blasé as it seems, I'd had enough of all the glitz and glamour. During those manic years of hit after hit I'd constantly get phone calls saying, 'This tour is coming up,' or 'You've got to do *TOTP*.' Far from being excited, I'd actually think, 'For God's sake, I just want a day off!'

I was probably about nineteen or twenty when the records stopped, and it was a relief. I'd never been ruthlessly ambitious or fame-hungry so I actually didn't mind at all.

After the break-up from Robin I was single for a while, and over that period of time I had two one-night stands. I guess I was trying to be detached, just having sex for the sake of it, and I had mixed experiences. The first guy I slept with I never should have done anything with and I absolutely hated it. He was a tour manager we knew and for both of us it was a drunken fumble, a moment of madness. It was awful, as halfway through I just thought: *Oh God what am I doing? I don't even fancy you!* I think I was trying to convince myself I could be like that, but when it came down to it I didn't like it one bit and I just wanted him to leave.

Then in 1984 we went to Australia on tour. When we visited Tasmania we stayed in a hotel with a beautiful pool and one day Maureen and I were leisurely swimming up and down when two guys appeared. It turned out that they were both marines and one of them was just divine. After smiling at us for a while they came over to chat. I was convinced the gorgeous guy would fancy Maureen – she was the one everyone fancied. But when they got in the pool and starting laughing and messing around with us, it turned out the best one really fancied me!

We invited them to our show that evening and that night I took my gorgeous guy back to my room! We had a very quick and passionate romp – he just came to the room, we got down to it and then he left! This time I had no regrets at all, as it was marvellous! Because he was a marine he was really fit and his body was amazing.

In those days I'd never even heard about HIV, and the only thing girls worried about was getting pregnant. Because I was on the pill I assumed I didn't need to worry. How different things are now!

The next day I was grinning from ear to ear and my sisters were all horrified, in an envious kind of way. 'Coleen Nolan, that's disgusting,' they said. 'What was he like?'

My hunky marine did write to me when I got home but I never replied. What was the point? He lived in Oz and that was the end of my short venture into the land of one-night stands. Instead I set my sights on a drummer in our new Nolans band, a guy called Stewart.

It's funny, because he didn't exactly make a good first impression. When he first joined we nearly fired him after three days. He seemed weird, coming out with these odd off-the-wall comments, and quoting obscure lyrics from Frank Zappa, but gradually his weirdness became funny and he had me. Like most girls I found funniness very attractive. It was a good job really, as Stewart wasn't classically handsome, being very tall and skinny with dark hair.

Stewart was a great musician, but it's hard going out with a drummer because in my experience they can never stay still. They're always tapping their feet or rapping their fingers on tables. It drove me mad! But even worse, he wouldn't buy a T-shirt without his mum approving and when he went to look for a flat his parents had to come. It was nice that he loved his mum and dad so much and they were completely lovely. But it annoyed me that at twenty-three he wasn't more independent.

Stewart was generally very easy-going and kind, but I think a lot of the appeal was that our relationship was just easy. I fell into the same pattern as with Robin. He moved in and we got to see a lot of each other on tour. We did have some good times and as well as being funny he could be very thoughtful, always making an effort with birthdays or special occasions. But in my heart I suspected he wasn't the right man for me yet I ignored that inner voice and convinced myself I was in love with him.

After about two years it became obvious things weren't right between us. Having been so hurt by the break up with Robin, I now had the same sinking feeling that Stewart was falling out of love with me. It was incredibly painful. I was sure there must be something wrong with me. It was starting to turn me into a nervous wreck.

Inevitably Stewart called it a day in the middle of a week when we were on a cabaret tour. 'I'm not sure what I want,' he said. 'Maybe we should separate for a while.'

I nodded.

'Do you want me to leave the band?' he offered.

'No,' I replied. 'Don't worry about it. If it gets too hard I'll let you know.'

My pride stopped me from showing him how upset I really was, and he may have thought I really was okay with the split. I wasn't though, and it was about to get worse. Stewart had always got on really well with Bernie. She used to come and stay at mine a lot and I'd leave them downstairs chatting about Frank Zappa, who they both liked. They were always laughing at each other, and she would parrot off all the same stupid quotes.

On tour after our sound checks, and before the main performance, we'd go for dinner, just us girls, and leave the band
to jam or whatever they wanted to do. Now I noticed that
Bernie wanted to stay behind to listen to the band all the time.
Was my ex-boyfriend attracted to my sister? Bernie was exuberant, funny and a real party animal. *Is that what Stewart likes
about her?* I wondered. *Am I boring in comparison, as I don't drink
much?*

Watching them together became too much for me so I
called Stewart aside.

'You know how I said if it got too hard you'd have to leave?
Well, that moment is now. I don't want you to work with us
any more.'

Then he went down to the bar and told the others, 'Your
sister has just fired me!'

Thankfully Stewart did leave and then, when the tour was
over, quickly moved his stuff out, and I was able to avoid Bernie
for a good few weeks. Again I sat at home crying into Bill's fur.
'You're the only man I need,' I told him tearfully.

Thankfully when I rejoined my sisters for a summer season
at Bournemouth International Centre we had a different
drummer. But I was left reeling when just a few days later Maureen came up to me with a concerned look on her face. 'I need
to tell you something,' she told me, pulling me into a dressing
room. 'Bernie is seeing Stewart.'

I know we'd split up but that still hurt. But just like with
Robin, I didn't burst into tears or rant and rave. I think that's
often my problem – I never get that rage out. Inside I was so
wounded. It felt like such a betrayal. I remember thinking, 'I
must speak to Mum and Dad about it.' But when I did call
them it turned out that Bernie had spent the night before sobbing in their arms, telling them how awful she felt because he

was my ex-boyfriend, but that she just couldn't help her feelings for Stewart.

'Bernie is so upset,' Mum told me. 'She's devastated.'

I'm sure she was but Mum seemed to think that because I wasn't bawling and crying I wasn't bothered, which hurt me even more. All I wanted was for my mum to give me some sympathy too.

However, one good thing came out of the whole sorry business. When Maureen told me about Stewart and Bernie, every single feeling I'd had for him disappeared. I couldn't even be bothered to discuss it with him or Bernie. Instead, the very next day I went into the dressing room where she sat quietly, waiting for my reaction. I walked over like nothing had happened and said, 'Can I borrow your blusher?' She nodded dumbly, clearly surprised.

I kind of wanted to mess their heads up by appearing unaffected but it was hard not to say anything. Stewart came to Bournemouth to see Bernie in one of our shows and when I heard, I said, 'You are joking me!' But no, there he was, watching in the wings like butter wouldn't melt and Bernie gazing adoringly at him. At that moment I could happily have pushed her off the stage!

The first time Bernie and I spoke about Stewart was actually eight weeks later in September, when we went on a six-week tour to Russia and we ended up sitting next to each other on the plane. As we buckled in ready for take-off I said to her really sweetly, 'So how are you and Stewart getting on?' She nearly spat her drink out.

It was odd, because after that she'd always come to me to talk about their relationship while I'd be looking at her thinking: *I know! I've been there, done that, got the T-shirt!*

Four

'All right, gels!' said a young guy, with shoulder-length dark hair and a Cockney accent. 'You seen Dave?'

It was the summer of 1986 and Maureen and I had been in the middle of a cuppa in the canteen at Bournemouth International Centre when he'd come in, his blue eyes clearly scouring the room for someone. I'd immediately sat up and taken notice. He was gorgeous.

We assumed Dave to be a comic called Dave Wolfe, who was also playing at the BIC, and pointed him in the direction of the bar. Maureen and I watched silently as he headed off.

'Who was that?' she asked.

'I have no idea,' I replied, smiling. 'But I need to go into the bar to find out!'

So as good as my word, I washed down my tea and headed off to find Dave and his mysterious friend. I found them in the bar nursing bottles of Bud.

'This is Shane Richie,' said Dave, introducing us. 'He's a comedian too.' It turned out that Shane, who told me his real name was Shane Roche, was performing upstairs in the little cabaret room. The three of us talked for ages and I totally warmed to Shane. He was dead chatty and nice. Really funny and full of life.

We discovered we'd actually already met, five months earlier. 'I supported you last February,' Shane told me. 'At the Orchard in Dartford.' Embarrassingly, I really couldn't remember. But I knew I was interested, so that night I nagged my sisters to throw an impromptu party at the lavish house we'd rented for the summer.

'Let's have a do and I can invite him!' I pleaded.

My plan worked perfectly. Shane rocked up with Dave in tow and the two of us were soon laughing, joking and flirting outrageously. He came back to ours the second night too, and that was the first time we kissed, as we sat chatting together on the sofa.

That first kiss just blew me away. After that I was just feverish for Shane. I had an overwhelming feeling that this was the real deal, and my romances with Robin and Stewart immediately paled in comparison. Shane wasn't like anyone I'd met before. He was a year older than me almost to the day, and loud and funny and not at all shy. He made everyone laugh and he was great on stage. I'd already sneaked upstairs to see his show in the cabaret room. It involved topless dancers and was a bit naff, if I'm being honest, but he was very funny in it and I could see he was a very talented performer.

The day after our kiss I was walking on air and very excited, as Shane had asked me to meet him for lunch. As I gushed to Maureen, I noticed that my brother Brian, who was visiting, was really quiet. I was flapping, shrieking, 'Oh God, what am I going to wear?' when Brian took me aside. 'I've got something to tell you,' he said. 'Shane's engaged.'

Well, my heart just sank. The night before I'd asked him if he was seeing someone and he'd said, 'No'. How could he lead me down the garden path like that? I was absolutely gutted. Maureen looked at me sadly as I threw the skirt I'd had in my hands down on the floor with frustration. 'What are you going to do?' she asked.

So with a heavy heart I decided I'd still go and meet him at the BIC centre. When I walked in my stomach churned. There was Shane sitting with Dave. He just looked so handsome. While Dave was there I tried my hardest to pretend I was dead happy, but it didn't fool Shane. As soon as Dave left he said, 'What's up with you?'

'You tell me,' I replied, raising my eyebrows.

Shane looked at me blankly.

'You probably do know what's up with me,' I continued, as his face grew more and more concerned. 'Are you engaged?' I finally asked.

'Yes, but it's over!' he told me, sheepishly. 'I just haven't got round to telling her yet.'

'That's fine,' I chirped. 'We'll just be friends then!' I wanted to be principled, because I knew all too well what it was like when someone else made a play for your boyfriend. But it's hard when you really, really like someone. I kept looking at Shane's lips longingly, desperately wanting to relive the kiss from the night before. I wanted to stick to my principles but I wasn't sure I had the self-control.

Shane and I went for a stroll around Bournemouth while he tried his hardest to win me round. 'So you're not going to go out with me then?' he asked with a twinkle in his eye.

I shook my head, trying my hardest to pout even though I desperately wanted to smile. But then Shane dropped to his knees in the middle of the street. 'Pleeeease go out with me,' he howled, as two old ladies passing by turned to look, clearly wondering what all the commotion was about.

Later we sat down and he told me about his girlfriend. She

was a dancer and he'd met her working in Jersey two years earlier.

'She's not done anything wrong,' he insisted. 'I get on really well with her mum and dad and the reason I can't finish it yet is that I don't want to fall out with them. I want to let her down gently.'

It seemed like a valid explanation and because I liked Shane I was prepared to be patient. We saw each other every day after that and two weeks later we slept together for the first time. It was as electric as our first kiss. I kept having to pinch myself actually. Here was a guy who ticked all the boxes – he was funny, gorgeous, outgoing, talented . . . I just couldn't get enough of him! Eight weeks later we were in a full-blown relationship.

Every night I'd finish our show and then dash upstairs to watch Shane performing at 10 p.m. He'd even met my parents and they liked him straight away. They came down to Bournemouth and from the day he met my mum he used to call her Fag Ash Lil – she always found it funny. But Shane still hadn't done the deed with his fiancée! She used to call him on the backstage phone every night. I'd hear him chatting away. He'd put his hand over the receiver, roll his eyes, and mouth 'Sorry' at me.

Now I'd be like, 'You are joking me, right!' But he was so attentive and romantic that I was totally smitten. Eventually someone told his girlfriend what was going on and she called up to say, 'I know. I'm coming over.' He looked terrified at the prospect, so I said, 'Well, maybe that's not a bad thing, you will have to end it with her now.'

She came over pretty much on the last day of the season and he spent all sodding day with her. When I huffily asked why he'd felt the need to spend hours with her, he told me, 'But there's only one ferry back to Jersey. She was upset – I couldn't leave her stuck in Bournemouth all day, could I?'

I found out he'd finally broken up with his fiancée via my niece Amy – who was about six or seven at the time. She came running up, breathless. 'Aunty Coleen,' she gasped. 'Shane told me to give you a message. He says he's all yours.'

About bloody time!

Still, I was thankful to finally have Shane to myself. And once we were officially together it was time to meet Shane's parents. His mum, Lil, was a great shock when I first met her, as was Harry, his dad. They were both very Irish, with strong Dublin accents and lots of dirty language – every second word was effing. His mum had bleached blonde hair and turned up in a denim miniskirt and trainers and slouch socks. 'Bejesus, you're f***ing lovely,' she blurted out. Her swearing was never used offensively, it was just part of her language. I'm sure she would have spoken to the Queen like that too.

Harry was a big heavy-set man with jet-black hair; he looked almost Romany. He was a heavy drinker then, and I knew Shane had issues with his dad from his childhood, but he actually doesn't drink now, as he later had to have a kidney and liver transplant. Harry was really friendly; he made people laugh and he'd get you in a big bear hug. He was very different from Shane, who didn't drink a lot. I think at the time it disappointed Harry that Shane wasn't a real man's man, going to the pub all the time.

Even so, they were real salt of the earth people. And wherever Lil was, her sister Aunty Mary was never far behind – they were always together. She had a softness about her, she was romantic and really reminded me of Debbie Harry looks-wise.

So, after meeting the family and with the season now over we headed back to Hillingdon, and following tradition, Shane moved in. It's funny, after all he'd put me through, leaving me fuming while he whispered sweet nothings to his fiancée down the phone for eight weeks, he was incredibly jealous that I'd had ex-boyfriends living there with me previously.

'I'm not sure I can live here, because you've lived here with someone else,' he told me on numerous occasions.

Not long after Shane moved in the Russia tour came up. The prospect of leaving my boyfriend to go on tour for six weeks was very depressing, and even though it was an incredible country to see I was constantly counting down the days until I'd get to see Shane again. At that time it was really hard to phone home, so it was horrible. I missed Shane like mad. I wrote him a letter every day for six weeks, forty-two letters in all – which I know he kept for many years. That was our first big test and, if anything, it made us stronger.

Russia was very beautiful, with amazing architecture, and the concert halls were just stunning. Probably the best we've ever been in. But the food out there was terrible. Russia was a Communist regime at the time and we'd see queues everywhere, people lining up on the street to buy milk and bread. We lived on a diet of hard-boiled eggs, bread, cheese and tomatoes and bottles of Coke. We could get black tea but no milk. We all got tummy upsets and our bass player even got dysentery, but we battled on.

We'd have a party in one person's bedroom every night and we'd always name that room after an English pub, so if it was in Bernie's room it would be the Red Lion or if it was in Maureen's it would be the Crown. I can remember one night a bloke from the hotel told us we were making too much noise but we carried on partying regardless. Ten minutes later he came back with a guard carrying a gun. 'Bed now!' he demanded and we all scarpered!

When we arrived back in the UK Shane was there at the airport to meet me. He arrived wearing a big Russian hat, which I just loved, and he drove Bernie, Maureen and me back to mine and cooked us a proper British fry-up. I cried with relief when he served it. I'd hated the food in Russia!

Shane had a surprise for me too – he'd totally redecorated the bedroom because he hadn't been able to relax with the thought of two guys there before him. He'd painted it all and got new matching curtains, canopies over the bed, and bed-linen. He described it as peach, but it was actually orange! But anyway he was happy, and I loved what he'd done too.

Everything was great after that. I was absolutely besotted, and Shane was very romantic. He would shower me with flowers for no reason, and every time he went out the door he'd leave a little note saying, 'Just gone to the shop but I miss you,' or 'I love you!' We made each other laugh a lot. Everything was great.

I had my first Christmas away from my family that year. We stayed at my little house in Hillingdon and I very ambitiously announced that I would be cooking us a Christmas spread fit for a king. Everyone was in Blackpool and I was worried I might cry, but I didn't – I was too busy flapping! In actual fact I spent most of Christmas Day panicking in the kitchen and on the phone to my mother.

'How often do I baste the turkey?' I'd ask frantically one minute.

'How do I make the gravy?' I'd shout down the phone ten minutes later, precariously trying to strain the sprouts with my other hand. I was worried Shane would hate my efforts but in the end it was great.

'Mmm,' he said instead in an exaggerated fashion as I served up. 'Something smells *amazing*.'

I'd gone completely overboard when it came to the food. I'd prepared a starter and dessert as well as the roast. In actual fact I'd cooked enough food to feed about thirty homeless people, but Shane didn't say a word. Well, not until I carved the turkey and it gave birth – I'd left the giblets in. It was hysterical.

When I look back now I can't help thinking I was a bit like a little girl playing house. I'd done everything just like I knew Mum would be doing up in Blackpool. The table was all Christmassy, with a red and white tablecloth and a Christmas centrepiece of holly and candles. I'd put a Christmas album on and the room was illuminated by candlelight and the lights from our tree. Afterwards we smooched to Christmas songs and it was all very romantic.

Shane got me an amazing present too – he surprised me on Christmas Eve with an eight-week-old Maltese terrier, which I'd always wanted. He carried in this little furball, which he placed in my hands, and it was love at first sight. We called the new puppy Tyson after the boxer, who'd just won his first fight. At this stage I still had my old dog Bill, who thankfully also loved Tyson. At first he gave him a little growl and snap to let him know who was boss but after that they were as thick as thieves.

But poor old Bill, he didn't last long after that. He started to have strokes and then one day he ate through his own testicles. We came downstairs one day and they'd just gone. When I called the vet's I just couldn't say the word testicles on the phone. 'His, you know, bits have gone,' I told them and I was instructed to bring him in. Thankfully, apart from voluntarily castrating himself, Bill was OK.

But after that Shane refused to let him sleep in the bedroom any more. 'He's eaten his own knackers,' he said. 'Next time he might go after mine!'

In the end Bill got really incontinent and confused and I had to have him put down. I was heartbroken. It was just the saddest day for me. I felt like Bill had lived my life with me. He'd been through all my break-ups, and as silly as it sounds, I used to chat to him about stuff. I was devastated and so were my family. Having Tyson helped to ease the pain a little but I needed Shane a lot at that time.

Right from the first moment I'd met Shane I'd known I felt differently about him. I really believed he was 'the One'. But although I'd done everything career-wise, had my own house and had gone head first into a very whirlwind and serious relationship by the grand old age of twenty-one, I was still very young. I wasn't at all cynical – I let myself get swept up in love. But I also remember having this gut feeling that one day Shane could slip through my fingers. 'I don't think I'll have Shane for ever,' I said to Maureen.

It was just the way he was. He was full of ambition and really wanted to be famous. He gave his career one hundred per cent but I'd never had that burning ambition. Being in the business, I'd seen what it had done to other people's relationships. Being famous changed people and I was worried I could get left behind. But when I told Maureen she just said, 'Shut up!' At that point no one believed we wouldn't stand the test of time because we just got on brilliantly.

During the summer season of 1987, when I was twenty-two, my sisters and I played Blackpool while Shane was doing Weymouth. I hardly saw him for months and it was hard. We'd literally talk on the phone about twenty times a day.

Despite missing Shane I was having lots of fun too. I was living with Maureen and after the show everyone would pile back to ours for a party. We'd stay up all night and sleep all day. I did like a drink then! How ironic that the following summer the pair of us would be heavily pregnant and barely able to perform, let alone party.

Spending weeks apart meant there needed to be a big trust element between Shane and me, but even then I can remember hearing rumours. Everyone had a link in those summer shows, so gossip was always rife. The dancers in our show and the ones working in Weymouth with Shane would probably have worked together in the past, ensuring that tittle-tattle would filter back in dribs and drabs. And that year Shane was being linked to a dancer in his show.

'I think there might be something going on,' someone had said, but to be honest I just dismissed it. We were in the business of rumours and I'd been in the industry long enough to know it is the biggest for gossip. If you weren't seeing someone then you were gay and if you even looked at a member of the opposite sex then you were sleeping with them. The amount of things we'd hear – farcical stuff about ourselves. 'The Nolans sleep with all their crew' was one of our favourites. Our lot would laugh at that and say, 'If only.'

So for that reason I wasn't about to pay attention to hearsay, and I consoled myself with the knowledge that Shane and I were mad about each other. Plus I'd seen this dancer. He used to show me pictures of everyone partying after the show and there were a couple of him and this girl. They probably did flirt and fancy each other, but then I liked a flirt too. I always flirt with anything male. I don't think there's any harm in it as long as you know where the line is, so any Chinese whispers about Shane I was going to take with a big pinch of salt.

Once the season was over we went back to our little house in Hillingdon and all the rumours were immediately forgotten.

We were blissfully happy, just a young couple hopelessly in love. That Christmas we told my family we wanted to stay at home again. But then we actually surprised them on Christmas Eve by turning up at Denise's in Blackpool.

It was all Shane's idea. He was close to his family, but there was just him, his mum and dad and his brother Dean and they didn't celebrate like we did. Their Christmas revolved around the telly, whereas Christmas Day was always a big deal in our family so Shane was happy to spend it with me.

'Let's go up and surprise them,' he suggested.

I thought it was brilliant and it worked a treat. I can still remember walking into Denise's front room and everyone just glancing round and screaming with delight. Everyone jumped up and hugged us. It was great. But not long after we arrived Shane looked at me with horror on his face.

'Oh my God, I've forgotten your present,' he said. He seemed really upset. 'I can't believe it,' he kept adding. 'How can I have been so stupid?'

'Don't worry, it's fine!' I told him. 'We can get it when we get home.'

On Christmas morning we were all sat in the front room when Shane suddenly asked, 'Can I just put this video on?'

Oh Lord, I thought. *My family are going to hate him.* We were all telly addicts but Christmas was the one time the telly never went on. But before anyone could say anything he'd pushed the video into the recorder and pressed play. I sat there cringing as all my family looked on expectantly. Suddenly Shane appeared on screen stood outside our house. I looked at him confused, wondering what on earth was going on. 'Merry Christmas, Coleen!' the on-screen Shane chirped. 'Sorry I didn't bring your present but I couldn't wrap it.' Then the camera zoomed out and there he was next to a blue Ford

Sierra. My family were all grinning and at that moment I knew that they were in on it.

My family adored him. You couldn't not adore him! He was just so friendly with everyone and so generous. He was a real extrovert and the life and soul of the party, and they saw he was mad about me and I was mad about him. And they realized we were serious when we got engaged.

Lots of people have huge, planned, romantic proposals – ours was nothing like that! It was pretty much a spontaneous thing over a McDonald's meal during a shopping trip in Uxbridge. We weren't buying anything in particular, we were just browsing, and I remember looking in a jeweller's window and pointing to a little solitaire ring. 'That's nice,' I commented. Later we were sitting on a bench eating burgers and chips when Shane turned to me.

'Do you want to get engaged or what?' he said.

'Yeah, all right then!' I replied.

Whoever said romance is dead? So when we'd finished our McDonald's we went and bought the ring. It was gold with a tiny little diamond in the middle and cost £160. We both liked it, and while it was not the most expensive piece of jewellery in the world, it was all about what it stood for. I was absolutely delighted and couldn't wait to tell everyone.

When we got home the first person I called was Maureen, who was thrilled. After that everyone kept asking, 'So when are you going to get married?' and I realized I hadn't even thought that far yet! And I didn't think of it again for quite a while, because soon we had a lot more on our minds . . .

In March 1988 I discovered I was pregnant! We weren't using precautions and simply thought, 'If it happens, it happens.' We weren't in a rush. This time round there was no doubt in my mind about having the baby – it was a lovely surprise and I felt very happy. We were in a serious relationship and knew what we were doing.

I'd previously told Shane I suspected I might be pregnant, but as he was on tour with Cannon and Ball I did the test by myself. When it came back positive I literally whooped to myself and immediately called Shane to tell him. Cannon and Ball were the first people to share our happy news. Like me Shane was so ecstatic, he really was walking on air. We both were.

After I'd broken the news to Shane I headed to Greenford in Middlesex, where my sister Denise lived with her boyfriend Tom, a drummer whom she'd met at the London Rooms, where he was part of the resident band. Maureen was there too and my Aunty Theresa, so I took a deep breath and told them all. They looked at me a bit stunned but were ultimately thrilled.

But then my Aunty Theresa said, 'Oh Jesus, I don't envy you telling your mum and dad.'

Obviously Shane and I weren't married, and although people in the family knew we lived together, I'd be the first daughter to have a baby out of wedlock. Not that I cared what anyone thought, we were blissfully happy and that was all that mattered. So taking another big lungful of air I dialled my parents' number in Blackpool. It was Dad who answered the phone and I decided I wouldn't give him any opportunity to see my pregnancy in a negative light. 'I've got something to tell you, Dad,' I said. 'I've got some very good news that I'm very excited about. I'm pregnant!'

God love him, he was fine. 'Well, as long as you're happy, love, I'm absolutely delighted,' he told me.

It turned out Mum was at bingo, so Dad asked if I wanted her to call me or for him to break the news. I decided it might be best coming from him – and judging by her reaction I think that was the right choice! Apparently she cried and was dead upset. She was very religious, my mum, and it had taken her a while to get her head round us living in sin, let alone having a baby!

It's funny, because although my dad was the strict one when I was a child, it was him I preferred to tell things to in adult life. Mum was the one who didn't handle things as well and got upset if things weren't done 'the right way'. One of the first things she said to me was, 'So you'll be getting married then?'

'One day,' I agreed.

But there was no way it would be happening before my baby was born. *I'm not marrying him because I'm pregnant or walking down the aisle with a big fat belly*, I thought to myself. I hated the fact that everyone would assume it was a shotgun wedding even if it wasn't. The wedding would have to wait.

I needn't have worried. Soon there was another 'scandal' rocking the Nolan family. Five weeks later Maureen found out she too was pregnant. That was a big mistake! At the time none of us even knew she had a boyfriend, and she'd only been seeing Ritchie for two or three months.

I thought it was a fantastic thing for her. She was thirty-four and had always wanted kids, and when her previous relationship of eight years had come to an end I'm sure she was fearful it would never happen. Of course she thought she'd like to be married first, but I kind of felt like this was God's way of saying, 'Jesus! Just get this girl pregnant!' Terrified of our parents' reaction, she made me call them up. It was Dad who answered again.

'I've got some more news for you,' I told him.

'Well, you can't be pregnant again,' he laughed.

'No, *I'm* not . . .' I hinted.

'God, who's pregnant now?' he exclaimed.

'Maureen!' I finally revealed, filling him in. Dad was speechless and went off to break the news to Mum – who no doubt cried once more for her fallen daughters.

She wasn't the only one who was less than approving. Of course for the general public it was a massive shock, and it was in all the papers at the time. I can recall Jim Bowing writing a double page spread about how we should be ashamed of ourselves, had a moral obligation to young girls and were a terrible example. I just thought, 'Oh, shut up!' But yes, the terrible Nolan sisters were bringing much disgrace to their family. We weren't supposed to know how to spell 'sex', let alone be having it out of wedlock! However, it was quite obvious we were!

Shane was also a bit annoyed that all the focus was on the 'Nolan sisters' being pregnant. In the early days I was better known than him and I think it grated a bit. When we'd first got together there'd been a headline in the *News of the World* that said, 'Nolan's lover is hen party stripper.' It wasn't true, he only compèred them, but what wound him up the most was being branded 'Nolan's lover'!

'One day that'll be my name before yours,' he told me.

Shane needn't have worried; he was getting famous. He'd done telly with a few summertime and seaside specials and one *Live from the Palladium*. His profile was getting bigger but he was yet to be a household name.

Anyway, I had other things to think about – a craving for rice pudding first and foremost. I just couldn't get enough of it while I was pregnant. Then a couple of months in I discovered I was bleeding. I immediately went to the doctor.

'All you can do is go home and rest,' he told me. 'If the

bleeding continues for the next twenty-four hours then you may be having a miscarriage.'

I was really worried and went home to bed, too frightened to move. But thankfully the bleeding stopped and I made it to full term.

About three months into my pregnancy, a sheepish Bernie confided in me that she was having a hard time with Stewart. It had lasted for about two years on and off but now everything was going wrong. She'd cry on my shoulder, telling me all their problems and asking, 'What am I going to do?'

Then Stewart even had the cheek to call me up and say he'd chosen the wrong sister. I felt like vomiting when I heard that, but I thought if I tell her it looks like I'm bragging. So I spoke to Anne and said, 'I'd rather you told her.' But when Anne told Bernie she just said meekly, 'He probably does miss her.' I've never heard from him since.

Because I was expecting my first baby at the same time as Maureen, it meant we could constantly compare notes, which was great. Neither of us found out the sex of our babies. We wanted it to be a surprise anyway, but twenty years ago things weren't as straightforward as they are now – there was a lot more guesswork involved.

We both had good pregnancies, which was a relief, but knowing what Anne had gone through previously did make me nervous. And I remember even discussing Anne with my old doctor on Harley Street. I actually wanted him to deliver my baby but he talked me out of going private. He told me, 'At the end of the day you're having a baby. Why pay £15,000 when the treatment and outcome will be the same?' So in the end I opted for the nearby Hillingdon Hospital.

Our baby seemed to be in no hurry to enter the world, so when I was ten days overdue I was induced. From the first twinge to my baby arriving it was fifty hours, so I kept going into hospital and being sent home. After each false alarm I'd come back with a McDonald's meal. Mum and Dad were staying with us and would eye me, bemused.

'For God's sake, stop going out and getting takeaway,' Mum laughed. 'Just go and have a baby!'

Well, he eventually arrived at 11.20 a.m. on 2 December 1988. I loved giving birth, which is an odd thing to say, as if you'd heard me screeching and hollering and demanding gas and air you wouldn't have believed me! But I just felt so proud that I'd done it, because I'm usually such a coward.

Mum had previously told me, 'I don't want to be near you when you have a baby!' She knew what a wimp I was. I'd walk into the doctors' surgery for an injection and faint! But on the day I felt like the first woman in the world to have a baby. It was amazing.

Shane was frantic when I went into labour, as he had a gig, and he desperately started calling round until he found another comic to take his place. I kept winding him up, saying, 'But you missed the conception, why be there for the birth?'

As my contractions got stronger and stronger he was supportive in his own way. Typically he was cracking jokes and flirting with all the nurses and had them in stitches. It amused me up to a point, but then I thought: *OK, shut up now, I feel like I'm going to die, so let me die in peace.*

But then with one last, agonizing push, suddenly our baby was here. 'It's a boy!' the nurses told me, passing me my baby to hold for the first time. I was immediately struck by how tiny he was. And he was the ugliest-looking thing! He had really spiky jet-black hair that looked like I'd gelled it. He actually looked a bit Japanese, and it did cross my mind that Shane might question what exactly I'd been doing on tour in Japan! *What a funny-looking creature*, I thought, but I loved him instantly. Later, when I wrote my first impressions in his baby book, I put: 'You looked like a cross between ET and Gandhi.'

People do lie when babies are born. When Maureen gave birth to her son Danny five weeks later, I can remember Anne saying to me, 'Wait till you see Danny, he's absolutely beautiful!' Well, when I got there and went over and peered in the Moses basket at my new nephew, 'beautiful' was not a word that sprang to mind. He actually looked like a little piglet with an upturned nose and baggy eyes.

I turned to Maureen and said, 'Nice basket!'

'He's beautiful,' someone else cooed.

'No,' I replied. 'Stop lying. He's not beautiful and neither was Shane!'

Before Maureen had given birth she'd asked me what to expect, so I'd gushed about it being fantastic and 'the best thing I'd ever done'.

'You lying bitch,' she chastised me after it was her turn. 'It was absolutely horrendous.'

Compared to me, Maureen had had a terrible time. She had twenty-two hours of really heavy labour and was vomiting all the way through. She kept saying, 'I think I need a caesarean,' only to be told, 'No, no, it's fine.' Then Danny went into distress and she had to have an emergency caesarean. She didn't even get the chance to say goodbye to Ritchie. Her and Anne's experiences made me realize how easy I actually had it with my first-born.

On the day our son was born it was lovely to see Shane being such a proud dad. He couldn't stop looking at his boy and just looked completely made up. He didn't break down in front of me, but later he admitted that he'd gone out to the car and cried.

Mum, Bernie, Lil and Aunty Mary were all in the waiting room eating fish and chips. And as soon as my labour was over they all piled in. I was all woozy and happy. I couldn't get over it! *Look what I did*, I thought. *I've just done that!* I felt really proud of myself. Then I looked at my mum and thought: *She did this eight times with no anaesthetic! Mental!*

After a lot of deliberation we decided to name our son Shane after his dad. It was my idea, as it's a tradition in my family – my father was Tommy, so that was the name of my eldest brother, and Maureen was named after my mum. My brother Tommy has a little Tommy now too – it all gets a bit confusing!

While I was thinking of traditional names, Shane wanted to be modern and revealed he liked the names Blue or River. I nearly choked on my ham sarnie when he blurted that one out. I was horrified. Can you imagine either of those names with the surname Roche? There was no way I was agreeing to that – one sounds like a fish and one like a song. Even worse, if we'd had a girl he wanted to call her Mercedes or Paris – thank God that never happened. I used to wind him up, saying, 'If it's twins shall we call them Rolls and Royce!'

Shane always wanted to be different but I wasn't about to be swayed. I pointed out that our child would be going to a normal school, and when I was a kid having an unusual name had made me a target for bullies. 'You're called Colin! Euggh, that's a boy's name,' kids used to sneer at me. It drove me up the wall. No matter how thick-skinned you are, kids are cruel.

Coming up with ridiculous names may be the bloody trendy celebrity thing to do but I don't agree with it. You may want your kids to stand out, but with a daft name they will stand out for all the wrong reasons. So I put my foot down and told Shane our son wasn't being named Blue or River. 'I want to call him Shane after you,' I announced. Well, Shane liked that and relented – but my brother didn't.

'It sounds like an Alsatian,' he said.

But you can't please everyone, can you? Once you call them something you can't imagine them being called anything else. Maybe now, at twenty, Shane Jnr would love a name like Blue or River?

Our son's first Christmas came twenty-three days after he was born and we bought him so many presents! I gave him his last feed at 11 p.m. on Christmas Day but at 1 p.m. on Boxing Day he was still asleep. I called my parents in a panic and Dad answered the phone. 'Don't worry, he'll wake up as soon as he's hungry,' he said. He still sleeps like that now.

When he did eventually wake up he gulped the bottle down and then projectile-vomited all over the Christmas tree. It was like a scene from *Alien*. So I called my parents up again. 'It's because he was hungry and gulped it down too fast!' Dad said. 'Stop worrying!'

I decided immediately that I wouldn't breastfeed him. I made that definite decision that it would be a bottle and a dummy, as soon as he came out. I knew we'd be back performing that summer and it was too much. I never had that instinct to breastfeed. All of it put me off. But midwives still constantly rammed it down my throat. I had friends who were breastfeeding. But it turns out I was the only one that Mum breastfed.

I'd been doing the practical side since the day he was born. I'd pop up to Blackpool whenever I could, as there were more than enough people willing to help out. Mum was so devoted. She was so calm with both the boys – you could just hand her them. This was a woman who'd had eight kids and she always had old wives' tales.

'If he's teething put a bit of whisky on his gums or put a bit of sugar in his bottle to fill him up,' she advised.

'No, I'd like him to have teeth!' I said.

It amazed me that from the time she'd had us, times had changed so massively. I had no concept of how she'd managed without disposable nappies. 'Oh my God, where were these in my day!' Mum laughed. She had five kids under six at one point. I can't imagine scraping poo off that many nappies and boiling them and then waiting for them to dry before you had to do it all over again a couple of hours later! I think she was amazed that women moaned so much, with all the technology we had compared to the way things had been for her. She didn't have sterilizers, yet none of us were sickly babies.

She was very much a safe pair of hands. You could always leave grandchildren with Mum and she wouldn't have any flapping. 'Jeez, I've had eight of you,' she'd say. 'Get out!'

It was lovely actually, as she'd sing them all these Irish songs, lots of old ditties that she knew off by heart. There were fast, funny ones like 'Old Mother Clipper Clopper', 'Ooh Shalalala' and 'Horsy, Horsy' to make them laugh. And then there was the soft, lilting 'Give Her the Moon to Play With', and 'Brahms's Lullaby' to send them to sleep. Over the years I also sang all those songs to my three kids.

My dad was brilliant too. He did lots of baby-sitting. One time Shane Jnr had been crying for about two hours non-stop back in Hillingdon. I'd bathed, fed, winded him and fed him some more. Dad was staying with us and in the end he said, 'Coleen, sit down, have a cup of tea, and give him to me.' So he took Shane Jnr and laid him on his chest and within seconds it was like someone had flipped a switch and he fell straight to sleep. He was like a baby whisperer!

'I don't care how long you have to sit there, you're not moving,' I told him.

While I was a stay-at-home mum Shane was working hard, accepting every job he could to pay the mortgage and bills, and we really struggled. Before the baby was born I'd been paying nearly the entire mortgage, but we'd got a joint bank account when Shane Jnr arrived and now Shane had taken on the full brunt of being the breadwinner. And that left me being a full-time mum, something I thoroughly enjoyed, in fact I absolutely loved it.

However, things weren't quite so enjoyable when we really started struggling for money. At one point Shane was taking any work he could get – sometimes he travelled for miles to get £50. I felt lonely if Shane was away working, especially if the baby got ill. Everything was so new to me. Mum and Dad were so far away, and Maureen had also moved back to Blackpool, so I never had that security of knowing they were nearby.

Thankfully Maureen's ex, Pete Suddaby, who still lived in their house around the corner, was Shane's godfather and a devoted one at that. As soon as I phoned he'd always come round. Sometimes he'd pop in for a chat or take Shane Jnr off me and give him a bottle. I really relied on him actually; he was brilliant.

About seven months after Shane was born it was time for me to go back to work with a summer season in Blackpool, while Shane did a Butlin's tour, dividing his time between Minehead, Bognor and Skegness. It was never an option that the baby wouldn't go with me. Shane was a good dad, he adored his son, he'd play with Shane Jnr, he bought him toys and had a cuddle, but he couldn't have handled months of changing nappies and sterilizing bottles.

Before we'd headed our separate ways Shane and I had made a nice commitment to each other. We'd decided that the time finally seemed right to start thinking about getting married and we'd set the date for September 1989. So with exciting plans for my wedding in my mind, I headed up to Blackpool and moved into Maureen's home with baby Shane.

From days old, Shane Jnr was a little dormouse. He slept for twelve hours a night and never needed a night feed. Danny on the other hand was a really hungry baby and woke every three hours. I'd come down rested at 9 a.m. to find Maureen looking weary in the kitchen. 'Please tell me this isn't the first time you've been up?' she'd despair. 'This is my fourth time!' She was absolutely knackered, especially as we were doing two shows a day on top of being new mums.

That year was a really long summer season in Blackpool – about twenty weeks away from home. Once Shane had finished with Butlin's he started work as the warm-up man on Sky's *Jameson Tonight*, a live chat show that went out every night on Sky One, hosted by Derek Jameson. With his usual charm and charisma it had led to an actual presenting job, but he'd come up to Blackpool overnight on a Saturday and spend Sunday with us before going back Sunday night or very early Monday.

That summer was hard. I didn't have a minute in the day to think about anything but motherhood or work – we were doing two shows every night at 6.10 p.m. and 8.30 p.m. At least I was lucky enough to have a baby who slept at that time. Little did I know that when he'd reach the age of one all hell would break loose and my first-born would decide that he was never going to sleep again!

And, even with so much going on, before long we were back at our little home in Hillingdon and it was time to get cracking with the wedding preparations. Then, about six weeks before, I began to get a bad feeling about the whole thing.

It was all going ahead – we'd booked Ansdell Baptist church, in Lytham St Anne's, my wedding dress was chosen, the bridesmaids' dresses were picked out, but it was starting to get out of hand. Whenever I showed Mum the guest list she'd tell me I needed to invite Aunty Whoever who used to bounce me on her knee aged two. Suddenly we had all these relatives from Ireland coming, and old friends of Mum and Dad, yet now I couldn't invite my oldest mate to the church service.

'Donna and her mum and dad can come in the evening,' she'd tell me.

I could see Shane out of the corner of my eye, sitting there listening, his body clearly tense. To some extent I knew that this was what weddings were about, but it was beginning to feel a bit like it wasn't our wedding any more. It had escalated into this big event and I noticed Shane was going very quiet and didn't seem to want to talk about it.

'You just don't want to get married, do you?' I asked him one day. Shane didn't look at me and he didn't answer.

Horror reverberated through me. I knew instinctively that the wedding was off.

Five

When Shane didn't answer me about the wedding I just cried and cried. Like all girls I had had it in my mind that I'd have my big day, a lovely dress, all the frills. I was enchanted by the fairytale and now it had been snatched away from me.

'I do want to get married,' Shane said slowly. 'But I don't want to get married like this. I don't want to feel it's not our wedding and we've just got to turn up.'

I knew what he meant, but initially I also couldn't help thinking that it was just an excuse because he didn't want to marry me, and I felt so humiliated. Everything was literally under way and now this. I thought Shane might be making an excuse to get out of our relationship altogether.

'No,' he said, trying to comfort me. 'I still want to marry you and we will, but we'll do it our way.'

It was all well and good, but now I faced the daunting task of going up to Blackpool to tell Mum it was off. She didn't cry but she was upset and annoyed. 'That's ridiculous,' she said.

But weirdly my dad seemed pleased. 'I'm delighted, I think it's the right decision,' he commented. I never asked him why he felt like that; I almost didn't want to hear why, so I just moved on from it.

Thankfully there weren't any snide or pitying comments

from the rest of my clan. As a family they were just worried about me.

'Oh my God, are you all right?' Anne asked.

'He could have decided a bit earlier,' Maureen added.

But that was it really. They were very tactful considering.

It took me a while to forgive Shane for letting me down with the wedding, but after a few days of being very tearful about the whole thing, I did manage to think about it practically. 'Am I upset about the day itself or do I just want to marry him?' I reasoned. I decided if I had to get married the way he wanted then ultimately it would be fine, as we'd still be getting wed.

And Shane had an altogether different ceremony in mind. 'Let's elope to Florida,' he grinned. 'Just me and you.'

So that's what happened. We told everyone we were going on holiday to Florida for ten days and planned a simple ceremony for 8 March 1990.

Meanwhile our whole routine with Shane Jnr just went up the spout. Suddenly he'd go to sleep at eight or nine but the only way I could get him to drift off was in our bed. I'd tiptoe out of the room and then he'd wake up. He was really restless, and seemed to be making up for all that sleeping during the first year of his life by partying. Even if I did get him to settle he'd get up at midnight and stay awake until three or four in the morning. And I kid you not, he was obsessed by Michael Jackson. We'd sit there all night watching the video for *Moonwalker*, Shane Jnr glued to the screen and me trying my hardest not to doze off.

People told me I should wake him early in the morning to try to alter his sleeping pattern, but when you're shattered that's so hard. If I did wake him up he'd be a grumpy little git and that would be enough to keep him up all night again. So instead he'd sleep two or three hours in the day, and that's when I would sleep too. He only got away with it because he was very cute. He loved people, absolutely loved them. (The tantrums didn't come until he was two, and then boy did they come!)

While we were planning our secret wedding, Shane was busy co-hosting *Jameson Tonight* and during filming one night he met a guy called Robert Earl, who funnily enough was a man who'd helped Joe Lewis look after my sisters when we'd first come to London in 1974. He now owned a part in Planet Hollywood and he was massive. When Shane met him they'd got on so brilliantly that he'd confided about our plans in Florida. Robert was keen to help. 'Why don't you let me organize it,' he said.

Before we went, the only member of my family I told was Maureen and I think she was a bit worried. She's not a drama queen, so she didn't really express any reservations, but I have no doubt that she knew us eloping was Shane's idea rather than mine. 'If that's what you want to do then go for it,' she told me sweetly.

Apart from Maureen, Robert and Shane's best mate, Chris Gosling, who was going to be best man, we didn't tell anyone. Instead, pretending we were just going away for some quality time together, we left Shane Jnr, who was about fifteen months old, at home with Shane's mum Lil and headed for the airport like two giggling school kids.

Beforehand I'd gone shopping for a wedding dress, and I must admit I felt envious when I saw all these girls coming out in beautiful long dresses to choruses of oohs and aahs from their mums, sisters and friends. I was there on my own and longed to go the full hog too, but I felt I had to keep it low-key. *I'll feel like an idiot if I'm in a big meringue and it's just me and him,*

I thought. So reluctantly I bought myself a very simple wedding dress from a bridal shop on Oxford Street. It was a short off-the-shoulder dress, in satin, and was three-quarter length. It took me ages to decide whether to have a veil or not. But then I decided that if I didn't have a veil I wouldn't feel like a bride.

When we arrived in Florida we were met by Robert, who put us in touch with a brilliant lady who organized everything for us. We'd chosen to get married at a stunning place called Cypress Gardens in Orlando, and stayed at the lavish Sheridan Lakeside Hotel.

In the days before the ceremony we went to the county court to be sworn in for our marriage licence and shopping to buy our wedding rings. It was actually very exciting. Chris, or Goz as he was nicknamed, was an airline steward with British Airways and he arranged his flying schedule so he could be there a few days beforehand. The night before our big day he and Shane headed off to a lapdancing club on a stag night with all the lads from Chris's crew. While Shane and Goz were off gallivanting, I sat in on my own. I was dead happy and just stayed in our bedroom trying to get ready, even managing to glue my thumb to my finger trying to put on false nails. 'I shouldn't tell you this,' Shane had revealed, before he headed out for the evening. 'But Maureen and Ritchie are flying out to be here tomorrow!'

Maureen had really wanted to just knock on the door and then appear like a big, fantastic surprise, but when she phoned Shane to make arrangements he said, 'I've had to tell her.' She was really pissed off. They'd been on holiday in Barbados and they'd flown for hours in the hope of surprising me.

If she'd managed to surprise me that way, I know I would have cried. But it turned out that she cried when Shane told her that I knew! Shane always argued that he'd told me because he was going on his stag night and was worried she'd be trying to get in touch. But I suspect that ultimately, like a child, he just couldn't keep a secret.

As much as it took the shine off for Maureen, I can't tell you how happy I was. It was just great because I could make her my bridesmaid.

Shane and I hadn't bothered with sleeping in different places for the night before, and by the time Shane got in from his stag do at an obscene hour of the morning he was incredibly drunk and it was almost time for me to get up. So a few hours later I crept out of bed and had breakfast on my own. Then I got ready in the dark because he was still out for the count. In the end I had to shake him and say, 'Shane, you need to get up! It's our wedding day.'

When he was ready we got into a stretch limo and made our way down to a gazebo by a lake. I was excited, but if I put my hand on my heart, it doesn't compare to how I later felt on my wedding day to Ray. That was just so magical.

With Shane it was all a bit surreal and I just wasn't having that butterfly moment. However, it was beautiful. The only people there were Maureen, Ritchie and Chris and an American couple we'd met in a bar. The main thing I can remember about the whole ceremony is Maureen absolutely sobbing from beginning to end. I kept wondering: *Why is she crying that much? Is it because she doesn't want me to do it?* I think there was a part of her that was wishing the whole family could be there.

I didn't cry, but I did smile, and I was thrilled. Shane was very composed as well. I'm not sure if the way we did it made it feel less real to Shane too. It was quite an off-the-wall thing, it didn't feel like a proper wedding, and I often wonder if this meant he felt less married? But at the time he was happy; we both were.

After we'd exchanged our vows we went for a lovely meal and then on to a bar to dance the night away. Eventually we staggered back to the hotel, drunk as skunks, and slept in separate double beds! Thinking about it now, the elopement was the most romantic part, there was nothing else romantic.

We'd planned to break it to our families once we got home, but before we even left Florida, Linda called to say that the *News of the World* had been sniffing around.

'Have you heard your sister is getting married in Florida?' the reporter asked her.

When I confirmed it was true, she told me, 'You better call the others.'

My parents and almost everyone were absolutely brilliant. They were thrilled for us, although they said they were sad that they hadn't seen it. 'We can't wait for you to get home and we can have a party to celebrate,' Linda told me.

But my sister Denise was really angry. 'I'm not going to look at the wedding pics or speak to her again!' she ranted to Anne. But then Denise was always the most highly strung. She's just the absolute opposite of me. She's always been steadfastly family-orientated and has always said that the family comes first, that you should think of your family before yourself, but in the end she got over it.

We flew back three days after we got married, on Shane's twenty-sixth birthday. But the trip home was a flight from hell. A few hours into the journey the plane suddenly dropped. We'd been sitting there being nauseating newly-weds, holding hands and smiling, when the plane started a rapid descent and everyone looked at each other fearfully.

About ten minutes later the pilot came on and actually

announced that one of our engines had failed and we were going to divert to JFK, which was three hours away! Bizarrely there was total calm on the plane and everyone was deathly quiet. I was fine until the air hostess came down the aisle crying. It was her first flight and the poor girl was terrified, but it was hardly reassuring!

By the time we landed at JFK it was the middle of the night and everything was shut. There were no nappies or bottles of milk for families with babies and all the young kids were crying. We sat there for seven hours and it was awful. Then after a long wait we apprehensively got back on a plane. We'd just settled into the flight when, half an hour in, exactly the same thing happened again! Well, they hadn't said it was the same plane.

'Ladies and gentleman, we have engine failure again,' the captain announced.

'Happy birthday, Coleen,' Shane said, rolling his eyes. My twenty-fifth birthday was the day after Shane's and we were celebrating by flying back to JFK again!

This time they put us up in a hotel, but the next morning we headed back to the airport to find they were attempting to put us on the same plane for the third time! But there was no way we were getting on that flight, so Shane kicked up a stink and we flew back with BA first class.

Before the flight we'd grabbed a newspaper and had been amused to see the headline, 'Nolan weds lover in secret.' Then halfway through the flight I heard a man behind saying, 'Ooh, have you read this in the paper? That Nolan girl has eloped with her lover!'

The flight was fine but I was terrified all the way. I couldn't bear the thought of Shane Jnr losing his parents. When we got to Gatwick we actually spotted lots of irate-looking people from our original flight. When we asked them what had happened they revealed that once they'd landed at Gatwick they'd been bussed to Heathrow for their luggage. But then their cases had been at Gatwick all along! It was the perfect ending to a nightmare story.

After all the rigmarole of getting home, Shane missed two nights of *Jameson Tonight*, which was a lot of money for us to lose. Yet all the airline offered us was £10 compensation!

When we got back to the house, all tired and exhausted, we saw that Shane's mum, Lil, had delivered a bottle of champagne and two champagne flutes complete with a rose and a card. It was a lovely thought. Apart from that we didn't have a party or celebration. Shane was straight back to work so we just got home and carried on where we'd left off.

As I got used to life as Mrs Roche, I felt very grown up to be married with a kid. It was all very exciting and lovely, but looking back now we were so young. Not long after the wedding I went to Northern Ireland for three weeks touring. To my dismay I couldn't take Shane Jnr, who was now eighteen months old, so Lil offered to look after him once more. Shane was really beginning to build a name for himself and was busy doing loads of guest slots on TV shows like *The Les Dennis Laughter Show*, *Des O'Connor Tonight* and Noel Edmonds's *Saturday Roadshow*, so it also suited him for his mum to care for Shane Jnr. But I must admit, from the moment I left him, I found being away from my son horrendous. Lil would always baby-sit if I needed her, but she never listened to me. As much as I loved Lil and I didn't have any airs and graces, I was quite intimidated, as she'd just come into the house and take over. Even the few rules I had for Shane Jnr she didn't stick to. 'When I'm looking after him he'll do what I want to do,' she told me. And somehow I was never able to argue back.

If I got upset about something, Shane would tell me to confront Lil myself. 'If you and your mum have a row, you'll have a row, and that'll be it,' I told him. 'But if me and her do we might never speak again.'

Deep down I knew he'd never say anything. I knew that to him the sun shone out his mum's backside and vice versa. So when I headed off I just felt like a neglectful mother. It was during those weeks that I started to think, *I can't do this any more.* I had to resist the urge to call every five minutes, because I knew Lil would ring me if there was a problem. Plus the thought of calling and hearing my son crying in the background just killed me.

Some gigs on that tour were great, but some were awful. Some of the places in Northern Ireland that we played I'd only ever seen on the news, like the rough side of Belfast. But in fact it's really beautiful. I was shocked at how lovely it actually was. But we did have to be evacuated from some hotels while we were there because of bomb scares and of course that was very frightening.

We were usually playing in nightclubs or pubs. But then one night we were on at a place called Drogheda. We turned up to this tiny village, and when we got to where we were playing we were bemused to see a tiny pub. They'd built a little wooden stage but we had the band with us as well! It was so squashed.

'This is going to be terrible!' I whispered to Linda.

But then, unexpectedly, it turned out to be one of the best gigs we ever did. They were literally hanging off the rafters and they went ballistic. The Irish are so fabulous. They're just so welcoming. They couldn't do enough for us.

Whenever I spoke to Shane on the phone, he'd reassure me everything was fine with the baby but I still couldn't wait to get back. It made me realize how lucky I was not to be performing fifty-two weeks a year.

Like they say, when you have a baby your priorities change, and it was definitely getting to the point where I was losing all the enjoyment of working. But sadly we weren't earning enough to stop – especially not me. Even so, after a long three weeks it was a relief to get back home to Shane Jnr, and I didn't perform for quite some time after that.

The following summer my sisters and I did a season at the Sandcastle, a water park in Blackpool where they also had daily live entertainment. Keith Harris and Orville were headlining and we also had our own show, which our sister-in-law Linzie, who was a dancer, had choreographed.

I loved Linzie, who was married to my brother Brian; I thought she was fabulous. We were both twenty-six and got on so well. My birthday was 12 March and hers was the 18th, so we'd even had our twenty-first birthdays a week apart, which was great. She'd been going out with Brian for years and was a huge part of the family. She was very like us. She was a dancer and very down to earth. She just fitted in. We had loads in common really.

Everyone was looking forward to the opening night in July but then a couple of days beforehand Brian told us Linzie was really unwell. 'She can't come in as she has a nasty cold,' he said.

We assumed we'd see her the following day, but then Brian called to say he was really worried. He'd had four doctors up to the house because Linzie couldn't breathe properly when she was lying down. She'd been diagnosed with a virus and prescribed antibiotics. But as the days passed nothing seemed to help. Instead Linzie was getting weaker and weaker. Eventually Brian took her to hospital, but then on the Thursday night we had a phone call saying her lungs had collapsed.

When I went to visit Linzie in intensive care on the Friday I was shocked. She looked so frail and ill. Not like the Linzie we knew and loved, who was happy, vivacious and full of life.

And then on Saturday Brian called with some devastating news. 'Linzie's not going to make it,' he sobbed down the phone.

To our utter shock Linzie died later that day. It turned out that the viral infection she'd caught had attacked her heart.

I just couldn't get my head round it. Linzie had been so young and healthy and had never been ill in her life. She worked as a dancer and aerobics teacher but the doctors actually said that could be the reason why she couldn't beat the virus. Her immune system had never had to fight anything before, so when it got into her heart she had no immunity. It was the biggest shock, and still is to this day. She and Brian had only been married a couple of years and had only moved into their house two weeks before. They'd been so happy.

It was the first time I'd ever lost anyone like that and I was just devastated. In fact it is one shock I don't think I'll ever get over. She was such a lovely girl. Unfortunately Shane had booked to go to America the day after Linzie died, as he'd bagged some comedy slots at a club in Oregon for a couple of weeks. I was absolutely bereft and he was worried about me.

'I won't go,' he offered.

'No, I want you to go,' I insisted. 'You being here is not going to change anything.'

I was completely wrapped up in my own grief and anger and assumed he'd be back in a fortnight. So I got on with the show each night, trying my hardest to keep it together. But then Shane called to say he'd be staying a few more days. A comedy booker had spotted him and wanted him to do some shows on the West Coast. Well, a few days turned into ten and Shane still wasn't on his way home. It was a running gag on the show. I'd go to work and they'd say: 'When's Shane back?'

'I don't know!'

'Any news?'

'I don't know!'

I was starting to feel like I was on repeat. Everyone in the summer show was asking, and they weren't the only ones. My family wanted to know what was going on: 'What do you mean you don't know?' they'd ask. They just couldn't grasp that.

My sisters and friends were saying, 'If that were my husband . . .'

I'd always reply, 'Oh it's fine . . .'

Then on the phone privately I'd tell him, 'Shane, I'm finding it really hard.'

But he'd say, 'Not much longer, Princess.'

Then each day he'd call so full of enthusiasm about the career opportunities in the States that I hated to rain on his parade. If I told him I was unhappy he'd say, 'Well, I'll come home if you want me to.' But I hated forcing people to do things they didn't want to do. *I won't be a nag*, I thought.

While he was in LA Shane called to say he'd been introduced to a renowned comedy acting teacher called M. K. Lewis and he'd enrolled on a course. I later found out that he actually always knew he'd be doing that course, as it had all been arranged before he even met his teacher! He was doing his acting course during the day and he did get comedy gigs in the evenings. But for a hell of a long time he didn't tell me when he was coming back – it was always 'only a couple of days'.

During all this time I'd been renting a little house for the summer and I was struggling to cope. As well as my dog Tyson, I now had a little Shih Tzu called Dylan, but within two weeks of me being in Blackpool the pair of them had wrecked the place. It wasn't their fault – sometimes I'd be out of the house for eight hours a day. I'd come home to discover they'd pooed and chewed everywhere, and, to make matters worse, two-and-a-half-year-old Shane Jnr was having tantrums to beat all tantrums all day, every day.

I was tired and grieving, doing eight shows a week and screaming at the dogs.

'You'll have a nervous breakdown,' Maureen warned me.

She was right. I just woke up one day and thought, *I can't cope*. So I called up the RSPCA and asked them to re-home the dogs. When Shane eventually returned in September he went mad about Tyson and Dylan.

'I hope you're joking,' he said.

'No, I'm really not,' I replied testily. 'I'd had enough.'

But I couldn't stay cross for too long. While he'd been away Shane had got me a rather unique love token. A tattoo of a heart on his backside, with 'Co' written in it. I had to laugh – my first thought was that he got as far as the 'Co' and couldn't bear the pain of having the whole of 'Coleen', although he refused to confirm it. And now that he had one he was desperate for me to have one as well. 'Are you getting one with my name on?' he suggested.

I've never been tempted. The only names I'd have are my children's and I thought: *Even if Shane is for life I don't want his name on my arse.*

But later on, through all the pain of us splitting up, the thought of that tattoo kept me going. I kept thinking that whoever he slept with he still had my name on his arse. He should have got 'Princess' really, then he could have related it to any girl.

Back in Hillingdon, life soon got back to normal and after a while I decided I'd like to extend our family. 'I'd like to have another baby,' I said, testing the water with Shane one night.

'OK,' he agreed. He might not have been jumping up and down with enthusiasm, but Shane was always very obliging in that way. He felt it was a woman's right to have babies. So we set to work and Jake was conceived in December 1991 (it must have been a good Christmas that year!).

When the time came for my twelve-week scan I left Shane asleep in bed and went to the hospital alone. While I was there I found out the sex of the baby, so I rushed home again to wake Shane and tell him.

'It's a boy!' I enthused.

'Oh great,' he replied, smiling sleepily, before drifting off again.

I was thrilled, and immediately came up with the name Jake. 'It's manly and reminds me of cowboys,' I said. (This was long before *Brokeback Mountain* put cowboys in a rather less macho light, of course!)

In the spring of 1992, when I was halfway through my pregnancy, the Nolans went back to Japan for a three-week tour to promote an album we'd released out there called *Playback*. It was the first time a Western artist had covered Japanese songs with English lyrics – there were some very odd translations! I may have been twenty-seven, but in the eyes of our audience I was still a fourteen-year-old girl, and the fact that the youngest Nolan was now married and pregnant worried our promoter.

'Can you pretend you're fat and take your wedding ring off?' he asked.

Charming! So reluctantly I took my rings off and kept

schtum about my baby bump. It was completely farcical. Interviewers would constantly ask, 'Are you married?' or 'Do you have a boyfriend?'

'No,' I'd chirp, all wide-eyed and innocent, while all the time I was sitting there five months pregnant.

But then we were booked for a TV show where the two hosts were known to be quite crazy and outrageous. 'Coleen, they'll pick on you and call you tubby,' the promoter said breezily. 'But just go along with it and say you're fat.'

Well, that was going too far. So instead I pretended I was ill and let my sisters get ridiculed in my place!

'You know you've got a half-sister,' Mum announced.

Linda and I just looked at each other in complete shock. Mum wasn't one to drop bombshells, and this huge revelation was the last thing we'd ever expected to hear from her. The pair of us were back in Blackpool after our Japan tour and had spent the afternoon sitting talking to Mum. She was never usually one for volunteering things (her catchphrase was always, 'You'll find out soon enough'), but that day she was being very open and telling us about her life with Dad.

'Why did you never leave him, Mum?' I asked her, referring back to the days when he'd been a drunken bully.

'Where would I go with eight kids?' she said. 'Anyway I loved him too much so I'm glad I never did.'

Then all of a sudden Mum paused, deep in thought, before dropping the bombshell about Dad's love child.

'It was when I was pregnant with Denise back in Dublin,' Mum continued. 'I found out your father was seeing this woman. I asked around to find out where she lived and then went round and knocked on her door. When she answered she was heavily pregnant too, and your father walked up to the door behind her. So I told him, "You need to go home."'

I was shocked but also intrigued, as there was part of me that was quite excited. 'I've got a half-sister somewhere,' I thought. 'I wonder what she's like.'

'How come she never got in touch?' I said to Mum. But she didn't know. Maybe Dad's mistress put her up for adoption or she never knew about us? We never found out any more and I don't even know her name. I've thought about trying to find her, but God almighty, I wouldn't even know where to start. I don't know the other woman's name or anything about her. Would Dad's name be on the birth certificate even? Maybe it just said father unknown? It just amazed me that Mum would keep that quiet for so long. I'm so the opposite of my mum – I tell everyone everything as soon as I find it out.

A few weeks later we joined Anne, Denise, Maureen and their families to go on holiday to Disneyland in Florida. I was still pregnant with Jake, and Shane's lack of chivalry didn't go unnoticed by my sisters. While we were standing queuing in line, Shane Jnr, who was now three and a half, would easily tire and want to be picked up, but Shane would barely hold him for five minutes at a time, telling him, 'You need to get down now.' But within minutes his little legs would be getting tired again, so I kept heaving him up.

More than once Maureen took him out of my arms, saying pointedly, 'Let me carry him, it's ridiculous. *You're pregnant.*' Not that Shane took the hint!

During that trip Anne called me into her room one night. 'I've got something to tell you,' she said.

'I think I already know,' I told her, assuming Mum must have also told her about our half-sister.

'Know what?' she asked, her face really pale.

'About our half-sister!' I said.

'No, that's not it,' she said. 'I've known about that for years. I've got something else to tell you.'

For a minute I couldn't even imagine what it could be. Maybe she's pregnant, I thought.

But then she just said it straight out: 'Dad abused me when I was a child.'

I remember saying, 'Dad abused you?' and feeling really puzzled. It wasn't the fact that she was abused, but who she was abused by. I was just so shocked.

'Yes,' she said. 'Dad used to touch me, when I was eleven.'

Oh my God. Dad? I thought. *How can that be right?* Yet I knew there was no reason for her to come out with that and say it if it wasn't true. So not for one second did I feel angry or think: *You're a liar.*

But it was so very hard for me to imagine. I just felt sick and stunned. I couldn't imagine my dad doing that. Of all the things he did wrong, of all the times he was violent, I'd never got a glimpse of that. I'd even lived with him on his own all that time when my sisters were on tour, but he never did one thing that wasn't right. So it was really hard for me to imagine the man I knew being the monster she knew.

'Have you told the others?' I asked.

'Yes,' she nodded.

You know what's really, really sick and sad? I sat down with Shane afterwards and burst into tears. *Why didn't he do it to me?* I thought for one grotesque minute. It's almost as if I was thinking: *Maybe he didn't love me as much.* God, why did I feel that? Yet at the same time I was so bloody delighted that he didn't do it to me.

Shane was speechless; he didn't know what to say either.

121

What can you say to someone who's just found out that their father is a paedophile?

After Anne told me I was constantly haunted by one memory of Dad beating Anne when I was small. He was particularly brutal to her, and I could clearly remember him hitting her repeatedly in the face, spitting, 'You *will* cry.'

But she just sat there saying, 'I won't,' while he continued to hit her in the mouth. One tear rolled down her face but her expression of defiance just didn't falter. If I'd been older I would have killed him for doing that to her, but I must have been five or six and I was just far too scared myself.

We flew home from that trip all reeling from the shock. But when we got back to the UK none of us marched round there to have it out with him. I wasn't going to storm over and shout, 'You abused Anne.' He was an old man and getting sick by then. He had recently been diagnosed with a lung disease called PSS (progressive systemic sclerosis). Even though Dad had given up cigarettes ten years earlier it was a smoking-related disease that obstructed his airways and was destroying his lung tissue.

Plus finding out the truth would have killed my mum. She might have stood by him and turned on Anne. *Which one of us is going to split up this family?* I thought. *Am I going to be the one who rips us apart?* None of us ever did. Our family was never one for vocalizing problems. They always got swept under the carpet.

I don't have any guilt for not speaking up, but I know Anne has. She wishes she'd confronted him, as she grew up with a terrible rage she just couldn't express, and even after his death she was still eaten up with hatred for what he'd done to her.

Shell-shocked and stunned by the awful ordeals Anne had endured, me and the other girls headed to Bournemouth to do

Me aged fifteen months.

Bernie's first Holy
Communion with
Linda aged nine and
me aged two.

Me aged seven, taking my
first Holy Communion
with Mum and Dad.

Above left Me singing 'Show Me the Way to Go Home' at a working men's club in Blackpool, aged four.

Above right Me (aged 3), Linda (8) and Bernie (11) singing a Mary Poppins medley at The Brunswick Club in Blackpool in 1968.

Mum, Linda, Bernie and me in Gibraltar on a rare day off while doing the cruise ships.

Me aged nine with all my sisters from left: Maureen, Linda, Anne, Denise and Bernie at our house in Ilford, Essex, when we moved to London.

The girls (from left Maureen, Anne, Denise, Linda, Bernie) when they worked at the London Rooms in Drury Lane.

Me and my best friend Donna outside my house in Waterloo Road, Blackpool, with my dog Bill.

School photo in London aged ten.

While on tour in Cornwall in 1982 I went horse riding nearly every day!

Wow, I look so young
and innocent. Well I
was only fifteen.

Singing a solo in Japan
aged fifteen.

A Japanese publicity shot, in our own clothes, which we always had to buy.
I want whatever Maureen's on!

Oh my God, so eighties!

Our first TV special for the BBC. We nearly died of nerves! We called these our nappy suits!

Japanese live TV show with the American teen idol Leif Garett. Whatever happened to him?

Me and my first love, Robin, on the Bullet train in Japan.

I honestly don't know what to say. I loved this photo at the time
but whoever permed my hair needed shooting!

a summer season. It was where I'd first met Shane, and now each night I'd waddle on stage the size of a house. My pregnancy was proving to be a good distraction from the news about my dad. Unable to find a way to process the harsh reality of what my father had done to Anne when she was eleven, I just filed it away in the back of my brain. It was the only way I could deal with it.

I'd seen him since. I'd gone up to Blackpool and walked nervously into the house, waiting to be overwhelmed by nausea and disgust for him. But all I saw was this frail old man smiling warmly at me and calling Shane Jnr over to see him. I knew I should feel repelled by him. I should have wanted him nowhere near my son, yet I didn't feel any of those emotions. He was still my dad, and no matter how hard I tried, the disgusting reality of what he'd done to Anne could never penetrate my brain. I'd sit there torturing myself actually trying to imagine what had happened to Anne, to play it out in my head, but it was no good, I felt nothing.

In the end I missed the last two weeks of that summer season. It was just getting a bit too much and I wanted to be back at home. Not that I got any rest! A month before I was due to give birth we moved into a brand new Tudor-style five-bedroom home. We'd managed to secure a massive mortgage on a gorgeous place just round the corner from our old home. Unfortunately no sooner had we signed on the dotted line than our finances began to flounder. At the start of 1992 Shane had been cleaning up with his stand-up and his presenting job on a TV show called *Caught in the Act*, earning up to £7,000 a week, but then the BBC axed the show and now we didn't have nearly as much disposable income. By the time we moved into our new home we couldn't afford to put down carpets!

Jake was born ten days after his due date, on 16 September

1992. As with Shane Jnr I had to be induced the night before he was born, as they said he was breech. 'If we can't turn him we'll have to give you a caesarean section or use forceps,' the doctor had warned. I was dreading it, as I was such a coward. But as I was lying in bed in hospital on my own, all terrified, suddenly I felt this colossal pressure in my tummy and it completely changed shape. Jake had just somersaulted in my belly and his head was down, ready to go!

This time I had Shane, my Aunty Theresa and Maureen at the birth. Poor Bernie was supposed to be on a date with her boyfriend of the time, the now famous producer David Ian, but they kindly stepped in at the last minute to baby-sit Shane Jnr.

As births go, Jake's was a lot quicker than Shane's. It was seven hours, and because he was a bigger baby, he was easier to push out. I remember the midwife saying to me, 'We'll have this baby out by quarter past.' I just didn't think she'd actually be right!

He weighed 8lb 2oz and was just adorable – your typical textbook baby. All chubby and just divine. But because he was delivered so quickly the doctors were worried that his blood could be slightly contaminated from the umbilical cord and he needed to be monitored and observed for twenty-four hours. So, to my dismay, I was told we would be going nowhere.

Shane, Mum, my Aunty Theresa, Bernie and Maureen were all waiting back at ours eager to celebrate, so I had to tell them to go ahead and toast Jake's arrival without me. Instead, at every hour on the dot the nurses would do a blood test on Jake and check his blood pressure and temperature and do a pin prick in his heel. I remember lying in bed seething as they kept waking my poor little mite up. It was awful. When it's your baby you are so protective and I just wanted to punch them!

By the time Jake was allowed out of hospital and we were

given the all-clear, Shane had gone back to work and Bernie had to pick me up from hospital. The others had all gone home too, so when Bernie dropped me off I realized it was just me, home alone in a house that we couldn't even afford to decorate, with two small children.

Suddenly it was all very overwhelming and I just sat there crying, wondering how I would cope with a hyperactive three-year-old and a two-day-old baby on my own. *I don't know what to do*, I thought. *Jake cries for milk and at the same time Shane Jnr needs the toilet.* It was just so scary juggling two children single-handedly, and such an anticlimax coming home to an empty house. You want a fuss when you've just had a baby.

Despite my new baby jitters, Jake was so beautiful. He looked like a cross between Winston Churchill and Mao Tse-tung. Shane Jnr idolized him, and even insisted he fed him his bottle. He was also a very good baby, sleeping for five hours at a time.

'You're blessed with that one,' my Aunty Theresa told me that first month.

But after Shane Jnr's early transformation from sleepy little koala to nocturnal party animal, I wasn't about to be smug. 'Aunty Theresa, he's biding his time,' I laughed.

When Jake was six weeks old, our old CBS writer Mike Myers got in touch asking me, Bernie, Anne and Maureen to do some recording, as he had some songs he wanted us to demo. I was eager to earn some spare cash, as we were struggling to meet the mortgage each month. Anne, Bernie and Maureen came to stay at ours so we could record together, and Denise, who was still living in Greenford with her boyfriend Tom, agreed to look after the boys during the day.

It was a gruelling two weeks. We were getting to the studio

at 9 a.m. every day and getting home at 1 a.m. – and then on top of this I was getting up to do night feeds.

Consequently I was walking round like a zombie. It didn't go unnoticed. A few days in, we were all sitting down having a cup of tea when Maureen suddenly said, 'Look, we've all had a chat and we've decided you can't keep doing this by yourself, so we're going to help.'

'I'll do the night feed tonight,' Bernie piped up.

'We'll take it in turns!' Anne agreed.

I was so grateful. So every night we'd carry Jake's swinging crib into a different room and we'd take it in turns to care for him. I'm sure any other woman would have said, 'His father will do it,' yet when all this was going on I didn't even consider asking Shane. *I wish he'd offer to help*, I'd think secretly, but that old fear of being a nagging wife always stopped me from speaking up.

And it was during that time that I realized how different men and women really are. If I was feeding Jake my sisters would immediately offer to make me a cup of tea. But on the whole men don't seem to notice things like that, or at least Shane didn't. He probably assumed I'd ask for help if I needed it, but yet he never worked out that I did.

Perhaps he was just too occupied with worrying about our money situation? Things were still looking pretty bleak financially, and Shane's next role brought in hardly any cash at all. In early 1993 Bernie's boyfriend David Ian gave Shane the opportunity to audition for a part in the stage musical *Grease*. He really wanted to get into acting and this was the perfect opportunity. When Shane joined *Grease* he had his eye on the lead role of Danny Zuko, but that went to the Australian actor and *Neighbours* star Craig McLaughlin and Shane eventually landed the part of Kenickie. It was the opportunity to shine on the stage Shane had longed for and he threw himself into it with gusto. But the money was terrible!

At that point we even had the bailiffs coming to the door when we fell behind with the mortgage or we put off paying a bill. But we always managed to keep them at bay by finding the money from somewhere. Once, though, they arrived at the door and as I stood there, trying to look forlorn, I just knew they weren't going away this time.

'Sorry love, we're going to have to take the car,' one told me.

I could barely hide my smile as I replied, 'Really? Well, if you absolutely have to then I suppose there's nothing I can do.' So I let them take Shane's battered old red Golf, which was so much more trouble than it was worth. So it was definitely no loss to either of us!

Meanwhile, as Shane's enthusiasm for *Grease* flourished, I felt our relationship was beginning to flounder. Having my second child and battling the baby bulge had left me feeling down about myself. I now weighed 11 stone, the heaviest I'd been, and was wearing size 14 to 16 clothes. Because we were strapped for cash I wasn't going out much, so I felt like the tired wife at home with the kids. And because I'd just had a baby we weren't having sex very often either. Shane was wrapped up in his own world and my family weren't around, so I just felt non-existent. I felt fat and ugly and although I'm not blaming Shane for that, he didn't notice that I needed reassurance. He was wrapped up in his rehearsals, and even when he did get a day off he'd sleep all day on the couch.

Once, when I hadn't seen him for a couple of days, I decided to buy a new dress and try to look nice. I thought: *Maybe he's not noticing me because I'm drab and feeding a baby and toddler?* So I treated myself to a pretty frock, a chiffony type in a cream colour with little flowers. It was quite figure-hugging and flared out, and I got some new shoes too.

That night Denise was singing with an orchestra at a country club in Greenford, doing a Judy Garland tribute. Some of my family were going, and Tom, Denise's boyfriend, was too. I remember feeling really nervous and even embarrassed that I'd made such an effort – in some ways it was a bit like going on a first date. I spent ages doing my hair and make-up.

Shane was meeting me there with his manager, Stan Dallas – one of the original Dallas Boys harmony group. I loved Stan; he was such a nice man and he was brilliant for Shane, they had a great relationship. When I walked in all self-conscious my family and friends instantly pounced on me, saying they loved my dress and telling me, 'You look gorgeous!' It was nice.

But then Shane came over with a wry smile on his face. 'Christ,' he said. 'What have you come as?' I felt as if I could curl up and die right there.

'Oh, I'm only joking, darling,' he laughed, and gave me a kiss, but it was too late. The damage had already been done and all night I felt like a silly, unattractive frump.

Then to top it all off Shane didn't sit with me, he went and sat with Stan. In the row in front of them was a woman who immediately started flirting with Shane. She was in her early twenties, a bit younger than me, and had on a cowl-neck top with no bra. She kept deliberately standing up and bending over to talk to him. *You're so winding me up*, I thought, watching her.

I was sensitive anyway, but that made me feel like even more of an idiot. I just wanted to go home, and I was really angry with the pair of them. When we got back later, I went mad at Shane.

'Don't be so stupid!' he said. 'As if I was flirting with her. She might have been flirting with me, but was that my fault?'

Things didn't get much better after that. Over that whole period I was down and insecure. Jake was still a baby and I was tired – I think I had a bit of the baby blues really. As Shane's confidence grew, mine was plummeting. Then when *Grease* opened at the Dominion Theatre he was lapping up the attention from screaming girls and all the rave reviews.

It would be wrong of me to suggest that Shane made no effort. We tried to have a holiday every year – one on our own and a family one – and while Shane wasn't a DIY man, if something broke down he'd immediately get it done, so I never wanted for anything really. While he was performing in the West End, and the money improved a bit, he used to get a baby-sitter every Saturday so I could travel to London to see the show. Shane would book us a suite in a hotel and we'd go out with the cast or have a meal just the two of us. It was lovely.

But even so, that was just one night out of seven. Sunday was Shane's day off and invariably he'd be so knackered he'd sleep all day. Apart from my Saturday date with him, it just got to the point that he had his life and I had mine. I loved being a mum and worshipped my two boys, but my life also felt lonely. We never really talked about it, but I was convinced I'd become a bit of an afterthought to Shane. And one night I felt my fears were confirmed.

Shane had come home after the show with his mate Goz, who had now left the airlines to be his PA, but there was no 'Hello Princess,' or effort to find me as he walked in the kitchen. What he didn't know was that I was sitting in the family room and listening to the conversation.

It took fifty long minutes before Goz piped up with, 'Where's Coleen?'

'Dunno,' I heard Shane reply in an uninterested fashion.

I just crept up to bed and cried. It felt as if he honestly didn't care. He clearly had this great exciting life now and I was the boring wife with two kids, with nothing to talk about.

The thing with Shane was that he'd always shower me with materialistic gestures like presents, flowers, jewellery, but it was the stuff that cost nothing that he couldn't give me, like time together, compliments or affection. I'd got to the point where I just wanted him to walk in and say, 'You look great!' or 'Why don't the four of us go to the park?' But that just wasn't happening.

I felt unattractive, unloved and non-existent. It seemed now like I was just a housekeeper and mother. I had no idea where the sexy Coleen that Shane had once been unable to keep his hands off had gone.

Not long after Shane opened in *Grease* I went to Weymouth for the 1993 summer season. By now Jake was ten months old, and I took both the boys with me. I was still feeling very low and vulnerable, so in a way it was nice to get away and do my own thing. To be a singer once more rather than Shane's boring wife who had nothing to talk about bar nappies and colic.

But it was during my time in Weymouth that I allowed my head to be turned.

Throughout those summer seasons you get very close and build up strong bonds with people, so I must admit that when a man I met started paying me attention I was very flattered.

The guy in question was a keyboard player (what is it with me and musicians? I could have had a full orchestra by now!) and was very attractive. There were some very pretty girls per-forming in Weymouth, and I never thought anyone would be interested in me. As far as I was concerned I was the fat dowdy one on the end. But he did notice me and I couldn't believe it.

I don't even know how it happened, it just did. At first we simply talked but then I noticed he was always very complimentary. 'God, you look gorgeous tonight,' he'd tell me, looking me up and down and smiling. Well, when you're so vulnerable that's like someone giving you the Miss World crown! So I started making a real effort to look nice. For the first time in ages I had that bubble of excitement, those little butterflies in my tummy. *I think this guy likes me and actually thinks I'm attractive!* I thought. It felt really good.

My musician seemed quite grown-up. He was softly spoken and not at all a Jack the lad. I think the big attraction for me was that he wasn't loud like Shane. He was very quiet and kind and a good listener – something I needed.

During the show I'd hired a nanny, which meant I could go out after the show with the other performers. We all used to sit and chat in a group in a hotel bar or go for walks along the beach. Weymouth was beautiful, and it seemed like a long way from home.

He had rented a town house with some of the other musicians so I often went back to their place. And it was there one day as we were having a cup of tea together that he leaned in and kissed me.

Six

As I kissed my musician, it was like a sexual awakening. Adrenalin was pumping through my body. I knew what I was doing was terribly wrong, but I was literally shaking with exhilaration. *I am still attractive*, I thought to myself. After that we ended up kissing most nights after the show. I was completely infatuated with him, craving him every time I saw him and just living for the moment, burying thoughts of my husband in the back of my mind.

But it was possibly one of the most horrendous times of my life as well. It was a terrible deceit to live with and I had these awful feelings of guilt.

The tour was only eight weeks long and Shane would often come down on the Saturday night after his show. That was really hard – I did still love him but I didn't want him there. I wanted to stay in my bubble. Although I tried to keep him away from my lover, once, after my affair had begun, I can remember him sticking his head into the auditorium to greet the band. 'All right lads,' he said. I just felt awful, incredibly guilty. I didn't like my two worlds colliding one little bit. Thankfully that was their only encounter, as I did my very best to keep them apart.

But Shane wasn't a fool either. I think he knew then that I

wasn't myself. After he'd left I felt so bad I needed to talk to someone, and one night I confided in Bradley Walsh, who was headlining in Weymouth. At that point my affair wasn't exactly a secret. Everyone knew, and I think the other members of the band and crew could all see that we really cared for each other. Bradley and I got on very well, as he'd previously dated my sister Bernie, so one day when we were sitting outside on the prom, I told him, 'I feel so guilty, but I have all these feelings for him.'

'I'm not being funny, Coleen,' Bradley replied. 'I get on great with Shane, but you don't need to feel as guilty as you do. He's not so innocent either.'

'Well, you might be right, Bradley,' I sighed. 'But I can't make a fuss about rumours, particularly after what I've been doing.'

Like summer seasons previously, people were always hinting about things and at that point I was hearing lots of rumours that Shane was messing around. A lot of the gossip centred around a girl in his show but it was never anything concrete and I knew first hand how often such rumours were untrue. But even if it was true and he was pulling everything in sight, I was as much to blame, and I should have told him how I was feeling rather than cheating on the father of my kids.

I can give a million reasons why my affair happened but I can't justify it. Ultimately I should have sat down with Shane and told him how I was feeling. I should have said, 'I'm vulnerable, this needs to change.' But we just didn't communicate. I didn't want to have to ask Shane for affection, even if that was exactly what I needed. The sad truth is I was scared to say anything. I didn't think he fancied me any more. I was just the mother of his children. He loved me but he didn't fancy me. Yet my musician did.

Despite it being a very sweet affair, he had made it very clear that once the summer season was over we would be too. And that was fine. He didn't lead me on or promise me the earth. We both knew the score. So I endeavoured to enjoy the lovely moments and not think about the repercussions.

I continued to see him at the show in the evenings and it was wonderful. I felt I could go out and be flirtatious and sexy – because at last someone thought I actually was. But all the while Shane was sensing something. For a start I wasn't so needy. As a result he suddenly became very attentive during his visits. It made me bristle. I kept thinking: *I'm not sure it's not too late*.

It was such a turmoil of emotions, and my last day of the season was horrendous. I didn't want to go home. My affair had lasted five weeks and I was heartbroken. I'm not sure if I was in love, but I definitely loved the fact that someone made me feel special and attractive. If he'd asked me to run off with him I don't know if I would have. But he never did. Either way I'm pretty sure it wouldn't have lasted.

So it all ended very amicably. He was really sad and so was I, and it took all my strength not to sob on his shoulder as we bid each other goodbye. We decided we'd stay friends and go back to our lives and I wouldn't tell Shane. I honestly couldn't bear hurting him. It was a bit cowardly, but I think if I'd fallen out of love with Shane then I would have told him.

So I packed up and drove home to Hillingdon. I had the boys in the car and on that two-hour drive I tried my hardest not to cry. I was devastated that it was over but I was also devastated about what I'd done. Suddenly the bubble had burst and the guilt hit me with a vengeance. I hated myself. I kept thinking: *God why did I do that? Why didn't I just talk to him?* The truth is I did still love Shane, I was just crying out for affection.

When we arrived home the house was empty, as Shane was in London performing in *Grease*. So once the boys were asleep, I began to unpack everything and then I ran a bath. *It's time to forget the summer*, I told myself, soaking in the tub. *I need to concentrate on making things right with Shane.*

So I did, slowly managing to erase the affair from my mind and getting back to family life.

But I was more of a person in my own right and Shane noticed. He kept saying, 'Are you all right? You seem different.'

'I'm OK,' I lied. 'I think it's just the summer season being over. I miss everyone.'

Although I'd vowed not to see my musician again, I did speak to him on the phone once or twice when Shane was at work and that's how he found out. He came back from work one day and asked me, 'Did anyone phone tonight?'

'Um, Maureen?' I replied.

'Anyone else?' he asked.

'No,' I insisted, beginning to feel anxious.

'Are you sure?' he asked, staring at me.

'Yes!' I answered, alarmed by his tone.

'Well, if you are sure, then what the fuck is this?' he shouted, hurling a tape on the floor.

It turned out Shane had been so suspicious that he'd bought a bugging device and had recorded my calls. He'd caught me red-handed and it was the most horrendous night of my life to date.

I looked at him with tears in my eyes. I just knew I couldn't deny it. 'I'm sorry,' I sobbed.

We stayed up all night as Shane raked over every little detail of my affair. I just couldn't stand the pain on his face; I thought my heart was going to rip out of my chest and explode. I'd stopped smoking for nine months but that night I started again. It was all a huge reality check. *Oh God, I don't want to lose my husband and for my kids to come from a broken home,* I thought. *What on earth have I done?*

After screaming at me for hours, Shane stormed outside. When I looked out of the window I saw he was sitting in his car and crying, his whole body shaking with sorrow. I was just so devastated for him. I felt like such a bitch for hurting him.

Later he came back in and the two of us cried all night. We'd cry and then we'd row, and then cry some more. 'You starved me of affection,' I wept, trying desperately to explain my reasons. But when I saw the pain on his face it just sounded lame. I thought: *I have to stop making excuses for being a cow.* I vowed then that it would never happen again. If I ever felt that way in the future I'd tell him. I have to say it was a wake-up call for both of us.

Shane didn't trust me for a very long time after that, and for eight weeks I had to go to the show with him every night. Thankfully Denise was brilliant and was always on hand to baby-sit. During that time Shane was watching my every move, and I mean *every* move! If I said I was going to the supermarket and I'd be an hour, but then happened to be ten minutes late, he'd be straight on the phone. I spent months doing whatever he wanted me to do to convince him. It was good in a way, as he became everything I wanted him to be. He was attentive and interested in me once more. It made me think: *I nearly blew this.*

In time it was clear that Shane was beginning to trust me again. It took lots of talking but I think he eventually realized that I'd been with him for eight years and had only slipped that one time. I wasn't the type of girl to go and have an affair. Once he'd accepted that, he was fine and everything returned to domestic bliss once more.

I think the whole thing gave Shane a big fright. Suddenly he was more interested in me. Those three years from 1993 through to 1996 following my affair were possibly the best years of our marriage. We were closer than ever. Shane made such an effort and I did too. We talked more and I decided to give up work completely, as we didn't need the money. By now Shane was doing really well in *Grease* and had recently taken over the lead role of Danny Zuko, which was considerably better paid. It seemed ridiculous for me to slave away when I could be a full time mum and wife for him.

I was so proud of him for landing the part of Danny. When Craig McLaughlin was leaving, they knew Shane wanted to do it so they asked him to audition. But Shane told them that the only way he'd try out was if they let him do a live show. I always thought that was a very ballsy thing to do, and when I watched him that night he was absolutely brilliant. I was convinced his gamble had paid off. Then a few nights later I walked in to find Shane sitting in the kitchen with his manager, Stan. They were smiling at each other triumphantly.

'What's going on?' I asked.

Stan took hold of my hand and said, 'How would you like to go to bed with Danny Zuko tonight?'

I immediately thought: *Ohh, I get to sleep with John Travolta!* But joking aside, I was so thrilled for him. When it comes to stage presence and professionalism Shane is brilliant and he works so hard.

As 1993 started to draw to an end, life was good, and the following year *Grease* went from strength to strength. It was drawing in massive crowds and the critics were raving about Shane. We had money to do up our house, Shane was sweet and attentive and we had a lovely home life. It was one of the happiest times of my marriage.

While Shane Jnr had been mad about Michael Jackson as a tot, at eighteen months old, Jake's passion was *Grease*. He was absolutely obsessed, and Shane even bought him a dinky T-Birds jacket, which looked adorable. We'd take the boys to see the show and Jake would sit on my knee in the box, just mesmerized. He knew all the moves and would sing along with his cute baby babble.

Meanwhile the money was rolling in for Shane. He was signed up to be the face of Daz's Doorstep Challenge adverts, where he'd turn up on housewives' doorsteps and challenge them to put Daz to the test against a rival brand. He was also hosting a bingo show called *Lucky Numbers* on ITV. Both of these Stan had successfully used to raise Shane's fees on *Grease*. As a family we didn't want for anything, and we were so happy. Another blissful year passed, while Shane's career continued to flourish. He was now a real household name and started presenting a new game show for ITV called *The Shane Richie Experience*, in which three engaged couples would compete to win a wedding.

At the time there was gossip about Samantha Janus, who was playing Sandy with Shane in *Grease*. I know there was nothing going on between them but Sam was beautiful, a leggy blonde with a body to die for, and I could see exactly why people were whispering. She and Shane had a fantastic on-stage chemistry. People in the show and my friends and family were always saying things like, 'Does it not worry you, the chemistry between Shane and Sam? If it was me I'd worry,' or 'Does it bother you if you call and he's in her dressing room?' But it didn't. I trusted Shane.

Were there other girls sniffing around? I don't know, but I never had any reason to suspect it. I was really contented and so was Shane. We were living the dream.

In 1995 Shane and I tuned in to watch a Channel 4 documentary called *The Dying Rooms* and were left completely shocked. It was about the appalling conditions in orphanages in China and showed how they were packed full of little girls who were being neglected. They were strapped to beds and literally left to die. It was awful and by the time it ended Shane and I were both in floods of tears. Seeing the terrible plight of those children we both immediately wanted to do something about it. I'd always said to Shane that I wanted to have my own kids and then I'd like to adopt.

'I really want to go for it,' I told him. 'Perhaps we could give one of those little girls a new life?'

'Yeah,' Shane nodded in agreement. 'Let's do it.'

So I started to make enquiries and contacted Social Services. We had some friends who had adopted and they suggested we should also call the Catholic Adoption Society. They were fabulous but quickly told us our chances of adopting a little girl from China were very limited. 'Although this is all going on in China it would be virtually impossible for you to adopt a girl because you already have two boys,' the lady on the phone warned.

I just thought, *Christ, these children are not wanted, we're offering lots of love and a good home and yet it's still so hard!*

The call was disheartening but I put the phone down determined that I still really wanted to adopt. If we couldn't help a child from China then perhaps we could help one closer to home? So I asked Social Services to send me all the adoption forms but as I waded through the mountains of paperwork and began to take in the full reality of what lay ahead – months of meetings with social workers and the like – I began to get despondent. For instance, one of the numerous stipulations was that if you were more than two stone overweight or smoked then you couldn't adopt. I knew I'd be ruled out on both those counts and it was really frustrating. It seemed like there was no point applying unless you were perfect robot parents.

So I've got to go on a crash diet and stop smoking before any of this? I thought, really annoyed by the ridiculousness of it. *Does it really matter that I'm two stone overweight when there are children being left in orphanages to die?*

Meanwhile Shane's time was consumed by *Grease* and I didn't see how he could fit in the numerous meetings and checks we'd need to go through to discover if we'd cut the mustard as adoptive parents.

Then in January 1996 Shane got a call saying that *Grease* was moving to Manchester and we put our plans to adopt on hold indefinitely. There was a real buzz about the show and the producers wanted him to continue in the lead role. It meant being away from his family, but the fee was unbelievable – double what he was on in London – and initially Shane was only asked to go there for three months.

When we sat down and talked about it I was really encouraging. 'It's not for long,' I reasoned. 'You'd be silly to turn it down.'

Seeing as Shane Jnr was going to school full-time, I didn't really see the point of uprooting him for three months. Boy, was that a mistake! Unfortunately three months actually turned into nine! And suddenly everything was about to start going horribly wrong.

In the April of 1996 Shane and Goz rented a beautiful farm-house in Mobberley, Cheshire. It was right out in the country-side and even had stables and a heated indoor swimming pool.

'I want you and the boys to feel at home up here,' Shane said. 'You're going to love it.'

Meanwhile we'd just sold our home in favour of buying a new place that was being built from scratch in Denham in Buckinghamshire. But when moving day came and I turned up at our new place with the boys and our new dog, a golden retriever called Harley, it was far from finished. All we could do was dump all our belongings and furniture in a couple of rooms and then move into a hotel. It was an absolute nightmare for the school run and we couldn't take the dog, so Shane's godfather Pete had to take her. We lived like that for a week, and thank God friends would have us round every night to cook us tea. Finally after a week we moved in, although it was still pretty much a building site.

On Shane's opening night I travelled up to Manchester to celebrate with him. The show was brilliant and afterwards there was a party. It's so bizarre thinking back, as at the show I couldn't take my eyes off one girl. I wasn't at all like that normally. Over the years Shane had worked with so many dancers and leading ladies and I didn't think anything of it. Shane's character Danny Zuko was always snogging the face off Sandy. People would ask me, 'What's it like watching your husband kiss another woman?'

'Well, it never bothers me!' I'd say. 'There's about two thousand other people watching!'

But at the after-show party for that opening night I can distinctly remember examining this one girl. There were loads of people there but she just stood out to me. She had really long dark hair and was wearing a skin-tight white dress. I just thought: *Ooh, look at her. God, she's gorgeous.*

As I was studying her Goz wandered over and said, 'You all right, Col?'

'I'm fine,' I replied. 'But who's the bitch in the white?'

He laughed his head off. Well, it must have been female intuition because that turned out to be Claire, the girl Shane had an affair with. At the time I had no reason to suspect, but I think the affair started pretty quickly after that party. And the next two years were probably the worst of my life.

Shane always called me twenty times a day and we were always in touch. It was just the way he was. If he stubbed his toe he'd call me. But a few weeks into his Manchester run I noticed he didn't seem that keen on me coming up to see him with the boys. 'I might come up next week,' I'd say. But he always had excuses as to why I shouldn't. 'I'm so busy . . . I'm hardly in the house . . .'

It perplexed me. By the time the summer holidays began there seemed no reason for me to stay at home, not when Shane had a lovely big farmhouse we could all enjoy as a family. 'I'm going to come up,' I told him firmly. 'The boys are on their holidays and they want to be with their dad.'

It was all sorted but then Shane called to say he was really busy. 'Why don't you go to Blackpool and see your family,' he said. 'I've got things on all week.'

Reluctantly I did, but then one week turned into two, then three . . . until ridiculously we ended up spending four weeks in Blackpool. Every time I called Shane he put me off. In the end I just lost patience. 'I don't care what you're doing,' I said. 'We're coming.'

As I headed to Manchester I kind of knew something was going on. Shane's behaviour had just changed so much. He was usually suspicious and very jealous with me, but all of a sudden he didn't seem to be bothered. The fact that he'd let me stay in Blackpool for four weeks was really weird.

Blackpool was just over fifty miles from Manchester – barely an hour's drive away for us.

I kept saying every day, 'But when are we coming over?'

'There's no point,' he kept arguing. 'I'm out every day. You'll just be on your own.'

Not wanting to think the worst, I buried my head in the sand and put any strangeness down to the fact he just had this separate life. I knew that was what summer seasons were like. When you're working together so intensely away from home for weeks on end everyone on the show becomes very close, like a family with in-jokes and little routines.

When we arrived at the farmhouse Shane seemed pleased to see us. 'Hello darling,' he grinned, kissing me and grabbing both the boys up for a cuddle.

'It's good to see you,' I smiled.

I tried to put my worries aside, but when you've spent ten years with someone you know when they're acting strangely. *It's only for a few more weeks*, I kept telling myself. But then Shane signed up for another three months.

I wasn't best pleased. As each week without Shane passed, a niggling doubt was setting in. It was as if Shane was beginning to filter me out of his line of vision again. He wasn't noticing me any more, and the attentiveness was waning. Absence certainly wasn't making the heart grow fonder.

To be honest, though, I had plenty of other things to worry about, like effectively being a single mother to our two boys and the fact that my dad was not at all well. I was now in complete denial about Anne's abuse and was more concerned with thoughts that my dad wasn't going to last for ever. One thing was preying on my mind. At my sister Maureen's marriage to her husband Ritchie the year before, Dad had taken my hand

and smiled sadly. 'My one regret in life is that I never gave my baby away,' he'd told me. It had really made me think.

So one weekend when Shane was back home I made a suggestion. 'I'd really like to have our marriage blessed,' I told him.

'Yeah, that's a great idea,' he replied. 'But you'll have to organize it.'

Well, that I could do! After weeks of wondering if my husband still fancied me, I was thrilled he'd agreed.

When I called Mum and Dad to tell them, they were delighted, so I set about arranging the whole thing in about six or seven weeks. This time I was going to go to town with the big dress and the whole caboodle. Shane Jnr and Jake were pageboys, of course, and Anne's youngest, Alex, was a flower girl. I also asked Bernie and Maureen and Goz's girlfriend Jo to be my bridesmaids.

We held the service on 18 August 1996 at Our Lady Star of the Sea church in St Anne's. I wanted it to be intimate, so I only invited sixty-eight people and it turned out to be such a lovely day. I'll always remember Dad glancing at me proudly as he walked me down the aisle. But the icing on the cake was seeing the way Shane's eyes lit up when he saw me heading towards him. Suddenly it felt like we were head over heels in love again. He was so attentive and loving that day.

After the service everyone headed to the Imperial Hotel in Blackpool for the reception and Shane was constantly by my side. 'I love you so much,' he kept whispering in my ear. 'You look so beautiful.'

We did all the usual toasts and ceremony and Shane gave a really funny speech. It was followed by a grand announcement. 'I haven't told Coleen this yet,' Shane said, smiling at me. 'But seeing as we didn't have a honeymoon the first time round I've booked us two weeks in the Maldives!'

Everyone whooped and applauded Shane, and I was literally walking on air. I'd had so many doubts over the last few months and now I felt like the blessing had given our marriage a new lease of life. But do you know what, I never heard another word about that trip to the Maldives. And before the reception was even over, reality set in once more and my happiness began to dissolve. Shane announced he was taking the boys swimming in the afternoon and I was left alone to look after the guests. Everyone kept asking, 'Where's your groom?'

'Oh, somewhere,' I'd shrug.

It's hard to describe the loneliness, confusion and overwhelming sadness I felt. It's funny, as just a few years later, when it was all out in the open, I sat down with Claire and discovered it was nothing short of incredible how he'd juggled us both. On the day of our blessing Shane had told Claire he was off to see his kids in Blackpool, thinking she'd be none the wiser. But then she saw it in the paper! Naturally upset, Claire confronted Shane and he immediately insisted that we were living out a charade of being together for the kids. His audacity was breathtaking and the more he got away with lying to the pair of us, the more confident he must have felt.

The next day Shane went back to work and I headed back south with the boys. As the weeks passed he seemed less and less enthusiastic about us coming to visit and wasn't very keen on heading home to see us either. It made me very suspicious and sad, remembering how when I'd first met Shane he'd travelled from Weymouth to Blackpool, no matter how done in he was, just to spend one day with me.

The boys were kind of used to not having their dad there; Shane Jnr was at school and Jake was too young to really notice. But although they still had me and I was their routine it made me sad to think Shane was missing out on spending time with them.

By now I'd managed to push Shane into agreeing to come home every second Sunday. But he was always shattered and slept the whole time, so it's not as if we managed to have any lovely long lunches or spend any proper time together.

So when, after another three dreary months without my husband, he called to say he'd been asked to sign for another three months, I raised my concerns.

'I've never asked you not to do anything, but I don't think you should sign that contract,' I told him. 'I just feel our lives are growing apart.'

I thought that was the end of it really, but then in October, Shane came in one day and revealed that he'd agreed to do the extra stint. I was cross, but the damage was already done and Shane had committed to the show. In hindsight what I should have said was, 'I don't want you to sign that contract because our marriage will be over.' Perhaps then he might have taken me seriously, but I was always a bit scared of dishing out ulti-matums. What if I had stopped him and he hadn't got any more work? Would he have blamed me? *He's clearly loving* Grease, I eventually decided, *so maybe I should just let him have his moment.* Still, as Christmas drew near I had a heavy feeling in my heart. What on earth was becoming of my marriage?

By now Shane Jnr was almost nine and had been a member of a local football team in Hillingdon for a while. I loved seeing him play. It was fabulous. Like watching all these little ants run-ning around after the ball! But I was also feeling quite isolated and lonely, so it was a relief when some of the other mothers took me under their wing. First I'd become friendly with two girls called Carol and Jane, and then Vicky had joined our little gang. Over the following weeks, as life with Shane got bleaker and bleaker, those girls would prove to be the most amazing friends. I don't know how I would have coped without them and they're still my best friends to this very day.

Carol was about eight years older than me and very much the loudest one of our group. She was tall, with short black hair, a real sun-bed worshipper, never wore make-up and had a gob as big as the Dartford tunnel. She had a wonderfully raucous laugh and a rasping voice from smoking. I always knew when she was at the football matches because I could hear her before I saw her! She was a real salt-of-the-earth girl, reliable, loyal, and immediately made me feel totally welcome.

She'd been through absolute hell with her husband. They had two kids and had been married for twenty-odd years when he went off with her best friend of thirty years! But although she'd had it tough she never moaned, and I never felt she was envious of my life or anyone else's. Carol was also magnificently common as muck – a party wasn't a party unless she flashed her bra at everyone. It would happen so often that we'd just look at each other and say, 'Oh Carol flashed her boobs again! Bless her heart!'

Jane had two sons and was a proper Cockney gal, the same age as me. She was a very attractive, sexy woman with short auburn hair, who always wore make-up. She had a soft, kind nature and never had a bad word to say about anyone. She'd been with her husband Michael since they were thirteen and they were the perfect example of teenage sweethearts who'd lasted the test of time. You just knew when you met them that they were mad about each other – always had been and always would be.

Like Carol, Jane was a nutter who really liked her wine. She'd always be the last one dancing at a party.

Vicky was a tall, attractive blonde whom I met after the

others. Like Jane, she and her husband Nigel were childhood sweethearts and did everything together. She was very sensible and educated, with four very clever kids. She was a real lady and very loyal.

So that was our little gang.

We all had very different personalities but somehow the four of us just gelled. There was Vicky at one end of the scale and Carol at the other, and I was somewhere in between all of them. I could sit and be sensible with Vicky or be loud with Carol. It was great. But much as I loved my whole new set of friends, I wanted Shane to be involved in my world. Yet he had his new life too and didn't want to give it up.

After he'd signed the new contract I'd emphasized that it was really important he came home every week. But before long it seemed to be a struggle for him to even manage every other weekend. If he did the atmosphere was weird. He'd want to sleep all day and had very little to say to me. He wasn't himself at all. I thought: *Christ, it's all happening again.*

All of a sudden things that made me laugh seemed to irritate him. I could tell I was totally getting on his nerves. In hindsight it was eerily similar to the way Robin had treated me when he was having an affair. I'd walk into a room and he'd walk out. I knew the warning signs were there but I didn't want to acknowledge them, so in my head I found a thousand excuses to justify Shane's behaviour. *He's just used to his own space at the moment*, I kept telling myself. *It's the upheaval, once he's home for good it'll be fine.*

I wasn't the only one making excuses either; Shane always had a reason if I asked where he'd been or why he couldn't come home – he was busy working, he was tired, he'd been out with his mates. He seemed to want me to think I was just being paranoid, silly or a nag. But deep down I knew it was much more than that.

I kept asking, 'Is there something wrong? Have you fallen out of love with me?'

It wasn't that our sex life had completely vanished or that he was a bad dad, neither of those things were true. It was more silly things. I'd visit him in Manchester and when it was time to go home, I'd say, 'I don't want to go, I miss you so much.' And instead of saying, 'I miss you too,' he'd just say, 'Oh you'll be back in a couple of weeks.'

I'm sure he didn't want to leave me. Part of him loved being the family man and father, but the trouble was he also loved his single life back in Manchester with his bird. Because I didn't know what was going on really, I assumed there was something wrong with me and I was full of self-loathing. Sometimes when the boys had gone to bed I'd drink a bottle of wine by myself and wake up the next morning feeling even worse.

And then, when I got invited on a hen night, Shane's reaction made me very uneasy. When I'd broached the subject of going on one a couple of years earlier he'd been very unhappy about it. 'Oh God, I know what hen nights are like,' he'd frowned, recalling his earlier years as a hen night entertainer. 'I really don't want you to go.'

At the time I was still trying to do anything to pacify him after my affair, so I told my friend it wasn't worth me going and upsetting Shane. But when a couple of years down the line I told him Carol had invited me to her friend's do he didn't bat an eyelid.

'You should go, you'll have a great time!' he enthused. It was all very odd.

I did go and have a laugh but I couldn't get the change in Shane's attitude out of my mind.

'I can't believe it,' I told Carol. 'He was thrilled I was going. I just don't get it.'

But although Carol had been through all the pain and humiliation of being cheated on first hand, she was always the one who discouraged me from jumping to conclusions. 'Stop winding yourself up,' she'd tell me. 'He might genuinely want you to go out and have fun.' So I brushed the doubts to the back of my mind.

Christmas passed, with just a few snatched days with Shane before he headed back to Manchester. We were now in our new home, a massive £1 million six-bedroom mock Tudor house in Buckinghamshire. But though it was beautiful, the size of the place made me feel lonely and isolated. Thankfully at the end of January 1997 Shane's run in Manchester finally ended, and to my great relief he was coming home. In my head it was Shane living in Manchester that was the root of all our problems. Now that he was coming back, I really hoped things would change.

Well, somebody came home who looked like Shane but it wasn't him! Whatever I said he didn't care, he was just going through the motions. I'd hoped having Shane home would mean we could spend more time together, but he immediately started doing anything he could to get out of the house. As soon as he got back he was suddenly off making an album for two weeks with some musician friends.

'It's a girlfriend and wife-free zone so we can get some work done,' he told me firmly.

I later discovered that Claire was there most of the time.

He also had a habit of disappearing off late at night. It would get to 10 p.m. and we'd be watching TV when he'd suddenly announce, 'I'm going round to Spongo's.' His musician mate

Paul Spong lived in Beaconsfield, ten to fifteen minutes from our house.

But it was very odd, as Shane had never been a big social-izer or 'going out with the lads' type.

'At 10 p.m. at night?' I'd ask.

'Yeah,' Shane would snap. 'You got a problem with that?'

And just the way Shane was on a daily basis became more and more strained. I'd walk into the sitting room in the evening and, whereas before he would have said to me, 'Oh Princess, sit with me and watch this film,' now he'd get up as soon as I sat down, as if I was repellent. It was as if he couldn't even bear to be in my company for more than a few minutes. Worse, I would catch him just looking at me sometimes, as if he didn't like me, let alone love me. I know now that at that point he didn't fancy me – because he really fancied Claire – but at the same time he was riddled with guilt. But the only reason I understand that is because of the affair I had.

I noticed Shane had stopped complimenting me too. When he was home sometimes I'd have moments of insecurity (like we all do) and say, 'I feel fat.' Instead of telling me I was imag-ining things and that he still found me attractive – the correct response, as men should know – he would reply bluntly, 'Why don't you try losing some weight?' Comments like that sowed the seeds of doubt even further in my mind, but then suddenly there would be other times, especially on holiday, when we were a normal, blissfully happy couple once more.

In March 1997, after our birthdays, I noticed Shane had started wearing this big silver ring. When I asked to see it he held on to his finger protectively. 'Why do you want to see it?' he asked. 'It's just a ring a fan sent to me.' Shane always had a way of making me feel like an idiot for questioning him, but I was constantly in a confused state.

However, he must have seen that the stress was getting to me, as a few weeks later he announced that he'd booked me in for four days at a posh spa called Grayshott Hall. I was really excited, thinking he'd be coming with me, until I heard he was sending me on my own! 'I went there not so long ago,' he explained. 'So I've booked all the best treatments for you.'

It was a nice thought, but as I was packing I noticed Shane had left the ring the fan had given him on the bedside table in our bedroom. Seizing the opportunity, I quickly grabbed it and dropped it into my bag. I don't really know why. I just wanted to have a better look at it.

So Shane waved me off and I headed off to Grayshott Hall, which was beautiful. But once I checked into my room I remembered the ring. Locating it in my bag, I started scrutinizing it, turning it round and round in my fingers. Suddenly I spotted something on the inside – really small letters inscribed in the middle. 'My love always, L,' they read.

Who the hell was L?

After that, all the beauty treatments and massages in the world weren't going to help me relax for those four days. By the end I was pulling my hair out so I called up Linda, who'd said she'd collect me, and I asked her to come and get me as soon as she could. 'And bring some chocolate biscuits,' I instructed.

Then I sat in the back of her car and scoffed the whole packet in five minutes flat. I've always been a comfort eater!

I later discovered L stood for Louise (Claire's stage name), and in a double blow I also found that Shane's thoughtful gesture was in fact very much recycled.

He'd actually booked me into Grayshott just weeks after going there on a romantic break with Claire. So all the staff must have already met his dolly bird. Of course he expected me to be happily unaware of this and I was at the time, but today I still find it very humiliating to think about.

Naturally Shane claimed L was just a love-struck fan and I had no choice but to accept that. The last thing I wanted was to drive myself mad seeing every girl Shane met as a potential threat to me. Even so, bit by bit over the next few months I started to turn into someone I didn't recognize. Shane was still off leading a separate life he told me absolutely nothing about, and when he was at home he'd look through me as if I didn't exist. It made me lonely, suspicious and constantly on edge. There had to be something up, and I was pretty sure that something was actually a 'she'.

One day I told him: 'Shane, I am sure you are having an affair and I am asking you to tell me the truth. I won't say I will not leave you because I don't know what I will do, but I just need to know.'

But he became impatient and snapped that there was no one else. 'I just need time to readjust to being a family man again,' he said. 'You've got to stop being paranoid.'

I knew he was lying but I just couldn't prove it. So I set about trying to.

I cannot tell you how hard it is being in the situation where you think your husband is cheating but you don't have any concrete proof. It was always 'deny, deny, deny' and then he'd convince me I was going mad.

One day Jake, who was by now almost five years old, was playing in the basement when he came upstairs to find me. He was clutching some photos. 'Mum, who is this lady with Daddy?' he asked. When I took the pictures out of his hands my blood just ran cold. There was Shane with his arms around a pretty dark-haired girl. She was laughing, and he was leaning in against a fireplace as if he was going to kiss her. As I studied them I was shaking.

'That's just a friend of Daddy's,' I told Jake, trying not to alert him to my horror. 'Now it's almost bedtime, so are you going to come and eat something?'

Later, after I'd settled Jake and his brother into bed, I grabbed the phone and dialled Carol's number. As I told her what had happened my voice started to break.

'Right, darling, I'll be round in two minutes,' she said.

True to her word she arrived quick as a flash. But as soon as I opened the door I burst out laughing. She was standing there on the doorstep with a plastic bag on her head.

'What on earth?' I asked.

'When you called I was leaning over the bath dyeing my hair,' she explained. 'I'm trying to cover up the grey bits.'

God bless Carol – she listened, consoled me and then headed home, her hair now a gothic shade of witchy black.

Not long after she'd gone the phone rang. It was Shane, who was now performing in *Grease* back at the Cambridge Theatre in the West End. 'Hello darling,' he said. 'I'm on my way home.'

'OK,' I said flatly.

'What's up now?' he said sounding irritated.

'I'll tell you when you come in,' I replied.

'I'm not putting the phone down until you tell me,' he insisted. Not wanting to give him time to make up an excuse, I immediately hung up.

Forty-five minutes later Shane arrived. 'What's up with you?' he asked as soon as he walked in.

'You tell me,' I replied, slapping the pictures into his hand.

'Oh that's just Claire,' he laughed dismissively. 'She's the best friend of one of the dancers in the show. She's mad about me. She was at a party and all she wanted was a whole roll of pics.'

'How come you've got them?' I asked.

'She sent them to me!' he said incredulously. 'Did you find them down in the basement with all my stuff from the show? They're in a box I haven't even looked at from when I cleared out my drawers after Manchester.'

Then he ripped them up and binned them. 'Come here, silly,' he said, cuddling me. But I wasn't convinced.

And it seemed Shane's behaviour also left my family and friends divided. Not long afterwards, Linda and her husband Brian moved in with us for a few weeks as they had a break in their tour and didn't have a house at that time. At this point Linda was touring the country doing *Blood Brothers* and Brian was her manager and PA and drove her everywhere.

On many an occasion I confided in Linda about my worries and suspicions but she never said a bad word about Shane. I think she could see the desperation in my eyes. She knew I so badly wanted a plausible excuse for Shane's behaviour and she didn't want to hurt me. While Linda was there, Bernie also came to stay for a couple of nights, and one evening, when Shane was out, and after I'd gone to bed, I was surprised to hear a heated argument going on between her and Linda in the kitchen. My bedroom was directly above them, so when I heard raised voices I opened the door to earwig. It was only after a couple of minutes I realized they were actually rowing about Shane and me.

'But I've heard from my friend on *Grease* that Shane's seeing a dancer behind her back!' Bernie was saying.

'Oh, come on, Bernie, you know what gossips are like!' Linda replied. 'You should know better than to believe this stuff.'

'But he's seen her in Shane's dressing room and he takes her out to dinner,' Bernie was insisting, getting louder and louder. 'I can't stand the fact that every time I see him he's all nicey, nicey, "Hello darling", with me. I just want to scream at him that he's messing my sister around!'

'Well, you can't,' Linda snapped. 'And if you can't stand him you shouldn't be staying in his home.'

It just descended into a massive argument, while I listened completely stunned. So I lay awake until Shane got back. 'Bernie has heard that you're definitely having an affair,' I challenged.

Well, he just went mad. 'I can't believe you or your sister would listen to idle gossip,' he yelled at me. 'If that's how she feels she should leave.'

We all went for a Sunday lunch the next day and everyone was supposed to be coming back to the house, until Shane said, 'I don't want Bernie to come.' So I had to ask Linda to go over and tell her.

You'd think that after so many incidents and accusations Shane might have been on his best behaviour, but sadly not. At times I actually felt as if he was twisting the knife. Rather than being nice to me, at times he was very volatile. I remember one day I was sitting in the front room with Linda and Brian when Shane yelled at me, 'Coleen, there's a shit in the hall.' We had dogs again now and the little buggers were always pooing everywhere. It was like an episode of *The Osbournes*.

'Well, I didn't do it,' I remarked. Linda and Brian chortled, but then Shane burst into the room with a furious look on his face.

'You think you're so fucking funny,' he spat at me. It was horrible. When Shane shouted I felt intimidated. I hated loud arguments, and whenever he raised his voice it made me feel really timid.

Looking back now, I can see that every time Shane treated me like that, he sapped my energy a little bit more. Every time he shouted at me, every time he lied, every time he neglected me, another little piece of my self-esteem would evaporate. And in that respect it's no wonder it took me so long to leave. I just felt worthless and anxious. Who on earth would want me? On that occasion his behaviour really upset me and he knew it.

By then I'd taken a part-time job in a health food shop. I didn't need the money, but being at home miserable all the time when the boys were at school was driving me mad. I'd work from 10 a.m. to 3 p.m. four days a week and had this lovely lady boss about the same age as me, with beautiful red hair. I'd tell her all about Shane and she was a good agony aunt. The day after he'd been so vile, predictably a big bunch of flowers arrived. 'I'm sorry, Princess,' the card read.

'They're lovely,' my boss said looking at them. 'We'll just put them in the bin, shall we?'

Not long after that Shane's London run of *Grease* ended and I invited Vicky to come with me to see his last show. Shane had told us there was a party at a private club after the performance, so we met up with Carol, who'd also been out in London, and headed over there for a drink and a dance. It was a while before Shane arrived with Goz, and seeing as it was his party I left him to do his schmoozing while I chatted with the girls and some other friends of ours who'd just turned up.

I'd driven that night, but I was having such a laugh that when a friend from the show, Robert, offered to drive my car home so I could have a few more drinks I was happy to accept.

'I can wait for Shane then,' I agreed. 'I'll get a lift back with him and Goz.'

When the party began to wind up I went over to Shane and Goz to tell them Robert was driving my car. 'I can come home with you,' I smiled.

'Sorry darling,' Shane said. 'There's not enough room with all the stuff I cleared from the dressing room.'

'Oh, OK,' I replied. 'I'll see you at home in a bit then, shall I?'

By now I'd been drinking, but thankfully there was just about room for me to squeeze into the car when Robert drove everyone to mine. Back at the house the party continued in the kitchen, but as we sat drinking and chatting I suddenly looked at the clock. *Bloody hell, they've been a long time*, I thought. In the end Shane and Goz didn't arrive back until two hours after the rest of us.

'Christ, what took you so long?' I asked when they finally walked in the door.

'We had to drop two of the girls home,' Shane replied. Carol, Vicky and me just looked at each other. I don't know if he was taking the piss out of me or if he'd genuinely forgotten what he'd said just hours beforehand, but I couldn't believe it. So there was no room for his wife but plenty of room for two random girls. But typical me, not wanting to make a scene or be confrontational, I simply said, 'Oh, right,' and headed off to bed.

I just lay there for ages thinking: *What does he mean, he dropped two girls home? Oh my God!*

With so much suspicion on my mind, I tried to get Shane's attention back to me by constantly trying it on with him. At that time I just turned into a nymphomaniac. It was all to do with insecurity and pride. I wanted him to see that sex was best with me. I could swing from the chandeliers if that's what he wanted. I'd do whatever it took to make my husband notice me again.

Seven

So did Shane refuse my advances?

Don't be ridiculous! When I gave him the full seductress routine he was loving it! For a while we were at it like bunny rabbits, and I enjoyed the intimacy of having physical contact with him, because it was the only affection I could get. Having said that, we actually had a nice little spell in the autumn of 1997 when it looked like things were getting back on track. Now that *Grease* had ended we were able to take the boys to Disneyland in Florida again and we were very happy for those few weeks.

The kids' excitement was infectious and we just had a fantastic time together as a family. One day we took the kids to the Animal Kingdom, and as we were sat together on a safari ride, the boys whooping with excitement at the giraffes, I caught Shane looking at us all with real affection and pride. 'I love you, Co,' he told me. 'I love all of this.'

I knew I had him back at that moment. He was really looking at me, feeling love for his family and celebrating what he was blessed with. If only I could have kept him in that zone, but sadly not. Soon he was back at work, swallowed up by the bright lights of fame and fortune and fawning sycophants.

In November Shane's new show *Boogie Nights* opened at the

Savoy Theatre. While *Boogie Nights* was running Shane often didn't get back until obscene hours of the morning, even though I knew full well the show finished at about half ten. And even on his nights off he'd disappear out late at night. I had no proof of anything going on, but his late-night mystery excursions were slowly but surely destroying me. I can recall one night when I was in the kitchen and saw he had his coat on ready to go out.

'Please don't do this,' I begged him.

'Oh, give it a rest, Co,' Shane snapped.

Crying, I slid down a cupboard on to the floor but Shane just stepped over me and headed out. I just lay there sobbing my heart out and then I went to bed.

But I was determined to catch him out. From the non-jealous wife I used to be, who refused to listen to rumours, I was now becoming an absolute freak. Every time Shane was out I'd turn into Jessica Fletcher, snooping round looking for evidence and going through the pockets of all his jackets and trousers. It became a ritual, a desperate need to find something. At the same time I felt I was behaving like a lunatic. I would often sit with my head in my hands, afraid that I had lost my mind because nothing made sense any more. I needed something to confirm my suspicions and to show me that I wasn't a paranoid mad woman. I even roped Carol, Vicky and Jane in.

By now they were all pretty convinced too. Every week they would come over, armed with bottles of wine, and we would sit in the kitchen getting pissed. Then we'd spring into action like Charlie's Angels. We'd take a room each, crawling around on our hands and knees, looking into every nook and cranny, scouring the bin, searching for clues to my husband's cheating. It was tragic but hysterical. As Christmas 1997 approached I honestly thought I'd reached my lowest ebb. But then Shane suddenly surprised me with a really touching gesture.

He'd booked the boys and us a holiday to Lapland to search for Santa! We flew out just before Christmas and spent four or five amazing days going on reindeer sleighs, husky dog sledding and messing about on ski-doos, which were like big jet-skis on the snow. It was so magical for the kids, and a proper family time. I came back from that trip feeling really happy. *He wouldn't do something that thoughtful if he was having an affair,* I told myself.

But I obviously spoke too soon. The minute we arrived home after the holiday Shane announced he was just bumming over to Goz's house.

'Now?' I asked looking at the clock. It was past 10 p.m. 'Can't you do it in the morning?'

'Jesus Christ, Co,' he snapped. 'I'll only be an hour.' But that night I waited up and I was sitting in the kitchen when he came in at 2.15 a.m.

'What are you doing up?' he asked, looking at me incredulously.

I stayed seated and was quite calm as I spoke. 'Shane, I know something is going on,' I said. 'If you don't love me I can deal with that. Human nature is a funny thing and people fall in and out of love all the time. But please, like me enough to tell me.'

After I'd said my piece Shane very calmly came over to me, took me by both hands and put his face really near to mine. 'I swear on my life nothing is going on, Coleen,' he said, looking me straight in the eye. 'But I do think you have a problem. You need help. Your paranoia is out of control.'

So I headed up to bed feeling sheepish. *There's no way he'd swear on his life,* I told myself, as I brushed my teeth. *He's definitely not having an affair. He just wouldn't say that if he was.*

163

It's funny, as years later I used to watch Shane playing Alfie Moon in *EastEnders* and it would send a shiver up my spine. He would be exactly the same. The same earnest eyes convincing you he was telling the truth, the same look of utter devastation and sorrow when he cried. It was only then that I came to realize what a brilliant actor he was and thought to myself, *Oh God, that's what he used to do to me*.

That year I was determined to enjoy Christmas, so I was thrilled when Shane made another thoughtful suggestion. 'Why don't we go up to Blackpool and surprise your family with the boys for Christmas?' he enthused.

It was a lovely idea. By now my dad was very ill, so it meant a lot to be able to spend time with him. But I can honestly say it turned out to be one of the worst Christmases I've ever had.

It all started on Christmas Eve, the day we planned to travel up to Blackpool. At the crack of dawn we were cuddled up dozing in bed when suddenly Shane leapt out and started getting dressed.

'Where are you going?' I said, rubbing my eyes.

'I've got to go and see Stan,' he replied, pulling on his jeans.

'At 8 a.m. on Christmas Eve?' I asked, puzzled. Why on earth did Shane need to see his manager today of all days?

'It's business,' he replied, throwing on a top, then he was out of the door.

Getting up, I busied myself with packing for our trip and wrapping the last of the presents, and tried not to focus on how long Shane was taking. Eventually he rolled up four or five hours later, not saying a word about his meeting, and we piled into the car. It was weird, but I put it to the back of my mind. I wanted to enjoy Christmas with my family, not get paranoid about what Shane was up to. Plus, I didn't dare make a fuss after he'd sworn there was nothing going on.

After a gruelling four-hour drive from Denham to Blackpool we finally arrived at Linda's, where we'd arranged to stay. Linda and Brian were just serving dinner and it turned into a really nice evening. Shane sat next to me and laughed and joked, rubbing my leg affectionately under the table. As I smiled at him and he grinned back, loosened up by the mulled wine we were all tucking into, I caught a glimpse of the Shane I'd known from years gone by. The Shane who adored me and had shared my excitement and enthusiasm for Christmas. It was nice to have him back. So that night as Linda and I put all the presents out for the kids I was feeling optimistic.

Christmas morning was lovely too. 'Santa's been!' Jake squealed, running into our room and clambering on to the bed, with Shane Jnr in hot pursuit.

'He never has!' Shane yelled back. 'What did he leave you?' The boys' enthusiasm was completely infectious.

To my delight Shane had very generously bought me a computer. Computers have never been my strong point, and because Shane Jnr was starting to use them at school I'd recently enrolled in a beginners' course at the local college so I could help him with his homework. If there is one thing Shane loves it is buying presents for people and seeing their reaction. I could tell he was completely made up that the boys and I were so thrilled with all our gifts.

But as the day wore on I noticed Shane's mood was darkening. He'd had a cold coming on for a few days and it was now hitting him with full force. By the time we went out to meet the rest of the family for Christmas dinner he was in a right old strop. 'My bleeding throat is killing me,' he moaned. 'I feel lousy.'

Everyone was delighted to see us, but when we walked in it seemed to pain Shane to even force a smile. As the meal progressed I noticed that everything I said seemed to annoy him. He just kept biting my head off. At one point there was a conversation going on, which admittedly I was being a bit slow getting to grips with, but suddenly Shane lost patience and shouted at me: 'Are you thick or what?'

Everyone looked completely shocked at his outburst and then my brother Brian stepped in. 'That's enough, Shane,' he barked. 'You're going over the top, so stop it.'

Everyone shifted uncomfortably in their seats and I felt this burning lump in my throat. It was just so embarrassing. Really hurtful and humiliating.

We'd planned to go back to my parents' after the meal, but then just as dessert was being served Shane stood up from the table and picked up his coat. 'I don't feel at all well,' he said meekly. 'If you don't mind I'll go back to the flat for a lie down. If I feel better after a couple of hours I'll come round.'

'OK,' I told him, concerned. 'Try to get some rest.'

Later, back at Mum and Dad's, I was still worried about Shane; so I called his mobile, but it was busy. I tried to call for over an hour, but the phone was engaged constantly. Why on earth was Shane nattering on the phone if his throat was hurting so much? I tried not to think of the inevitable answer, that he was on the phone to another woman. *Maybe it has a fault or something*, I told myself, but I just felt agitated all evening. When we finally got a cab back to Linda's, I marched in, to see Shane sitting on the sofa watching TV and looking miserable.

'How are you feeling?' I asked.

'Not great,' he replied hoarsely. 'My throat is killing me.'

'Shane, I've been trying to call you all evening,' I said. 'Why have you been on the phone?'

'I was talking to Stan and Mum,' he replied.

I just stood there staring at him. He'd claimed to have seen

Stan the previous day, and I knew he'd called his mum that morning. It made no sense, and I didn't buy his excuses for a second.

'To be honest I just want to go home,' Shane carried on.

'Well, we may as well,' I agreed, pursing my lips. So that night we drove back to London, barely saying a word to each other.

It was a pretty dismal Christmas all in all, but then, a couple of days later, things got even worse.

A letter had arrived addressed to me but I didn't recognize the handwriting. Tearing it open, my stomach lurched. 'I hope you enjoyed your Christmas,' it read. 'As it's the last one you'll have as a family. You need to know your husband is seeing this woman.' It was anonymous, and contained a newspaper cutting of a girl called Louise Tyler who was a dancer in a panto, *Snow White*, playing over in Surrey. I gawped, staring at the picture.

My first thought was that it might be the same girl I'd seen in the photos with Shane, but to be honest with it being black and white and her wearing a Snow White wig it was pretty hard to tell.

I was sitting opposite Shane at the table as I opened the letter and, shocked, I handed it to him without a word. He immediately snorted. 'Surely you're not going to believe that?' he said. 'It's just some nasty letter made up by a fan.' Then he ripped it all up and chucked it in the bin.

I swallowed hard. I really wanted to believe him. I loved Shane and wanted to stay married to him. He was the father of our children, and a kind, devoted one too.

A few days later I tried to find a programme from *Grease*, as I wanted to study the pictures of the girls in the show. I couldn't find one but I did find something else. It was a publicity shot of a pretty girl and it was signed, 'To Shane with all my . . .' and she'd drawn a heart and signed it Claire. I thought she looked very like the girl in the photos with Shane but I couldn't be sure. When I showed it to Shane he just looked at me exasperated.

'Oh, Coleen, she's just a dancer in the show,' he scoffed.

'But this is the girl in the photos,' I said. 'The one you said was a friend of a dancer – now you're saying she is a dancer?'

'No darling, you're not listening,' Shane said, waving his hand dismissively.

'But . . .' I started.

'Oh fuck it, I don't have time for this,' Shane interrupted me. 'I've got to go to work.'

And with that he was out of the door, leaving me standing there aimlessly, my eyes prickling with tears. I knew what he'd said, but now he was trying to convince me I couldn't even recall the sequence of events properly. By now, after a good eighteen months of this kind of stress, I was so done in brain-wise that everything was muddled in my head. Feeling as worn out as I did, I so badly wanted to believe him.

Obviously for months I'd been confiding in my friends and family about Shane's behaviour, but despite telling them my fears I didn't want them to believe them too. I knew what they all thought, even though they weren't cruel enough to say it. They wanted to tell me, 'For God's sake open your eyes, he's having an affair.' But they didn't because they could see the desperation in me. They knew I wanted to hear that I was over-reacting, so they listened without condemning Shane.

Before I faced up to the inevitable I needed to hear it from Shane himself. And as it happens it was only a few weeks later that I did. Bizarrely, in a stroke of poetic justice, after Shane had rumbled my affair by recording my phone calls, that's exactly how he got caught out too. I hadn't actually meant to bug the phone, but unbeknown to me the computer Shane had bought me for Christmas was picking up all the calls to the house. During those few weeks I'd had it almost constantly plugged into the phone line as I attempted to master the internet, and friends kept telling me that their calls were being automatically answered by a recorded message from an American lady.

When I investigated further, while Shane was abroad in Crete doing a show, I finally worked out that there were thirty-three calls all recorded on the computer's hard drive. Curious, I scanned through them, eventually stumbling across a call made by Shane at 11 p.m. one night. He was clearly talking to his mate Spongo, but I could only hear what Shane was saying.

'Hi mate,' he sighed. 'I'm just a bit down. I really wanted to see her tonight but she's going out with her mates.'

Don't panic, I told myself. *He could be talking about anyone.*

'Hello Princess!' the next one began. For a second I relaxed. Shane always called me that, so I just assumed he was talking to me. But then his next sentence confused me. 'Are you in-between shows?' he asked. 'What time do you finish? I'll try and come round.'

What show? I thought. It didn't add up. I hadn't been in a show for ages, and more importantly I'd only had the computer since Christmas, not even a month in fact. There was no way he was talking to me.

'I really miss you,' Shane continued, in that affectionate tone I knew so well.

Caught red-handed! Strange though it seems, my first reaction was to feel jubilant. I was so calm I actually went, 'Yes!' As shocked as I was, it was a huge relief to know that it wasn't me imagining things at all. I wasn't going insane, and I wasn't paranoid. I felt such a rush of different emotions – anger, fear, sorrow and vindication – all mixed up.

My sister Denise was staying with me at the time, so feeling triumphant I barged into the spare room to tell her. She was halfway through getting changed and looked startled. 'You have to come and listen to this,' I ranted. 'I've caught the bastard.'

Denise had previously told me not to jump to conclusions, but this time all the colour just drained from her face. 'Oh my God,' she said. 'I can't believe it.'

As the truth began to sink in, I put the kettle on and started pacing round the kitchen. I couldn't keep still as I tried to take it all in. Who was she? How long had it been going on for? It must be the girl from *Snow White*.

Denise was so worried she called her boyfriend Tom and told him to come round. I was just manic. I didn't really know what to do with myself. Anger started bubbling in my stomach. Shane had sworn that it was me who was the crazy one. I was bloody flying round that kitchen, but then I had to pull myself together.

Realizing I was supposed to be looking after Vicky's four kids as well as my two, I raced to pick them all up from school and bring them back to my house. I didn't want them to know something was up, so I had to act my socks off until 6 p.m., but inside I was just dying – I wanted to sit down and sob, I wanted to punch something, but instead I put on my best poker face to protect the children.

Although it wasn't fooling Vicky – she walked in and instantly knew. So we put a video on for the kids and I told her everything. 'What are you going to do?' she asked.

'I don't know yet,' I replied. 'Shane's in bloody Crete and I haven't been able to get hold of him all day.'

I don't think I could have got through that period without Vicky, Carol and Jane. It didn't matter what time of day or night I needed them, they'd be round. They were just bloody fantastic all the way through.

After not hearing from Shane all day, the phone finally rang at 11 p.m. When Denise answered, it was Goz. 'Hi Den, I need to speak to Coleen,' he told her. 'Shane fainted. I don't want her to worry but he's in hospital with suspected food poisoning.'

'I don't think Coleen would care if he never came out of hospital,' Denise replied calmly. 'She knows, Goz. She caught him on the answerphone.'

So Goz went off to tell Shane and it wasn't long before he called me, crying his eyes out.

'Hello,' I answered.

'I'm so sorry,' Shane croaked. He sounded really rough.

I didn't say a word, I couldn't. Where would I even start? For months I'd been trapped in a horrible state of paranoia, wondering what I'd done wrong, wondering if my husband loved me, convinced I'd turned into a jealous, snooping psychopath. I'd cried so many times that I wasn't even sure I had any energy any more. I certainly couldn't cry now. I just felt numb, as if I'd been drugged.

After a long pause Shane continued. 'Talk to me, Coleen,' he said. 'I'm so sorry. I promise you it's over and I regret it. I don't know what happened. I love you and I don't want to lose you. I love you and the kids. Please don't make any rash decisions.'

'You let me think I was going crazy, Shane,' I eventually replied. 'And you lied to me. How can I ever trust you again?' And with that I ended the call.

★

I made my way up to bed but I couldn't really sleep. My mind was just racing. I didn't know what to do, so I tried to take the emotion out of the situation. *People have affairs*, I thought, *I had one*. Was I willing to throw my marriage away and break up my children's home because Shane had made a mistake? He'd forgiven me once, so maybe I should do the same. Could I really deal with a marriage break-up at the moment? Did I want to be on my own? The thought of going through all that just seemed so all-encompassing.

'What'll probably happen is there will be lots of tears and then we'll go to marriage guidance and be stronger than ever,' I consoled myself. 'As hurt as I am, I can't really cope with any other option right now.'

When Shane came home the next night I guess I really should have given him what for, but unfortunately for me I'm just not confrontational. I've never been a screamer and shouter. Anyway, it was difficult because the boys were up, so we had to go through a charade of being happy to see one another and acting normally for their sake. It was the longest three hours of my life.

Once the children were in bed, Shane and I sat down in the kitchen together. There was silence for half an hour. Neither of us knew where to begin. Plus when he walked into the kitchen he looked terrible, really pale, his eyes red from crying. He looked like a lamb to the slaughter.

'Do you want a cup of tea?' I found myself saying. He looked relieved and just came over and hugged me.

I stood there, my body rigid. As much as I wanted to sink into his arms, I knew I should be giving him the cold shoulder. So freeing myself from his embrace, I moved over to boil the kettle for the tea.

'I'm not sure I want to be with you any more, Shane,' I told him, tears beginning to stream down my face. 'You've made such a fool of me.'

Shane sat at the table, his head in his hands and sobbing, absolutely distraught. But I just didn't know if I could forgive him for all the lies. 'The thing that is so mortifying for me, Shane,' I managed to sniff, 'is that after twelve years together and me asking you, you still didn't tell me the truth. How can I ever get past that?'

He couldn't answer, he just cried and cried.

'So is her name Claire or Louise?' I asked.

'Um, both,' he admitted. 'She was a dancer from *Grease* who I met in Manchester.'

After pouring the milk and handing him a mug, I avoided eye contact, staring out of the window instead.

'I'm sorry, I didn't mean to hurt you,' he continued. 'It just got out of hand and every time I tried to end it she said she'd go to the papers. I couldn't let that happen.'

I just listened, not really looking at him. My whole body felt tired and I was mentally drained.

'I'm so sorry, Co,' Shane said, his voice breaking. 'I don't want to lose you.'

He told me he had lied to this Claire too, that he had told her we hadn't had sex for a year and slept in separate rooms. I didn't know what to say, so I just stared at a little white speck on the floor for ages.

'Oh come on, you'll never leave me,' Shane suddenly said. When I glanced up I saw he was trying to smile through his tears. I know he was just trying to reassure himself we'd be OK, but I couldn't give him that comfort.

I decided to sleep on it, but the next day after a restless night I knew I didn't want to make the decision lightly and throw everything away because of one mistake – particularly one I'd also made. So I sent a letter to Claire at the theatre where she was working. I wrote that I wanted her to know that I knew she was having an affair with my husband and that Shane had told me things that he had been saying to her. 'We do have sex,' I told her. And I also told her that I didn't blame her, that Shane was the one with the responsibilities and that she had been fooled by him, just as I had been. I finished by writing that I envied her, and if she ended up with my husband then she was lucky because he was great.

I'm not really sure why I wrote it – it was quite cathartic, I guess, and also I wanted her to see that her actions were hurting a real person. But at that time, I genuinely thought that Shane and I would get past this rocky patch and grow old together. I just couldn't get my head round any other outcome.

I never got a reply to my letter, but Shane assured me he loved me and would break up with Claire. Over the next few days he cancelled any work and followed me round the house like a little puppy. 'I just want to be with you and the kids,' he kept saying. 'I love you and I'm so sorry. We'll get counselling.'

I was still being funny about physical contact, but then Shane stood in front of me and took me by the shoulders. 'Co,' he said, his brow furrowed with emotion. 'None of this is your fault. It's nothing you did. You are a brilliant wife. I just went a bit mad and fell into the single man trap.'

Later, on the phone, Carol asked me what I thought I'd do.

'I still don't know,' I sighed. 'I just can't really work out how I feel. It's such a mess.'

'Don't make a life-changing decision based on pride,' she advised. 'It's hard being on your own, believe me.'

It was good to hear my friend almost giving me permission to give Shane a second chance. I knew that deep down I wanted to, but I was embarrassed. The thought of everyone thinking I was a mug was almost as humiliating as Shane's infidelity itself. But the truth was I didn't want to split my family up. I wasn't sure I could survive alone and had never imagined I would have to. I had planned for our future to be together. I didn't want to be a thirty-four-year-old single mother. If that was my future I didn't want it. It looked too bleak. Instead I was determined to fight for my marriage.

'This is not going to be easy for me, but if you promise it's over then I'm going to try and forgive you,' I eventually told him. 'But Shane, don't you *dare* hurt me again.'

Shane immediately cried with relief. 'Oh Co,' he said, burying his face in my hair. 'I love you so much and this time I won't mess up. I promise.'

True to his word, Shane was every bit the attentive, loving husband I'd missed. He took me out for meals, showered me with presents and told me I was beautiful. The late-night excursions ended too, and I began to see a bit of light at the end of the tunnel. Ironically some of the happiest times were when I found out about the affair and he absolutely put me on a pedestal. If we went out I could do no wrong, he constantly said I looked great and he wouldn't leave me alone, to the point that I'd end up saying 'Get off!' He was always hugging and kissing me and I'd think: *He really does love me*.

At that stage he'd be jealous if I noticed another bloke – even one on telly. If I said, 'George Clooney . . . he's gorgeous!' I'd get 'All right darling, leave it out' in reply. And if I flirted with anyone he got *really* jealous – it was kind of reassuring in a strange way. Then on Valentine's Day he bought me the most amazing bunch of flowers – a big spray of red roses.

We still had some very happy times – still made each other laugh. He'd constantly tell all my friends he loved me. But although we were back on track and seemingly happy, I wasn't about to trust him one hundred per cent. I couldn't check his mobile because he had a code to lock it, but whenever he was out of the house I'd go through his pockets and paperwork.

And it was when I scrutinized his February bank statement that I started to get suspicious again. Just before 14 February I noticed some pricey transactions at a florist. But instead of one payment there were two. I wondered if he'd been charged twice by accident, but that didn't make sense, as the sum was different on each. The only explanation I could come up with was that Shane had sent out two bunches – one to me and one to his mistress. Outraged, I persuaded Brian, Linda's husband, to call up the shop pretending to be Shane.

'I'm sorry, Coleen,' he said after he'd got off the phone. 'They said there were two bunches and they went to different addresses.'

I was livid – particularly as I'd had the cheaper bunch! When Shane stepped in the door I could hardly speak through anger. 'Who did the other flowers go to, Shane?' I seethed.

'I sent one to my mum,' he insisted, without even flinching. 'Come on, Co, I've learnt my lesson.'

I didn't believe him, so I just walked out of the room, clenching my fists so tight with fury that my nails left red marks in the palms of my hands.

That night after I'd read Jake his bedtime story, I sat and stroked his brow as he drifted off to sleep, tears prickling in my eyes. My heart just felt so heavy and I hated myself for being so weak. *I've just let him get away with it again*, I thought. *He knows I won't kick him out. He's having his cake and eating it and there is nothing I can do.*

Pathetic or what! Why on earth didn't I just read him the riot act, call my solicitor and take him to the cleaners? In truth, because I loved him. As our relationship disintegrated in front of my eyes I felt a terrible sense of failure. I'd said my marriage vows to Shane all those years earlier intending for them to be for life. *I'm not going to be a statistic,* I thought. And there was something else spurring me on too. A mix of stubbornness and pride. Another woman was trying her hardest to steal my husband away from me. 'I'm not giving him to you that easily,' I imagined telling her in my head. 'We exchanged marriage vows and he's the father of my kids.' But still, I hated what I'd turned into. Why was I driving myself mad looking through Shane's receipts and belongings, yet turning a blind eye to his affair when the evidence I found confirmed it?

Agonizingly, not long afterwards I found a receipt from a jeweller's. Feeling sick with apprehension, I immediately went into the shop and made a fantastic story up on the spot about a mix-up with presents. They took ages tracing the receipt back for me and I felt so guilty. Lo and behold, it was for a little china ballerina. *Well, that's not for me*, I thought bitterly. *But it's the ideal gift for his dancer girlfriend.* Leaving the shop I felt suffocated, as if I couldn't breathe, thinking: *Shane claims he loves me but he kept on hurting me nonetheless. I need some space. I can't bear this any more.*

Back at home I confronted him. 'I don't want to hear your excuses, I just want you to move out,' I told him. 'You need to go away and live somewhere else.'

Of course Shane stalled for days on end, but eventually in June 1998 he announced that he'd rented a bedsit in Pimlico. 'It's only temporary though,' he insisted. 'I'm coming home.'

'Do you want me to pack a case for you?' I asked, ignoring his comment.

'No, I'm just taking the clothes I'm in,' he said. 'I'm not staying there permanently. Every couple of days I'll come back and see you.'

'No, Shane, you're missing the point,' I told him. 'The point of a separation is that I don't want to see you!'

But Shane refused to take a thing. 'It's like you're getting rid of me,' he sulked, his eyes welling with tears. So as per usual he pretty much got his own way. He could pop home for clothes whenever he wanted and was constantly on the phone to me. The space I so badly needed and craved just wasn't happening at all.

'Where are you?' I'd ask, hearing noisy traffic in the background.

'I'm outside the bedsit,' he'd say. 'I can't get a signal inside. It's so horrible. Just one mattress on the floor.'

'You don't have to phone me, Shane,' I told him, but he never listened.

It didn't take long for the papers to find out that Shane was living somewhere else. 'Shane and Wife Split After 8 Years' the headline read. But there was worse to come. About three days later I drove to the shops to get some milk and on my way back I noticed a guy standing outside the gates of the house.

'Hello,' he said, approaching the car. 'I'm from the *News of the World*. Sorry to turn up like this, but do you know your husband has been having an affair with a dancer called Louise Tyler?'

'Yeah, I do,' I replied.

'Oh,' he said, looking surprised. 'Well, I just want you to know it'll be in the paper on Sunday.'

'Thanks,' I replied and drove into the drive.

As soon as I got inside I called Shane. 'We're going to have to tell the boys,' I said. 'They have no idea what has been going on and they need to know.'

'You'll have to do it,' Shane replied, his voice breaking. 'I just can't.'

The only reason I let him get away with that was because if I did it myself I could guarantee it would cause the minimum amount of hurt for our sons. So later, when they were home from school, I called Shane and Jake up to the bedroom. They bounded in all happy and I sat them on the bed. 'I've got something to tell you,' I said gently. 'You know a lot of your friends' mummies and daddies don't live together? Well that doesn't mean that their mummies and daddies don't love them.'

They both nodded so I continued, 'Me and Daddy are not going to live together, but we both really love you.'

The pair of them sat there and said nothing for a minute, but then Shane Jnr, who was nine, curled up into a foetal position. He tucked his head into his knees and let out this high-pitched whine. He sounded like a wounded animal, and at that moment I felt like my heart smashed. After everything I'd gone through, that was the worst possible moment for me, but it also made me grow stronger. *I will never ever hurt them again*, I thought. I decided that no matter what Shane did I'd never stop them seeing him.

Well, the poor little mite howled for ages and I just held him. Jake was still a bit too young to really understand, but then he started sobbing because Shane was, and the three of us huddled up together on the bed and had a good cry. When the tears eventually stopped I beckoned them downstairs. 'Come on,' I soothed. 'Let's go and put a video on. Everything will be fine.'

'Why don't you love Daddy any more?' Shane Jnr asked me sadly.

'Sometimes adults fall out of love,' I explained. 'But we'll never stop loving you.' He seemed to accept that, and the three of us settled down to watch a film. But then half an hour later

Jake suddenly started crying again. I put him on my lap for a cuddle. 'Don't cry,' I said. 'It'll be OK.'

'But who's going to buy us videos now,' he wailed. Bless him, that's what worried him the most.

'I expect Daddy will,' I laughed, and after that everything was fine.

Although I'd told the boys, I did give Shane one more chance. When the *News of the World* story broke I was absolutely inconsolable. Seeing my humiliation spread all across the papers was awful, and worst of all there were pictures of Claire. It was the first time I'd been able to study my love rival properly, and it was torturous how many people called and texted me that day. That evening Shane came round and begged my forgiveness.

'Please let me move back in,' he pleaded. 'I can't live without you, Co.'

'Ssh,' I snapped, hearing the boys' footsteps on the stairs. 'Not now.'

Shane Jnr and Jake were so happy to see their father that all the anger and hurt dissolved and I didn't have the heart to send him away. I had so much on my mind. Not least my dad's health.

I'd phoned him every day around that time, and he was such a calming influence and never judged. 'Only you can decide what you want to do,' he told me. 'I love you, so whatever you do it's fine with me.'

But in the past few months he'd really gone downhill. He couldn't go out much, and if he did he'd only manage to walk about three steps before he'd struggle for breath. Now he was on twenty-four-hour oxygen and in and out of hospital all the time. Over the next few months I had several frantic calls telling me to get up to Blackpool quickly as Dad had taken a turn for the worse. I'd immediately drop everything and race up north.

Shane, to his credit, was great when this happened, immediately sending me off to pack and ordering me a car to take me straight up to Blackpool. But to our amazement, each time Dad would pull through. 'Dad, I'm not having a laugh,' I'd joke. 'But if you keep doing this I'll have to stand on your oxygen pipe!'

In fact when my dad had first got really ill, Shane had demonstrated the kind and loving side of his nature. When my father had first gone on to twenty-four-hour oxygen, getting up and down the stairs at the house in Waterloo Road had been too much for him, so Shane had helped my parents with money towards a bungalow. He could be incredibly generous, and had once got Anne and Brian out of terrible debt when they faced losing everything. Whenever people needed help there was never any doubt that he'd step in.

While I was haring back and forth to Blackpool, Shane was touring the UK with *Boogie Nights*. And as if my worry over my dad wasn't enough, one weekend in August I was horrified to see a kiss-and-tell story in the paper about Shane sleeping with a random girl he'd met on tour. It was a big double-page story saying she had spent the night with Shane and gone back to his hotel. The only thing that redeemed him was that she said he'd been drinking vodka and tonic.

'But you don't drink vodka and tonic,' I said.

'Exactly,' he replied. I felt slightly appeased but not totally convinced, so I still went nuts. *How can I ever trust him? I* thought. *Every time I give him another chance he makes a mockery of me.*

Then, about a week later, Carol and I went to see him in

Boogie Nights and as Goz walked out of the dressing room, Shane said really casually, 'Goz, get us a vodka and tonic.'

I was gobsmacked. I honestly didn't know if he was incredibly cocky or just so stupid that he couldn't remember which lie he was telling to which girl. As we walked out, Carol said to me, 'You don't have to say anything. I know what you're thinking.'

'I know what you're pissed off about,' Shane remarked later. 'You're annoyed that I asked Goz for a vodka. I was just winding you up, you know what I'm like!'

I wasn't convinced, and, devastated, I immediately started snooping again. A few weeks later I discovered a jewellery receipt for a gold ring with a sapphire. Shane hadn't given me any jewellery for ages and it was long past my birthday so it was fairly obvious who that was for. Unfortunately that day was also Jake's sixth birthday, so when Shane arrived at the party I quietly confronted him. 'Did your girlfriend like her ring?' I whispered in his ear.

Shane glared at me and fumbled in his pocket. 'There's the fucking ring,' he hissed, slamming it into my hand. 'You've ruined the surprise, you may as well have it now.'

When I looked at it I could immediately see that it wasn't meant for me. It was really garish and modern and not the sort of thing he'd get for me at all. So staring moodily at him, I put it back into his pocket and walked off. *It's Jake's birthday*, I told myself. *You need to deal with it another day.* Although soon I had something all the more pressing on my mind. About a week later I was at home when the phone rang.

It was Brian. 'Dad's not good, you need to get here now,' he said.

Straight away I arranged to leave the boys with Vicky and raced to the station to jump on a train. At the other end Brian met me and drove to the hospital, but after we'd parked up and raced to the entrance we saw Tommy standing outside, looking really lost.

'I'm sorry,' he said. 'Dad died about twenty minutes ago.'

So my dad had finally passed away, aged seventy-three. The news left me winded but I didn't cry. I just went and sat on my own for a while with a million different thoughts charging through my mind. Mum and Dad had been together for fifty years, and I couldn't believe all they'd been through. Dad was a drinker and nasty and at times I just wanted to say, 'Oh Mum, just leave him!' He was awful to her and must have made her feel worthless, like a piece of shit on his shoe, but in those last few weeks of his life the only person he wanted near him and the only hand he desperately wanted to hold was Mum's.

'Where are you?' he'd gasp. 'Maureen, where are you?'

Observing those last heartbreaking moments of tenderness between my parents, I'd admired them for staying together.

On the other hand my marriage was practically over, and it made me sad that Shane and I just couldn't survive the tough stuff. *I wonder if anyone will be there to hold my hand at the end?* I thought sadly. *I wonder who I'll be calling out for, if anyone?*

Losing Dad was the first big loss I'd had to face up to since Linzie had died seven years earlier, and it continued to be the weirdest mix of feelings and emotions. At times Dad had been a monster. He was a bully and a drunk. I knew he'd made Mum's life hell and sexually abused Anne. His behaviour repulsed me. But I also loved him.

He'd been a fountain of knowledge for me. He'd been so wise, so kind and so patient. And in later years, once he'd mellowed a bit, he'd been like a real mentor to me. Without him there was a massive void in my life. Bereft, I headed home to the boys. *They're all I have left to be happy about,* I thought sadly. *I won't have Shane much longer.*

Shane Jnr really didn't want to go to the funeral, but Jake desperately did so I took him up to Blackpool on the train while Shane Jnr stayed with Vicky. Shane was performing in Manchester with *Boogie Nights* and when I called to tell him what had happened he was really kind to me. 'I'm really sorry darling, I'm so sorry,' he kept saying over and over. And he promised he'd come to the funeral.

He turned up about 9 a.m. on the morning of the funeral, looking awful and clearly having had no sleep. I wondered if he'd been with Claire but had no fight left to make a fuss. So silently I put on my dress and applied my make-up, then the three of us headed off to the service, which was at St Kentigern Catholic church in Blackpool.

I can't remember much about that day, but I know I was coping all right until we got into the church. At that point my eyes started streaming. It was seeing the coffin that did it. Suddenly it was all so real. *I'll never see my dad again,* I thought. Blowing my nose, I sat down and managed to hold it together until it was my turn to get up and read. I'd chosen to read the words from the Celine Dion song 'Because You Loved Me', as they completely summed up how I felt about Dad. But halfway through I was overcome with emotion and Maureen had to get up and finish reading them for me.

Frantically I mopped my eyes with my hanky and tried to compose myself. I don't know why, but I'm funny about crying in front of people. After all that had happened with Shane, my pride had been hurt. I couldn't bear the thought of people feeling sorry for me and I'd got it into my head that crying was a sign of weakness.

Crying aside, the service was fabulous. Tommy and Brian

did eulogies for Dad, and Anne's daughter Alex read a poem from all the grandchildren. The church was packed out and all Dad's family from Ireland were there. In fact there were even people standing out in the car park. *He was loved*, I thought to myself, looking around at the sea of faces. *They just loved him.*

After the service we headed to the crematorium, which I was touched to see was crammed full too. As the committal ended we filed outside to 'That's Life' by Frank Sinatra. It was a brilliant choice, so perfect for my dad.

Afterwards we held a traditional wake at the Tangerine Club, the former home of Blackpool FC, where we'd once performed as kids.

Eight

The evening of Dad's funeral Shane headed back to Manchester to perform in *Boogie Nights*. 'Are you going to be OK?' he asked, stroking my face.

I knew it hurt him to see me so upset, but I think he was also quite relieved to have a reason to escape the sombre atmosphere. Shane can't really cope with thinking about death and tries to block it from his mind. My eldest brother Tommy is a bit like that as well.

Meanwhile Jake and I stayed up in Blackpool for a couple of days to be with Mum and the rest of the family. Mum was being very brave. It was typical of her really; she'd always been a very strong person. She'd have her weeping moments but they were very fleeting. 'We all have to go some time,' she said philosophically. 'Your dad had a good life.'

I hated leaving her, but after a couple of days Jake and I had to get home to Shane Jnr, who was staying at Vicky's. Mum insisted she'd be fine. 'I've got lots of people here to look after me,' she told me. 'I promise I'll be OK.'

It was actually really touching to see how many people were there to support her. As well as her family she had lots of friends rallying round her. Mum was very religious, so she had a big social circle through the church as well, and everyone was bending over backwards to help their beloved Maureen. The house was full of flowers and people were constantly popping round with cards and meals to keep her strength up.

In a way it was a small mercy that Dad had gone first, as I'd always thought Mum would be the one who'd cope better with the loss of her partner. When Dad was alive it had always been a running gag that he'd stay at home while she went out socializing. 'I haven't seen your mother all day,' he used to tut when I called up. 'She's out on the razz again.'

Arriving back in Denham, I was thrilled when Shane Jnr greeted me with a big hug. Both my boys were a real support to me and definitely gave me something to focus on, but to be honest I didn't really know what to do with myself a lot of the time. I felt bereft in every way. I couldn't even begin to compute my feelings, with no idea where one emotion ended and another started. It just seemed as though my life was crumbling. I'd lost my dad and I knew I was about to lose my husband too and I was scared of what the future might hold. *If Shane and I divorce how will I cope with being on my own?* I worried. *How will it affect the boys? Will I be able to find work?*

I couldn't work my life out any more and it frightened me. Ever since I'd first met Shane twelve years earlier I'd had a little plan mapped out in my head for us, and eventually for the boys. But now that future had been smashed. Losing Dad had somehow brought that reality to the forefront of my mind. My tummy ached with anxiety and I felt panicky all the time. I couldn't sleep properly and I had an overwhelming fear of everything.

I held it together in front of the boys but there would be times on my own when I'd really sob. Yet when I cried I felt guilty. Halfway through my sobs I'd realize I wasn't crying because I'd lost my dad, I was crying about Shane. *What's wrong with me?* I thought. *Why can't I get upset about Dad?*

Shane was still touring with *Boogie Nights* at this point, and coming and going from his bedsit in Pimlico. When he popped in, I couldn't bring myself to question him about Claire and whether they were still seeing each other, whether she visited the bedsit, whether they were even in contact. My mind ached from every thought process and I simply didn't have the strength to add any extra stress.

I was getting up, playing the smiley, happy mum, but once I'd dropped the boys off at school I actually slept all day. Later I'd force myself up to collect them, smile for a few more hours, put them to bed and then cry all night, snatching a few hours' sleep before the alarm went off. Although I was forcing myself to interact with people, in my head I felt very isolated and alone.

Previously I'd tried to keep the sex up with Shane, pouncing on him the moment he came round in the hope he wouldn't go elsewhere for it, but now I had no libido at all. I felt dead to the world.

Sometimes I was so down and desperate I couldn't even make myself get out of bed. But as I got further into that stage Vicky used to come round. On a Sunday she'd always have a roast dinner already cooking and she'd just walk in the house, say, 'Get up,' and make me pull myself together. Then she'd drive me and the boys back to her house for lunch. She helped me so much at that time; I knew then she'd always be there. All of those girls would be. I could really count on them, and if they didn't hear from me they'd just turn up.

I don't really think I'd acknowledged that I needed help before, but then, during a routine visit to the doctor's with one of the kids, my GP noticed how pale my face was and the grey bags under my eyes. 'How are you feeling?' he asked, concerned.

'Um, not so good,' I found myself confiding. 'Everything is a bit of a struggle at the moment.'

On his advice I reluctantly made an appointment to see a counsellor. I think it saved my life. I always tell people that now – even if you're happy you should consider counselling. It's amazing for sorting your head out. But beforehand I was very sceptical. My pride had been kicked and I never cried in front of anyone any more. There was no way I was going to start bawling in front of a stranger.

'But I won't know what to say when I go,' I said to Carol.

'You will,' she said. 'As soon as you walk in you'll know.'

When I arrived at the counsellor's office the following day I felt awkward and embarrassed. But when I walked into the room I was greeted by a petite blonde lady in her early sixties. Immediately she put her arm around me. 'Come and sit down and tell me how you are,' she said, in a lovely warm Scottish accent.

Well, for the first twenty-five minutes I sobbed before I could even say one word! 'Take your time, Coleen,' she told me.

'I feel guilty,' I eventually managed to sniffle in a small voice. 'I don't cry for my dad when I cry at night. I cry about my marriage.'

'But Coleen,' she replied kindly, 'there's only so much your brain can handle at one time. At the moment the person you're grieving for is still alive. Mentally you can't cope with grieving for two things at once.'

Suddenly I realized that she had a point and the guilt lifted a little. Although I still had a very long way to go.

Back at counselling the following week, I began to tell her

even more about Shane's behaviour recently. I explained about his late-night disappearing acts, his insistence that I was mad, the web of lies he'd spun and the moment I'd finally caught him out. 'The thing about Shane,' I explained, 'is that he does love me. We're still best friends, but he just wanted it all.'

'Do you honestly think he loves you?' my counsellor replied. 'He's not your friend. If your friend treated you like that you wouldn't give them the time of day. The only difference between you and a battered wife is that you have no physical bruising, but you are mentally battered.'

I was quite shocked by how blunt she was.

'I want you to do a test with Shane,' she continued. 'All I want you to say is, "The counsellor said it would be a good idea if we both went next week." That's all I want you to say.'

So the next time Shane called round that's exactly what I said. 'Oh yeah, that's a good idea,' he replied. But he never mentioned it again and the following week I arrived on my own.

'Surprise, surprise, no Shane,' she said.

'What was the point?' I asked.

'I'm trying to say to you that surely if he truly loved you he would have come with you to counselling?' she said.

I sat there nodding. I knew she was right. Yet I still couldn't quite summon up the energy to give Shane that final shove. I still had that incredible fear of my kids being from a broken home, and pride was also getting in the way. I didn't want to hand him to Claire. *She's not having you*, I thought. *I'm not giving up that easily.* Plus whenever Shane burst through the door engulfing me in a bear hug and calling out to the boys it made me feel happy.

When our little family unit was functioning it was perfect. The boys would come hurtling down the stairs from their rooms with excited screams of 'Dad!' and Shane would wrestle and tickle them until they could take no more. When calm was restored, the four of us would cuddle up on the sofa and watch kids' videos. It was bliss.

I viewed my life with Shane as a massive rollercoaster ride that never ended. One minute I was on top of the world, the next I'd plummet. And every time I wanted to get off he'd do something fabulous that would make me go round once more. Consequently my brain had turned to mush after all those heady highs and dark descents.

Then, to illustrate the point, a few weeks later when Shane had finished his tour, and just as I assumed that he and I were pretty much done with our marriage, he surprised me by suggesting that we go on holiday to Menorca for ten days without the boys. I jumped at the chance. I was still feeling low and really needed to get away. It also gave me a little glimmer of hope. Perhaps Shane and I could work through our problems after all?

And as it turned out, the two of us had a brilliant time. We stayed in a lovely boutique hotel with only about twenty rooms, which was very private and quiet. We spent our time lying by the pool, looking up to see all the mountains and trees surrounding us. It was stunning. Shane was attentive and kind and I began to feel a bit more human. He was actually noticing me. He took me for lovely meals every night and we went on beautiful walks, taking in the stunning Menorcan coastline.

'I love you, Co,' Shane constantly said.

But although he was being affectionate and saying everything I wanted to hear, towards the end of the holiday I started to feel a bit suffocated. I longed for the safety blanket of a normal, secure relationship with my husband, yet I couldn't just slip my blinkers back on and forget everything he'd put me through. And the more attentive he got, the more I felt like screaming, 'Just get off me!'

On our last night, as we tucked into tapas and sangria at a quaint little restaurant perched at the top of a cliff overlooking the sea, I decided to be honest about my feelings.

'Shane,' I said, putting my hand on his. 'I have to say something to you.'

'OK,' he answered.

'When we get back home I think we need to separate for a while.'

His face fell and he looked hurt.

'I don't mean for good,' I continued. 'Not a divorce. I just need some space.'

'But I want to move back in,' Shane protested.

'No,' I said firmly. 'I need to do this. I just need a few weeks.'

I guess at that point I was halfway to leaving him. But I still felt fragile and scared for the future. Whenever I contemplated life as a single mum a massive fear hit me. I kept looking in the mirror and imagining conversations with people. 'Hi, I'm Coleen! Am I married? No, I'm divorced actually.' I hated saying it. Plus not every man is happy to take on someone else's children. *Who's going to accept me along with my kids?* I thought. *I might never meet anyone again.* It didn't help that Shane was still a big part of my life – he called me just as much as he used to and would come round to the house as well. I wondered how I would ever decide what I wanted.

Then one day in April Shane turned up in a terrible state. He walked into the kitchen and literally fell into my arms and broke down.

'What on earth is wrong?' I asked.

'I'm finding it so difficult,' he told me. 'I can't bear it. My head is all over the place. I feel so guilty about the way I've treated you. I need to go away, not with the lads, just on my own. I've decided to go go-karting in France. I'm just going to chill out and get my head around everything.'

My heart immediately softened. He couldn't stop crying and just looked broken. So I headed upstairs with him and helped him pack. He couldn't find his passport but after turning the house upside down I eventually located it for him. As he headed out of the door, he turned and looked at me really sorrowfully, like a little boy.

'You're not going to leave me, are you?' he said. His eyes were swollen from crying and he looked as if he might start again any second.

'I don't know, Shane,' I replied softly, rubbing his arm. 'But don't worry about that now. Just enjoy your break and try to relax.'

'OK,' he nodded. 'I love you, Co.'

I watched him walk to his car; he had his head down and his shoulders hunched forward. He looked totally defeated. It brought a real lump to my throat.

After he'd driven off I turned and picked up the phone. Dialling Goz's number, I bit my lip. Shane's vulnerability always brought out my maternal instincts. It made me want to look after him.

'Hello?' Goz's voice filtered down the line.

'Hi Goz, it's Coleen,' I said. 'Look, I'm really worried about Shane. He's just been here in a terrible state. When you take him to the airport later will you make sure he's OK?'

'Course I will,' Goz replied. 'And don't worry, Col, I'm sure he'll be fine.'

When he didn't call back I assumed everything was fine. And when, over the next few days, Shane didn't call either, I was relieved for him, realizing that it was doing him good to have some time to himself, to be alone with his thoughts.

But three days after Shane had left, the phone rang. 'Is that Coleen?' asked a woman whose voice I didn't recognize.

'Who's speaking?' I asked cautiously.

'You don't know me, but I'm Claire's mum,' she said.

My stomach lurched. 'Oh,' I replied, contemplating whether or not I should hang up.

'I just wondered if you knew where Shane was?' she said.

What was this all about? 'He's away,' I said. 'Not that it concerns you or your daughter.'

'I'm really sorry,' she said quietly. 'I'm not doing this to hurt you, but I just want you to know that he's in Tunisia with my daughter.'

I just held the phone to my ear, completely dumbstruck. I thought back to Shane's distress, the swollen eyes, the crying. A seething anger began to rise in my chest. *I packed for him and found his passport*, I thought. *But all the time he knew he was going to Tunisia with his girlfriend.* I heard myself breathing deeply into the phone receiver.

'I can't bear what he's doing to you and my daughter,' Claire's mum continued. 'I always promised I wouldn't get involved, but this has been going on for two years and I can't stand it.'

'I don't know what I can say,' I said flatly, trying my best not to give away my emotion with my voice.

'Did you know he told Claire you're only staying together for the kids?' she added. 'And that you have no sex life?'

'Well, that's a lie,' I scoffed. 'It happened two days before he went off on his little holiday.'

Now there was silence from her end. 'I hope you don't hate me,' she said finally.

'No, not at all,' I sighed. 'I think if it was my daughter I'd do the same.'

'And please don't hate Claire.'

Her words made me swallow hard. 'Please don't ask me to feel sorry for her,' I said. 'The only people I can feel sorry for right now are me and my children.'

Putting the phone down I gripped the kitchen table with fury, digging my nails into the wood until my fingers throbbed from the pressure. I wanted to scream at the top of my voice or smash every piece of crockery in the place. But the kids were in the other room, so instead I took a deep breath and picked the phone up again.

'Hi, Goz,' I said, forcing myself to sound upbeat. 'You know when you pick Shane and Claire up from the airport when they get back from Tunisia?'

'Um,' he said cautiously.

'Well, do me a favour and don't bring him back to this house. He is NOT to come back here.'

Predictably it wasn't long before Shane called. 'I'm coming home,' he said. 'I need to explain.'

'Don't you *dare* come into my house,' I told him. 'As unlike before I will not hold my feelings in.'

'Co, I'm coming home tomorrow,' he insisted.

'No, Shane,' I said. 'Unless you want your children to see me going mental at you, you will stay away.'

'I had to go with her,' he whined. 'I took her away to get her out of the country. I explained to her that I wanted to be with you. But I had to convince her over several days so she wouldn't go to the papers. I was crying because I knew I was lying to you.'

His voice was filtering down the line but I wasn't really listening. 'Shane, save it,' I snapped.

'But it's over and she won't go to the papers,' he droned on, talking ten to the dozen. 'I'm still going to stay at the bedsit if you don't want me there.'

'No, I don't want you here,' I said, and then I hung up.

Well, of course Shane turned up the next day while the boys were at school. 'I thought I said I didn't want you here,' I snapped.

'Oh Co,' he said, trying to put his arm round me. He had the same remorseful little boy lost look in his eye that he'd left with, but this time I was feeling far from maternal and pushed his arm away forcefully.

'Just get your stuff and get out,' I said, glaring at him.

'OK,' he said. 'I will in a minute.'

I was surprised, but relieved. He seemed to be accepting what I was saying, so I began to calm down. He asked me about the boys and then went as if to leave. 'Co,' he said, 'I still need to get you a car stereo, don't I? Shall we go now?'

I stared at him, knowing full well it was a diversionary tactic. Then I thought, *Why not? You can buy me the most expensive one in the shop after what you've done.* So off we went, with Shane trying his hardest to make me laugh and me staring out of the window stony-faced with my arms folded across my chest. When we came back later it was almost the boys' home time. 'Can I stay and see them?' he asked.

'OK,' I sighed. By now I was too weary to argue.

We both knew he wouldn't be clearing out his stuff that day. And that night, of course, Shane got his own way and pitched up in the spare room.

At counselling later that week I filled my counsellor in, frustrated. 'Each time he lets me down I just think "I don't want to be with you any more",' I explained. 'But it's so hard when the kids are involved. When he asks to see the boys he knows he's got me over a barrel.'

I was finally beginning to see some light at the end of the tunnel, but inside I felt so battered. The words 'It's over' were on the tip of my tongue. It was just a question of finding the strength to get the ball rolling. And typically another day would go by and I still hadn't gone to a solicitor.

Shane continued to breeze in and out to see the boys and me. He'd sleep in the spare room at the weekend but for those two days the four of us did everything together as a family, with seemingly no hint of the underlying problems driving Shane and me apart. But Shane's deception over the holiday really had been the straw that broke the camel's back. When I'd been on the phone to Claire's mum a light had just gone out inside me. At last I was toughening up. Finally I knew that I didn't love him any more and I didn't want to be with him.

'Shane, it's not going to work any more,' I told him repeatedly, but he clearly wasn't listening.

'Oh come on, Co, you'll never leave me,' he'd say. 'We love each other.'

So I'd roll my eyes at him and walk out of the room. *No, I don't love you actually*, I thought. *And it's only a matter of time before I work out what I'll do next.*

So I carried on like that, mulling over my options. Would I stay in the house? Could we crash with friends? Would I head back to Blackpool? Each day my conviction that I was leaving Shane was growing stronger. The fog was beginning to clear and the dark depression I'd experienced ever since I'd got wind of Shane's affair and my dad had died began to lift. I was getting my fighting spirit back. I would and could go it alone. Whereas previously, stricken with grief for my dying dad, I'd looked at my parents' marriage as an example of triumph over adversity, now I'd taken off the rose-tinted specs. *God, they spent fifty years together and despite everything Mum stayed*, I thought. *If only she'd left she could have had a fantastic life. She could have been with a man who showed her lots of love and affection, yet she stayed and put up with so much.*

Mum was very old-fashioned, and when I confided that I was planning to leave Shane she told me, 'You should stay for the children.' It was what she'd done, as most women did in those days. But I knew I couldn't at that point. I'd already stayed longer than I should have because of the kids. Although I admired the way Mum had just got on with it and had been brave and strong, she'd settled for second best. My father was brutal to her and his womanizing had even resulted in a love child.

Although Shane had never once laid a finger on me, the way he was heading there was every chance he could get another woman pregnant – just like Dad. Was I prepared to follow the same path as my mother and overlook all the rot in our relationship for the sake of my children and a handful of fleeting happy moments? *No*, I decided, *I'm worth more than that. Any woman is worth more.*

I was already aware that although I didn't cry in front of Shane Jnr and Jake, children are very perceptive, and there were days when I was irritable and despondent no matter how hard I tried to look on the bright side. I realized that if I kept going like this they would look back one day and think their mum was really miserable. And paranoid too! If I stayed with Shane I'd never be able to trust that he was being faithful, and that distrust would drive me mad again.

The following weekend I was lying in bed reading when the phone rang. It was very late, so I looked at the clock, concerned. Who on earth was calling at 12.30 a.m.? I grabbed the phone quickly in case it was Mum or another member of my family.

'Can I speak to Shane?' a girl said.

I didn't recognize the voice at the other end. 'Who is it?' I asked.

'It's Claire.'

I instantly dropped the phone on to the table like a hot brick. Jumping out of bed I stormed down the stairs. *God, she's got some bloody bottle*, I thought.

'Shane,' I called in a singsong voice, 'your girlfriend is on the phone.'

Then I went back to bed, turned out the light and shut the door. I was lying there in the dark, shaking with rage and too angry to sleep, when I heard the door creak. 'Co,' Shane whispered. 'Are you awake?'

I ignored him but he carried on regardless. 'I've had a right go at her,' he said. 'She's trying to split us up.'

'No, you've split us up, Shane,' I said wearily. 'But I'm not bothered any more, so do what you want.'

I was relieved when he headed back to his bedsit the following morning.

Well, a few nights later Shane was back to see the kids. It was getting late and we were sitting in the front room talking about the boys, when suddenly the buzzer went, alerting us to the fact someone was at the end of the drive. *Who's turning up at this hour?* I thought, puzzled, as I walked into the kitchen to look at the monitor that was connected to a security camera at the gates. When I saw the hazy outline of a small woman with brown hair I knew immediately that it was Claire.

'Shane,' I called, 'your girlfriend is at the gates.'

'What?' he said. 'I can't believe it.'

'Well, you'd better go and see her because if she keeps buzzing and wakes my kids I'll kill her,' I said, glaring at him.

So off he went to talk to her while I sat in the kitchen in disbelief. The girl had the cheek of the devil.

Ten minutes later Shane was back. 'She's gone,' he said. 'She knows it's over between us and won't accept it. But it's sorted now.'

'Oh, that's good,' I said sarcastically. 'Now, if you don't mind, I'm going to bed.'

That night I couldn't sleep. I knew I was on the verge of making our separation permanent but it frustrated me no end that I still didn't have all the facts. I'd known for months that the only way I was going to get to the bottom of Shane's deception was to speak to Claire myself, but it was the one call I really didn't want to face up to. *I have to do it tomorrow*, I told myself.

So the next morning I went through Shane's phone bill and found a mobile number he was calling every day. 'Is that Claire?' I asked. 'It's Shane's wife.'

'Can I call you back?' she asked.

'Make sure you do.'

About an hour later she called. 'I need to know the truth,' I told her. 'I want to know what he says to you, as he's always lying to me.'

Well, before long I discovered that Shane had deceived Claire as much as he had me. 'He told me from the start that you don't sleep together and that you just pretend everything is OK for the kids,' she said. 'That you didn't want to break up officially until the kids were older.'

'Well, none of that is true,' I said.

'He also said you knew about me,' she continued. 'But when you came to the theatre I'd be rushed out of the back door. When I asked why, he told me he didn't want to rub your nose in it.'

Suddenly I understood why Claire had so brazenly called the house and turned up at the gates.

'Last night he told me he was coming home,' she explained.

'Coming home?' I asked.

'We had a house in Pimlico, then we moved to Chelsea.'

'But he hardly took any of his belongings,' I said.

'He didn't need to,' she replied. 'He already had loads of clothes at mine.'

We talked for over an hour and a half, raking over all the rubbish Shane had been spouting. It was clear he had no intention of ending things with either of us. As I put the phone down I knew today was the day that I'd leave Shane. *Thank you God!* I thought. I actually felt euphoric. *You don't love him any more,* I told myself. *Now stop being an idiot!*

The kids were now on their summer holidays, so the next day I packed up everything we needed and bundled them into the car. Then we drove to Blackpool to stay with Linda and Brian, who now had a place up there. When I got there I called Shane. 'I had a conversation with your girlfriend yesterday,' I said. 'I know all about the house in Pimlico and you moving to Chelsea. And the room you told Claire you could do up as a nursery. I hope you live happily ever after.'

'But Co—' he started.

But I didn't want to hear another second of his bullshit. 'No, Shane,' I said firmly. 'Don't say another word. It's over, and I will never believe a thing that comes out of your mouth again. My advice to you now is that you make a go of it with Claire, or our marriage ended for no reason.'

When I told my Aunty Theresa about my conversation

with Claire she was gobsmacked. 'How can you talk to that bitch?' she asked.

'But he lied to her too,' I said. 'And she was in love with him.'

It was now very clear in my mind that Claire was also a victim of Shane's behaviour. There was only one person to blame for this whole sorry scenario, and that was Shane. I'd finally realized that he was never going to change. What he wanted was both lives. He loved coming home and being a family man but he loved the beautiful girl on his arm too. Well, he was never making a fool out of me again. I felt as if someone had lifted heavy chains from my shoulders. And I'm sure that was all because of my counsellor: she had built up my spirit, self-confidence and self-worth over the previous six months.

That night Aunty Theresa agreed to baby-sit the boys, and Maureen, Brian and my niece Amy took me out for a few drinks to celebrate the start of my new Shane-free life. After the pub we headed to a nightclub called the Waterfront, and on my way in I spotted a very handsome bouncer on the door. He was tall with dark hair and big muscles from working out in the gym. As Amy said hello to him, we smiled shyly at each other.

'Oh my God, that doorman's gorgeous,' I yelled in Amy's ear, struggling to be heard above the pumping music.

'Oh yeah, that's Dave,' she said as we headed to the bar.

Then for the rest of the night Amy and Maureen egged me on, telling me to go and talk to Dave. 'You need a fling,' Maureen nagged. 'Come on, Coleen, I want to see you let your hair down.'

So, fired up, Amy and I accidentally on purpose plonked ourselves in a spot next to the dance floor where Dave was on duty. Seeing us he smiled, so Amy pulled me over and introduced us. Then she disappeared, not so subtly, off to the bar.

I immediately warmed to Dave. He told me he was studying interior design at college and worked as a bouncer in the evenings. As we chatted I found myself getting more and more flirtatious, and I couldn't take my eyes off his bulging biceps. Dave told me he had an eight-year-old daughter from a previous relationship and I told him about Shane Jnr and Jake.

'I feel a bit guilty talking to you, as you're married,' he eventually said.

'Isn't it funny how you feel guilty but my husband is at home with his girlfriend,' I laughed. 'I wouldn't worry at all.'

At the end of the night we swapped numbers and made a loose arrangement to see each other again next time I was in Blackpool. I walked out of that club grinning from ear to ear. It felt good to know that a man found me attractive. *What on earth was I so scared about? I wondered. There is life after Shane after all.*

My friends and family were so brilliant through it all as well. If I was them I would have banged my head against a wall, saying, 'Are you mad?' at the way I'd accepted what was happening for so long, but they didn't. And in the end I was actually pretty proud of myself for not throwing the towel in straight away. I was willing to forgive, for my boys and my marriage. It was Shane who'd thrown it all away and I would never waste a single moment feeling guilty about it.

Over the next couple of days Shane continued to call me, crying and begging for me to come home. 'I'm sorry, Co,' he sobbed. 'I can't live without you.'

But I'd heard it too many times before. 'This is the situation, Shane,' I told him. 'I want a divorce and I need us to sell the house.'

'Don't be ridiculous,' he said indignantly. 'I'm not selling it. If you want I just won't come round for a while.'

'No, I don't want to stay in that house,' I insisted. 'It hasn't got one good memory for me. We either put it on the market or you buy me out, or I'm going upstairs to tell the kids right now why we are applying for a council house.'

When I headed back to Denham a few days later, the first thing I did was drive around the area looking for houses on the market. I didn't want to move far, as I wanted the boys to still go to the same schools. I immediately spotted a really nice one up the road and back home I called the number and arranged a viewing.

Before long Shane turned up on the doorstep looking forlorn. 'I've lost everything,' he said. 'You've left me and Claire won't talk to me either. She's still upset after she spoke to you and says she can't trust me.' He looked so miserable, and despite everything I did kind of feel sorry for him. It also struck me as ridiculous that now that I'd given Shane up Claire wasn't going to have him either. What a waste of our marriage.

'Leave it to me,' I told Shane, and a bit later I called Claire.

'What are you playing at?' I asked her. 'You've wanted my husband to yourself for three years and now I've ended it with him and he's all yours you decide you don't want him? You are being stupid. Are you telling me you broke up my marriage for no reason?'

Claire just listened, clearly shocked by what I was saying. 'You're right,' she finally agreed.

When I told my friends and family what I'd done they were stunned. 'I can't believe you gave her your blessing,' Vicky gasped. 'I admire that you could do that, but you're a stronger woman than me.'

I knew that most people couldn't understand my actions

and probably viewed it as an odd thing to do, but it was absolutely how I felt. And after all the humiliation of staying with Shane through thick and thin, I wanted to be dignified. I think it's because once I put my emotions to the side I can be quite logical when it comes to real life situations. I just started to think about it sensibly. *Even if it was one hundred per cent finished with Claire tomorrow, could I carry on and be with a man I couldn't even trust to go out and buy a newspaper?* I wondered. I decided that I couldn't.

A few mistakes I could forgive or forget, but there has to come a point when it is one more strike and you're out. We're only human, but there comes a time when you have to be responsible for your actions and break the chain.

My phone call clearly worked, because before long Shane was reunited with Claire and to my relief he seemed to be accepting that our marriage was over. In a stark turnaround he helped me put in an offer on the house I'd seen and I started making arrangements to move out. But while I was trying to be grown-up and move on, not everyone felt the same. Some of the other members of my family were absolutely astounded. I told everyone, 'I do not want this to affect my children. If I'm willing to be on friendly terms I want you to be too.' Though I have to admit, if anyone did that to my sister I'd want to kill them too.

In the meantime I was heading up to Blackpool whenever I could, to see Dave, and we'd been talking a lot on the phone. I'd already told him all about Shane, and although he didn't give me advice he'd just listen, which I appreciated. He was fairly quiet, a bit of a deep thinker, the polar opposite to Shane, and at my next counselling session I found myself gushing about him.

'I've met this really lovely guy,' I told my counsellor. 'He's really shy and sweet.'

'Dave is what will get you over this,' she said. 'He's the bridge to your new life.'

I realized she was right. I didn't see our relationship lasting long-term, as we were just too different, but for now Dave was just the distraction I needed. A few days later Shane called round, so I took the opportunity to tell him about Dave. His face fell and he looked really put out. 'Is it serious?' he asked.

'I don't know yet,' I replied. 'How's it going with Claire?' I asked, changing the subject.

'OK,' he said. 'But she's still really upset with me.'

'Why don't you take her away somewhere?' I suggested. 'You could probably do with a nice break together.'

Shane looked surprised, and if I wasn't mistaken a little look of hurt flashed across his eyes. I knew that my appearing to be so unbothered about his romance was painful. It hurt him to see I'd moved on. And if I was honest I kind of wanted him to feel like that. I wanted him to realize everything he'd lost.

'Maybe I could take Claire to Florida?' he suggested. 'And maybe the boys could come too.'

Ouch. Now it was my turn to feel the knife twisting in my stomach. 'Oh,' I said, winded by his suggestion. The thought of Shane and Claire going on a cosy trip with my sons to Florida – our habitual holiday destination – hurt. Then I remembered my vow that whatever happened I'd put Shane Jnr and Jake's wellbeing first.

'I'm sure they'll want to go,' I replied, taking a deep breath. 'But if you arrange it Claire is not meeting the boys at the airport. She needs to meet them before.'

A few days later Shane called to say that Claire had agreed and he'd booked the flights.

'Right, well, you'd better bring Claire round then,' I said. 'We need to introduce her to the boys.'

Shane seemed unsure. 'You call her and ask, will you, Co?' he said. 'The whole thing makes me feel a bit weird.'

You and me both! I thought. But I couldn't trust Shane to be adult about this, so I did call Claire.

'Get Shane to bring you round tomorrow evening,' I said. 'I need to meet you and the kids do too.'

'OK, if you're sure,' she replied. So that night I told the boys all about the holiday.

'Are you coming?' Jake asked.

'No darling, you're going with your daddy and his new friend Claire,' I said. 'And tomorrow she's coming over to meet you. She's really lovely and you're going to like her.'

'Can I draw her a picture?' Jake asked. So we got a pad and colouring pencils out and we drew her pictures. *I am actually quite insane*, I thought to myself.

The next day I tidied the house from top to bottom and did my hair and make-up carefully. I was pretty sure Claire wasn't the crowing sort, but I certainly wasn't going to give her any ammunition to slag off my home or my appearance. When they drove into the drive my stomach churned. Was I really about to welcome my husband's mistress into our home?

When they first walked into the kitchen I have to say I was flabbergasted. Claire just looked so young. I knew she was only about twenty-two, but she looked a lot younger than that, as if she was in her teens. She was tiny too. About five foot and a size 6. She could have been my daughter or Shane Jnr's girl-friend. She looked terrified, so I forced myself to smile warmly even though I was dying inside.

'Would you like a cup of tea?' I said. Claire nodded, looking really relieved, but Shane just stood there looking agitated.

'I can't handle this,' he said, his eyes darting from me to Claire and then back again. Then he picked up his coat and stormed out. Claire and I just stood there like lemons. 'So we meet at last!' I laughed.

The wounds were still too raw for me to talk to her about Shane, so I started telling her about Shane Jnr and Jake instead. I explained what they liked to eat, their favourite games and TV shows, so she'd have some common ground to chat to them about. Then I called the boys in and encouraged her to interact with them. I could tell they liked her. She was quite softly spoken and sweet, and when Jake gave her his picture she looked absolutely delighted.

'I was terrified of walking in,' she eventually confided. 'I thought you might punch me.'

'I don't have the energy,' I sighed. 'The only reason you're here is so the boys aren't affected and they'll be happy.'

After a couple of hours Shane reappeared to collect Claire, and later he called me. 'What did you think of her?' he asked. He sounded excited, almost as if he was dying for my approval.

'Shane, what I think doesn't matter,' I said, irritated. 'There is only one reason why I allowed Claire into my home and that is because of the boys. So don't you ever forget that.'

I knew my sons jetting off to Florida with Shane and Claire was going to be really hard for me, so the same day I waved them off I arranged to go up to Blackpool to stay with Dave. Although we'd known each other a very short time and it was a fairly casual thing, we were getting on brilliantly, and one day I decided to throw caution to the wind. 'Shall we go on holiday?' I asked. He looked stunned. 'Don't worry, it's on me,' I said breezily. And with that I went out and booked us ten days in Cyprus, to leave in two days' time.

I took great pleasure paying for it out of Shane's and my

joint bank account. I went to town – first class flights, a top hotel, everything. After all the holidays, gifts and meals Shane had shelled out on Claire with our money over the past few years, I thought it was the least I deserved.

That holiday was amazing. Dave and I did nothing more than relax on the beach and go out for romantic meals. He was so attentive to me, and as each day passed I could feel the tension ebbing out of my body bit by bit. On our last day, as I lay on the sun-lounger admiring Dave's rather impressive and now tanned six-pack, I smiled to myself. *Good riddance, Shane Richie*, I thought.

Catching me looking at him, Dave jumped up and pulled me up off my sun-bed. 'Come here, gorgeous,' he said, hooking his arm round my waist and dragging me into the sea.

It wasn't long before the two of us were messing around in the water like lovestruck teenagers. As I wrapped my arms around Dave's strong shoulders and we bobbed up and down in the waves, I felt alive and carefree. The whole holiday was proving to be a massive self-esteem boost for me. It had been so long since I'd felt like a sexy, attractive woman. But here I was cavorting in the sea with my hunky lover. It was great!

The next day, as we were getting ready to leave, I told Dave I was jumping into the shower. 'I just want to freshen up before the flight,' I said. 'It won't take me long to throw everything in my case once I get out.'

But when I stepped out of the bathroom ten minutes later, rubbing my hair with a towel, I was surprised to see my suitcase on the bed, all packed. I just stood there astounded. 'Oh my God, you've packed my suitcase!' I said.

'Sorry,' Dave replied, looking worried. 'I'd done mine so I just thought it might be helpful.'

'No, it's great,' I chirped. 'It's just that no one has ever packed a suitcase for me before. I can't believe it.'

But that was just the way Dave was. During that holiday he doted on me. It was such a far cry from Shane, who'd always left me to do everything and even got me to pack his bag when he went away with his mistress.

By the time we'd landed at Manchester and travelled back to Dave's place in Blackpool it was late. 'You go up to bed,' he said, unlocking the door. 'I'll bring you a cuppa.'

As I lay there in bed sipping my tea, I took pleasure from the feeling of calm and enjoyed this rare moment of being waited on. I wanted to savour the moment because I knew the next day I'd be heading home to run around after two little boys once more.

After a lovely lie-in, I wandered downstairs to find Dave hanging out my washing. While I'd been out for the count he'd washed all my holiday stuff. I was gobsmacked. The man really was a find!

Back in Denham two very excited boys met me. 'Mum, I went on the Rock 'n' Roller Coaster six times,' yelled Shane Jnr.

'Yeah, Claire screamed her head off, Mum,' Jake joined in.

'We saw a policeman at the airport with a real machine gun!' Shane Jnr added. Just when I thought they hadn't missed me at all, Jake came running up to me and engulfed me in a hug.

'I missed you, Mum,' he said, putting his head on my shoulder.

'I missed you too, babe,' I said, enjoying a warm cuddle. As lovely as my break with Dave had been, it was good to be back with my boys.

Just a few weeks later I completed on our new home, and

at the start of August, Shane Jnr, Jake and I were able to move in. Meanwhile, in a bizarre state of affairs, my estranged husband moved his mistress into our old home. In many ways it was the ideal set-up. It was great for the boys to have their dad living just down the road, and Claire to her credit was great with them. There were times when Shane Jnr and Jake would talk about her non-stop. All I'd hear was, 'Claire did this and she was so funny . . .' and I'd just have to walk into the kitchen and mouth, 'Bitch!' silently to myself.

But joking aside, the fact Claire was so wonderful with the boys meant a lot to me. I was acutely aware of how hard it could be for children to deal with their parents splitting up. I'd seen too many friends using their kids as weapons and emotionally killing them in the process. I used to watch them and vow that no matter what happened I would never do that with my kids. I stuck to this promise and it worked. To this day I am so relieved that the one good thing that came out of our split was how unaffected the kids were.

I actually ended up getting on great with Claire too. She was young and had never been in a situation like this before so she handled things very well considering, although it wasn't always easy for me in the beginning. I couldn't help feeling she was in too much of a hurry to erase all traces of me from the house. At first I was moving my stuff out bit by bit. I hadn't got round to collecting it all and still had a key. But one day when I called in to pick something up I found all my belongings piled in the hall in bin bags. Looking back now I'm sure she thought she was being helpful by finishing my packing for me, but at the time I was too raw to see that and was outraged. It was a good job no one was at home to see my disgust.

I was so annoyed that I called Vicky and Carol to the house

to see. 'I can't believe that cheeky bloody mare emptied everything of mine into bin bags!' I raged. 'How dare she?'

Well, Vicky and Carol just looked at each other with a wicked glint in their eyes and then suddenly started tipping everything out.

'What are you doing?' I asked.

'Putting it back!' Carol grinned.

So together we emptied everything back into my drawers and hung my pictures back up on the walls. When we'd finished I called Shane. 'Can you kindly tell your girlfriend that I'll pack my own stuff when I'm good and ready,' I said. 'She's already got my husband and my home, so tell her to blinking well leave my things alone.'

In hindsight I did feel bad for calling Shane, as I found out later that he'd really shouted at Claire, yelling, 'Don't you dare touch my wife's stuff!' The truth is he should have stopped her in the first place.

Also hard for me to handle initially were the collages of pictures she put up around the place. They were filled with her, Shane and the boys playing happy families in Florida and also snaps from the holiday in Tunisia, when Shane had told me he was going go-karting – seeing those felt like a slap in the face, they looked so happy together. I understood that her domestic bliss with Shane had been a long time coming and she was probably very excited but that didn't make it easier for me.

The hardest thing, though, was that Claire had a habit of vocalizing her belief that Shane would never treat her the way he had me. Whenever we chatted about the past and Shane's deception she'd pipe up with something like, 'The thing is, now I know he'd never do it to me.'

I found it very patronizing. *Oh, so you think you're better than me?* I'd rage in my head, but I'd force myself to bite my tongue.

I figured she was probably just insecure and trying to convince herself, but even so, one day I just decided I'd had enough of hearing how her precious Shane would never even look at another woman.

So that night I asked Shane to come round for a cuppa after the boys had gone to bed. When he arrived I started being quite flirty with him and he responded enthusiastically.

'You know, Shane, I could have you whenever I wanted,' I told him seductively.

Well, it was like a red rag to a bull, and that night I slept with him.

Nine

As we lay in bed, Shane nuzzling my neck, I felt very smug. *Ha*, I thought. *Never look at another woman indeed*. It was empowering to have manipulated Shane so easily, but the next day I did have regrets. Even though Dave and I were still fairly casual, it felt like a betrayal, and I knew it was unfair on Claire too.

I'd originally decided to keep the truth about our little tryst to myself, but almost immediately Claire wound me up again. 'He'd never cheat on me,' she told me all wide-eyed. I just snapped.

'Well, I know he would,' I replied. 'Because he did last night with me.'

Well, that shut her up, but then her face began to crumple, pain written all over it. I could tell she was trying not to cry. Suddenly I felt stupid and childish. 'I'm really sorry, Claire,' I said. 'I only did it because you were winding me up, going on about how he'd never treat you the way he treated me. I just thought it was a bit arrogant. But last night was a one-off and I promise I'll never do it again.'

Of course within a couple of hours Shane was screaming down the phone to me. 'How could you?' he yelled, a tirade of expletives blasting down the line. 'She's gone mental and now she's gone to stay with her mum. She says she's not coming back.'

I didn't feel particularly proud of myself, I have to say.

A couple of days later Shane called again. 'Co,' he said, miserably. 'Please will you phone her up? She won't take my calls.'

Sighing, I put down the phone and dialled the number he'd given me for Claire's mum. When Claire came on the line I apologized again. 'Shane was stupid and so was I, but I promise it was a one-off,' I told her. 'He really does love you and he's devastated that you won't speak to him.'

My words must have done some good, as a few days later Claire was back with Shane and peace and harmony were restored. After I'd smoothed things over with them, I hoped that was the last time I'd get caught up in any of their domestics. I'd learnt my lesson, and I wanted to go forward not backwards. Apart from the kids, my life with Shane was over and I wanted to make a go of it with Dave. There was no need for me to be involved in Shane's relationship with Claire too.

But much as I tried to mind my own business, it was easier said than done. They were always rowing, and before long to my absolute bewilderment I became their number one agony aunt! Whenever they had a big bust-up Shane would screech into the drive and appear on my doorstep scowling. He'd storm into the house and pace the kitchen, ranting and raving. 'She just does my head in, Co,' he'd moan. 'She's so bloody sensitive.' I'd make him a cup of tea and calm him down but no sooner would I have bundled him out of the door than the phone would ring.

'Hi Coleen, it's Claire,' a little voice would say. 'Has Shane been round?'

When I explained that he had but I'd sent him home again, she'd sigh, and then all her frustration would come pouring out. 'He's so hot-headed and he just doesn't listen to me,' she'd say tearfully. 'Was he like that with you?'

By the time I'd had a double whammy of whinging from the pair of them (not to mention trying to stay as neutral as possible) I felt like killing myself! And as the months went on I began to feel really suffocated. I'd left Shane behind but here I was, still slap bang in the middle of a three-way relationship (and I didn't even get any perks any more!). I started to wonder if I should move back to Blackpool. That way I'd be nearer to Dave and my family and it would put some distance between me and the world's most volatile couple!

When they weren't rowing it was actually a fantastic, smooth operation. After our initial teething problems Claire and I got on really well. It took me a while to admit it, but she was a very nice girl. I no longer felt any animosity towards her, and now that our feelings weren't so raw we could calmly discuss those years when Shane had been juggling the pair of us. I don't think Claire really grasped that she'd done anything wrong for ages, as she'd believed our marriage was a sham. But as we talked more and she began to understand how Shane had treated me, she just looked mortified. 'Oh God, I'm so sorry, I didn't know,' she said.

It was understandable. She'd been only nineteen and hardly worldly-wise when she met him. Shane had been effectively living the single life in Manchester, and he'd wooed her with flash limos, fantastic suites at hotels, posh restaurants and lavish gifts. All of which had, unsurprisingly, impressed her.

'Don't feel guilty,' I told her. 'You weren't to know. He can be very convincing.'

Funnily enough, the one person who hated Claire and me bonding was Shane. When he walked into the kitchen to see us nattering away, I could tell by his body language that it made him uneasy. And I suppose in a way there was a little part of me playing a game. I knew Shane so well, and I was well aware that the fact I seemed so at ease with Claire was killing him, forcing home the message that I was really getting over him. Although at that point he still hadn't grasped that it was final. There was no going back. For me it was just another little way of clawing some of my pride back – I knew he hated that it was over between us. I think he began to realize that we could have been the perfect little family but he'd lost it all for good.

Once I'd left Shane I tried to get him to start divorce proceedings, but despite my solicitor sending the papers out repeatedly, he just ignored them. He just couldn't comprehend that our marriage was finished. He seemed to think I was just trying to prove a point.

'Shane, I'm serious,' I'd tell him.

'No you're not,' he'd scoff.

He was costing me a fortune, but when my solicitor suggested getting someone to actually serve the papers to him in person I was a bit shocked. 'I don't know,' I said. 'He'll go mad.'

But in the end it seemed to be the only solution. So while Shane was up in Blackpool performing in *Boogie Nights* I had an official deliver the papers to him at the stage door. Well, predictably he phoned me up apoplectic with rage.

'Shane, it was the only way to show you that I'm serious!' I finally managed to butt in. 'You've got to stop stalling on me, it's just not fair!'

He eventually stopped shouting at me, but I could tell he still wasn't exactly in a hurry to accept it.

Later that night, at about 3 a.m., I was woken up by the telephone. Heart racing, I quickly answered it. 'Co?' a choked voice said. It was Shane.

'Shane, what's the matter?' I muttered sleepily. But there

was no answer, just the sound of Shane's sobs. He was in a terrible state, blind drunk, and didn't seem to know where he was. 'I can't deal with it any more,' he cried. 'I just want to end it. I want to walk into the sea and not come back.'

'Shane, please calm down, you're worrying me,' I said. 'Now can you find somewhere to sit? Good. Now take some deep breaths and tell me what you can see around you.'

When he started describing a public park it immediately occurred to me that he was in Stanley Park, just round the corner from Maureen's house.

'You need to go to hers now,' I told him. 'I'll phone her and tell her you're coming round.' Thank God he listened to me and did as he was told.

Maureen was brilliant, but then that's Maureen all over. She's always great in a crisis. She managed to calm Shane down and he eventually went to sleep on the sofa. Then the next morning she called our local doctor and managed to get Shane checked into a private hospital. When he was there Shane called me. 'I'm sorry I gave you a fright,' he said.

'That's OK,' I replied. 'You're really exhausted and down, so just try to get lots of rest, will you?'

It really frightened me that Shane had got himself into such a state, but it didn't really surprise me. When times got tough Shane would work himself even harder, and it was no wonder that he'd finally succumbed to nervous exhaustion. While I'd accepted the marriage was over, Shane had just tried to plough on without thinking about it, still being the happy-chappy Shane on the outside and working himself into the ground. I guess something just had to break. He was off the rails, drinking a lot and clearly exhausted.

After this episode Shane seemed to be better, and when he came out of hospital all rested and a lot happier, he did start filling in some of the divorce paperwork. But he still stalled at every opportunity, and my decree absolute didn't actually come through until 2003 – almost four years later.

Meanwhile things were still going well for me with Dave, and towards the end of the year I got a nice self-confidence boost when I began to be offered TV work. It had all started with a documentary I'd filmed with the TV presenter Trisha Goddard, called *Celebrity Heartbreak*. In it I'd talked about my break-up from Shane and it sparked quite a lot of interest, including a call from the producers of a new show called *Loose Women*, who invited me on as a guest.

My initial reaction was to say no. I'd never heard of *Loose Women* and the title sounded a bit dodgy! *What are they trying to say?* I thought. It wasn't until they sent me a tape and I saw that the title was very tongue-in-cheek that I changed my mind! The whole concept was that during each show a panel of down-to-earth celebrity women chatted with humour and warmth about anything in the news or their lives in general. It was a real girly show, full of gossip, and it felt as if you were chatting over lunch with your friends. The show was filmed in front of a studio audience and was hosted by a journalist and presenter called Kaye Adams, who seemed very sharp and witty.

On the morning I went on I was immediately struck by the friendliness of all the team at *Loose Women*. Kaye was really lovely too and put me at ease, so when it was my turn to chat I didn't feel at all nervous. I actually really enjoyed the whole experience. So afterwards I was thrilled when the producers asked if I'd like to come back as a guest presenter from time to time.

'Yeah!' I agreed straight away.

What a difference a year makes, I smiled to myself as I made my way home. Twelve months earlier I'd felt utterly redundant, as if there was nothing more to me than being Shane's long-suffering wife and mother to his children. But now I was finding my own way again and jumping at opportunities without Shane. It felt really empowering.

So gradually I began to go on *Loose Women* more and more, sometimes as often as twice a week. In those early days the show didn't have the small pool of presenters you see today. You actually never knew who you'd be beside on the panel, but the ladies I worked the most with tended to be Kaye, who was the anchor presenter, a journalist called Pattie Coldwell and the former *EastEnders* actress Nadia Sawalha, who were all great fun.

That Christmas Eve the boys bid goodbye to Shane and Claire and we headed up to Blackpool to stay with Linda and Brian, who were now renting a flat up there. On Christmas Day we joined the rest of my family for lunch at a local restaurant and Dave came along too. I think he was a little bit overcome by the bedlam of my family en masse, and didn't say much, but unlike Shane two years earlier, at least Dave sat there smiling and graciously laughing at my jokes!

Afterwards we all went back to Maureen's for more fun and games. I'd hoped Dave might loosen up a bit after a few more sherries, but he didn't. Again he sat there quietly, only speaking when he was spoken to. He seemed happy enough, but it made me uncomfortable and I found I was overcompensating. I was getting louder and louder and kind of turning into Shane!

I remembered what my counsellor had said, five months before, 'Dave is the bridge to your new life.' *Maybe I will need to move on soon?* I thought, but then I chastised myself for being so uncharitable on Christmas Day.

At the start of the new year I did a few more presenting slots with *Loose Women*, and my confidence was really beginning to grow. By now Kaye and I were getting on brilliantly. We'd just hit it off from day one and she's still one of my best friends today. Professionally I just thought she was a wonderful presenter. She made it look so effortless. One minute she could speak knowledgeably about politics and the next she'd be holding court about men's pants. I really admired the way she was so versatile.

Now that we'd done a fair few shows together, we were kind of in tune to each other's sense of humour and there was some good banter going on. The show was still finding its feet, and ITV kept experimenting with different air times, so we'd only do a six-week run and then it was all a bit up in the air until you heard about the next series. I really hoped it would carry on. It was nice to be able to do something else besides warbling for a change and I didn't have any immediate plans to go back to the singing.

That is until March 2000, just after my thirty-fifth birthday, when I received a call from my eldest sister Anne revealing devastating news. 'I've got breast cancer,' she told me.

I knew Anne had gone to the doctor with a couple of lumps in her breast. Over the years she had found numerous cysts in her boobs, but not once had they been anything sinister. But when she'd gone to her GP this time with two new lumps, the doctor had found a third one, the size of a grain of rice, which she was suspicious about and which had turned out to be cancerous. Anne was so matter-of-fact in telling me that I almost laughed. 'Nothing like breaking it to me gently!' I said.

'I'm fine!' she replied. 'They've caught it early. I'm going to have a lumpectomy to remove it and radiotherapy. They also gave me the option of chemotherapy so I'm going to have that too, just to be on the safe side.'

I didn't get upset on the phone to her, but when I hung up I burst into tears. Anne out of all my sisters had been like a second mother to me. I loved her and I was scared for her.

It couldn't have come at a worse time. For a while now Anne and Maureen had been making a living continuing the Nolans as a singing quartet, along with Anne's daughter Amy and her friend Julia Duckworth. They were booked to do a summer season at the Grand Theatre in Blackpool in July, and although Anne was convinced she could still perform despite the fact she'd be in the midst of chemo, we all knew she was going to find it very gruelling. So as a precaution it was decided that I should learn the harmonies and dance steps as well and be available to come in at the last minute if it got too much for Anne.

Over the next few months she had a really tough time. During the operation the surgeon removed lymph glands from under her arm, so it was a while before she got the movement back, which made performing difficult.

So as soon as the boys broke up for the summer holidays the three of us drove up to Blackpool and moved in with Linda and Brian. For the next few weeks I shadowed Anne all through the rehearsals for the show. When she started her six-month course of chemotherapy she was determined to battle on, but before long the chemo was taking its toll and she needed to rest. So I took over until she was well enough to resume, and gave her the money from the shows so she wouldn't have to struggle. It had been years since I'd performed on stage, but I have to say it was brilliant fun and I loved every minute of it.

Being back in Blackpool was also fantastic and it instantly made me realize it was where I wanted to be.

'I'm seriously thinking about moving back,' I told Linda.

'That would be brilliant!' she replied, her face lighting up. 'What's stopping you?'

So the next time I saw Shane I took a deep breath and told him I was planning to sell the house and move back north.

He looked completely crestfallen and his eyes filled with tears. 'Please don't take my boys away from me,' he pleaded. 'I like having you around, and Blackpool is miles away ...'

'I'm not doing this to punish you, Shane,' I said gently. 'I just want to make a fresh start. I can't put my life on hold for ever. You know you can see the boys whenever you like. Every weekend if you want.'

To Shane's credit, even though it was very sad for him, he eventually came round to the idea and didn't stand in my way. I was really grateful that he put my happiness first.

I immediately put the house on the market and began to look for a new place in Blackpool. Then ironically, just as I was moving to the same area as him, my relationship with Dave bit the dust. We'd had a fabulous ten months together, but once the initial lust had worn off we really didn't have much else. He didn't have a lot to say to me. I appreciated the fact he was a good listener, but when I tried to start a conversation he'd usually say, 'Oh well ...' and that would be it! 'No, but what do you really think?' I'd ask, finding myself getting very easily irritated. He was just the opposite of me, and when the chips were down we clearly didn't have a lot in common.

On top of that Shane was still calling me all the time. I'd left him, filed for divorce and was moving back to Blackpool, but he still kept hinting about reconciliation. 'We'll get back together one day,' he'd say. 'I know you want to.'

There wasn't a day when he didn't phone me. A lot of people, not least Dave, found it bizarre. If something happened, good or bad, I was the first person he'd call and I was kind of the same with him. We were still really close, good mates, and I was grateful I'd met him because of my two beautiful boys.

It was still difficult to think of my marriage in a bad light, and even now I find it hard ripping Shane apart for it, purely because he does have a great side to him. The first ten years we were together were fabulous. I was never suspicious, we had the best time and everyone loved us as a couple. But Dave quite justifiably couldn't bear him. And that was pretty much the catalyst for our love affair ending.

'He's still part of your life and I just can't handle it,' Dave explained. 'I think it's best if we call it a day.'

That's the most you've said in months! I thought wickedly. But joking aside, even though I knew it wasn't working, I was still gutted to lose Dave. It was too soon after everything that had happened with Shane, so at first I saw it as another failure. *I'll never find the right man for me*, I thought miserably.

Not that I could mope around for long – not with Miss bloody matchmaker Maureen Nolan on my case. After the show each night my sister and I would often join Amy and Julia and other performers doing the circuit at a late-night bar called the West Coast Rock Café. Following my split from Dave I hadn't really felt like being social, but if I dared to suggest going home Maureen was having none of it.

'The boys are safe with Linda, so stop being so boring!' she'd bark. 'Anyway, how will you ever meet someone nice if you become a recluse?'

So reluctantly one night I agreed to go out with Maureen. 'Oh Maureen, I can't bear it,' I whinged at her, after I'd endured thirty minutes in a dingy nightclub. 'It makes me so depressed. There are about four hundred men in this club and I don't fancy one of them.'

So, defeated, we headed for the West Coast. And it was that night I first clapped eyes on my future husband – even though my first impression was that I didn't like him much at all!

When Maureen and I arrived at the West Coast it was already packed out. Seeing Amy, we waved and then headed to the bar, where Maureen immediately found a spot next to a blond guy in his early forties who stood supping beer with his mates.

'Hiya,' Maureen greeted him. The man smiled at her and then glanced at me. Being polite I smiled too, but instead of acknowledging me he completely blanked me and turned back to his friends. To add insult to injury they all laughed! *Charming,* I thought. *There always has to be one prick, doesn't there!*

When Maureen and I had got our drinks we wandered over to where Amy was standing with some of her friends. 'See that bloke?' I said, pointing at the rude blond man. 'Who is he? He was a right tit when we walked in.'

Well, Amy just laughed her head off. 'What, Ray Fensome?' she said. 'He fancies you like mad! He's been asking me for over a year, "When's your Aunty Coleen coming in?" He's always fancied you, but he's quite shy, so he was probably just embarrassed.'

'Oh shut up, Amy,' I said, flapping my hand dismissively.

But I was intrigued, and for the next hour I was watching Ray out of the corner of my eye and deciding he was sort of nice-looking.

Amy and I were chatting when one of Ray's cronies headed over. 'This is Trumpet Trousers,' Amy said. I raised one eyebrow questioningly.

'Are you coming on to the Dutchman Hotel?' Trumpet Trousers asked.

'I don't think I will,' I told Amy. 'I'll be up early with the boys.'

But Amy was insistent. 'Please, Aunty Coleen!' she whined.

'OK, I'll come for an hour,' I agreed.

When we walked into the Dutchman, there was Ray propping up the bar. This time he grinned, and clearly now had enough Dutch courage to strike up a conversation.

'It's you, innit?' he said in a broad Yorkshire accent.

'Err, yeah,' I said, trying not to laugh.

'Love it, don't I? Nolan Face!'

For our first year together that's all he ever called me – bloody Nolan Face. It's funny, as now everyone in our family talks in Rayisms!

Ray told me he played guitar in the Legends show, which was a bit like *Stars in Their Eyes* – all lookalike acts imitating people like Robbie Williams, Elvis and Elton John. As one of the band he'd been on tour with the show a lot and had done corporate events all over the world – parties for Ivana Trump, Man U players' weddings, that kind of thing. He also admitted he had a girlfriend who lived in London, which I was gutted about. But I didn't let on. 'Oh, that's fine,' I told him. 'We'll just be friends then.'

I told him all about Shane as well (Ray had actually met him in Blackpool the previous year), and, despite the shaky start, we clicked immediately and chatted for hours. Then at about five in the morning someone suggested going for breakfast at a greasy spoon café. I hadn't been drinking much and was craving a cup of tea, so I tagged along with Amy and her friend Vee to the café. Ray and Trumpet Trousers, who were both really drunk, were walking in front of us swaying. Then I noticed Ray had disappeared. *Where's he gone?* I thought.

Then as I walked past a bus shelter a hand grabbed me. It

was Ray and he had a very wicked grin on his face. He pushed me up against the bus stop for a lingering kiss that literally took my breath away. *Ah, I like that!* I thought.

We caught the others up and arrived at the greasy spoon. After the excitement of the kiss had worn off and I'd had my tea, all I wanted was to go to bed but now Ray was being really silly and drunk. 'Where are we going after this?' he slurred.

'Well, I don't know where you're going, but I'm going home,' I remarked. 'Don't leave me with him please,' I whispered to Vee.

So when a cab arrived she said, 'Come on, Ray.'

'I'm going with Nolan Face,' he said.

'No, Ray, you're going in this cab,' Vee insisted, physically pushing him in.

Then after all the excitement I headed back to Linda and Brian's to catch a quick hour's sleep before the kids got up and tortured me.

I next saw Ray the following night in the West Coast and we just grinned at each other. 'Nice to see you sober for a change,' I sniggered. It wasn't long before he was pissed again, mind!

I'm not sure he even remembered the night before, but it didn't matter – soon enough we were seeing each other every night. We couldn't help flirting and it was quite obvious we really fancied each other. We were always laughing, chatting about our lives, what we'd done in the past. We had such a giggle about everything. He'd say his Rayisms to me, like: 'You want me, don't ya? Superb!' He was always taking the piss.

Nothing happened after that first drunken kiss, as his girl-friend was due to come to Blackpool. But as the evenings passed it was obvious we were getting closer and closer. We both knew something was happening.

'I'm going to end it,' Ray suddenly announced one day. 'I can't let her come here and be standing with her when I know I'll want to be with you.'

At that moment I just thought: *Oh my God! I could fall in love with this man! He actually likes her enough not to humiliate her.*

It was a defining moment for me, the way he was dealing with things. I knew it was a big gamble for him at that point. He didn't know if things between us would last or whether it was just a flirty, lusty thing. But if he'd lied to his girlfriend it would have been awful – for both of us. I'm sure subconsciously it would have made me think: *Oh God, who can do that to someone?*

So Ray called his girlfriend and ended it. He was so upset that he didn't speak to me for three days. I loved him for that as well. He wasn't making excuses, he was actually cut up about hurting someone. But the fact is he was man enough to tell her that we'd met and he knew he wanted to be with me, which I really appreciated.

Unfortunately, although he'd done the honourable thing this time, Ray had a bit of a reputation with the ladies. After all I'd been through already, I think a lot of people were worried he might hurt me. Apparently the year before, when he'd been single, Ray had been a bit of a lady-killer – but why shouldn't he have enjoyed himself? He wasn't committed to anyone. People were saying things, hinting I should be careful. Vee told me, 'Oh God, never Ray,' and Maureen's boyfriend had heard things too. But despite the rumours everyone liked him.

'I'm old enough to make my own mistakes,' I told them. 'Christ, we're not getting married, we're just having a chat.'

'But I can't believe you're getting involved with someone else who loves women!' Maureen laughed, as we got ready for our show in the dressing room. 'Just be careful you don't jump in head first.'

It was nice that Maureen and my other sisters were concerned, but I did think: *Jesus Christ, I'm thirty-five!* I was well aware that it could be just a summer fling, but at the same time I also had an excited feeling in my tummy. Inside I just knew that something pretty amazing was going to happen with Ray.

Once Ray had sorted his head out, we met up at the West Coast that night and headed back to his flat for a cup of tea. We sat on the couch, nervously nursing our mugs.

'So do you want to watch a video?' Ray asked.

'No,' I replied. 'I'd like to see your bedroom actually.' I even shocked myself!

'Oh, OK!' he said, and then we both burst out laughing. Next thing I knew we were kissing passionately and Ray was bundling me into his bedroom! That night was incredible. There was such passion between us, but also a wonderful connection. After we'd made love we lay there until 5.30 in the morning, chatting and laughing and telling each other our life stories. As he stroked my hair and whispered in my ear it just felt so right.

'I'm going to have to go,' I told him reluctantly, looking at the clock. 'I have to get back before the boys get up.'

So, exhausted, but absolutely exhilarated, I forced myself up out of bed and made my way back to Linda and Brian's. The entry to the stairs up to their flat was via the second-hand furniture shop below, but on that particular night I'd only taken a key for the shop. I didn't want to wake them up so I found a couch in the shop and fell asleep. At about 6.30 a.m. I was awoken by the sound of floorboards above me creaking and I knew Brian must be awake. So forcing myself up, I knocked quietly on the flat door. When Brian came down to let me in he burst out laughing.

'You either got up really early to get the papers or you've just got in!' he said.

'Don't talk to me,' I said, putting my head in my hands. 'I can't even speak!'

'It's Ray, isn't it?' Brian said. He'd met Ray the year before, when Linda had done a summer season at the Leyton Institute in Blackpool and Ray had been seeing one of the dancers. 'He was always telling Linda, "I fancy your little sister,"' he laughed.

Bashfully I told him I was off to bed. But just as I'd taken my make-up off and crawled in, two little boys peered round the door and said, 'Can we have breakfast now?'

So I heaved myself back up and resigned myself to the fact that I'd get no sleep that morning. That whole summer I had about two hours' sleep a night, but I'd always make sure that if I stayed at Ray's I'd be back at Linda's for when the boys got up.

Our romance was incredibly whirlwind. We were so into each other from that first night that even if we were apart for only an hour we couldn't wait to see each other again. I used to wake up every morning with a text from Ray. And the love declarations came at rapid speed too. Within the first couple of weeks we were having a laugh about something or other and I suddenly told him, 'God, I love you!' and he said, 'God, I think I love you too!'

Even before that I can remember Maureen's husband Ritchie telling me off for constantly texting Ray. 'Shut up, I love him!' I found myself saying.

'Give over,' Ritchie replied. 'You might be in lust, but you don't love him.'

But I was sure I did. I've always been one of these all or nothing type people. Plus I was old enough to know what I wanted. I was thirty-five and I knew what was right and what wasn't. It wasn't as if I was twenty-three.

It became serious quite quickly, and one day Ray told me he was worried about how Shane would react. 'What is Shane going to say?' he asked. 'I was drinking with him all last year and now I'm with his ex-wife!'

'Hold on,' I replied. 'Is this the same Shane who is living in my old house with the girl he had an affair with? You really don't have to feel guilty, and please don't tell me you're going to be put off by him, because otherwise I'm going to feel like my whole life is ruined by Shane.'

I did get tetchy in those first few weeks, and there would be times when I'd insist, 'Shut up about my ex. I don't care what he thinks!' I was worried – after all, Shane constantly calling me had ruined my relationship with Dave. *How come he can go on and have a life but I can't?* I thought angrily.

So eventually I told Shane I'd met someone and he was predictably scathing.

'Who?' he asked.

'I think you know him,' I said. 'He's a guitarist with the Legends show in Blackpool.'

'Oh please,' Shane replied. 'It's not Ray, is it?'

'Yes,' I said. 'It's going really well.'

'I can't believe you're going out with him,' Shane raged.

But the next time I spoke to him he'd had a complete change of heart. 'He's a great guy,' he admitted. Then Shane texted Ray saying that if he didn't take me out, he would come up to Blackpool and break his guitars.

For those first few weeks Shane was hot and cold all the time. I'd get nice texts and then nasty ones. In one text he told me to watch out because Ray was shagging everything the year before.

'Yeah, but the difference is he wasn't married and when you did that you were!' I quickly texted back.

In the end I just ignored him, though. I was really, really past the point of caring if Shane liked who I went out with.

The summer season was not just memorable because I'd met this wonderful man, but also because for some strange reason I was asked out all the time – often by blokes I'd known for years! They'd come over and say things like: 'Why don't we go out for dinner?' I was mortified. It was usually people I'd never flirted with and I'd never got the impression they fancied me. It was very difficult and very embarrassing. And more worryingly, a couple of them were married. I just felt sorry for the poor wives and demanded, 'Why do you think I'd turn into the other woman?' And anyway, I'd just met Ray and there was this incredible thing happening between us.

When I tell people how quickly our romance happened and how we built a future together at an alarmingly rapid rate I am aware that it sounds like a thirty-something single mum simply settling for what she could get but it was so much more than that.

When I fell in love with Ray I just knew instantly that he was The One, he had such an incredible affect on me. I really feel he saved me and changed me as a person. He got under my skin and into my head and took the time to suss me out like no man had ever done before. It made me realize that Shane barely even scratched the surface when it came to getting me, but Ray immediately made it his mission to understand how my mind worked. He wanted to know my passions, my secrets and my deepest fears and he loved me unconditionally.

He helped me to understand things about myself that I never knew before and pushed me to reveal how I really felt. I've always been non-confrontational and many, many times I've been walked all over but Ray has changed me as a person. He made me stand up for myself. He was solid and real, my rock and my best friend, and every time we hit a traumatic situation, to my utter shock he was still there, through thick and thin.

Within weeks of us getting together Ray revealed how broody he was, admitting that being forty-three he'd assumed he wouldn't get to have kids. I'd only just met him but it stirred up a weird feeling inside me. Time was ticking for me too, and realizing it was his last chance as well, I made an impulsive decision.

'Why don't we just go for it?' I said. 'Let's make a baby!'

Ray looked flabbergasted but also incredibly excited. I know people will say it was a ridiculous risk to take. And it's true, I could have easily ended up a single parent with three kids. If Ray had been twenty-six I might have felt differently, but because he was forty-three and desperately wanted a child it just felt right. I thought, if he's willing to take the chance … and take on two stepchildren and an ex-husband who's very much in the picture – then so am I. Every time we made love we'd say, 'Oh, we might have just made a baby.' And every time we were out together we'd say, 'Shall we go home and make babies?' rather than, 'Shall we go home and have a shag?' Thinking back now, it was a weird situation! But I never gave it a second thought; it just seemed so right.

As September drew near I was in the midst of house hunting and trying to sort out new schools for the boys. Shane Jnr was due to go to the same school as Maureen's son Danny. But two weeks before term started he came to me one night crying

Above left Oh my word,
I promise this maternity dress
was fashionable in the 1980s!
Here I was six months
pregnant with Shane Jnr.

Above right Me and my sisters
on Danny's christening each
holding our godchildren.

Mine and Shane's
wedding day in Florida
in 1990 when we eloped.

One of my favourite pictures of Shane and Jake aged four and three months.

Shane and Jake aged two and six. Trust me after this photo was taken they probably kicked the hell out of each other!

L–R: Maureen, Shane, Me, Bernie, Gos, his girlfriend Jo, Jake,
Shane Jnr and Alex. I went through with our blessing, even though
I knew it wasn't right. We did it for my dad.

Mum and Dad in mine and Shane's
house in Florida. They look so happy!

Ciara aged one week on her first outing to Bernie's house in 2001.
I don't look too bad but Ray looks shattered!

Ciara aged two at her christening with me, Ray, Shane Jnr, Jake, Shane and Christie.

Right The Nile charity bike ride in February 2007 when we cycled 400km in five days. My bum still aches at the thought! But we raised £150,000 for the Alzheimer's Society.

Below Me and Twiggy on our first day hosting *This Morning* in September 2001 – little did I know the heartache to follow.

Me and the film crew in the Maldives filming for a *This Morning* holiday slot.

Me and the Loose Ladies.
L–R: Jayne, Carol, Sherrie,
Me, Jackie, Andrea and
Linda winning *TV Choice's*
Best Daytime Show 2007.

Slimmed down and happy
with my new figure.

I wanted to keep going in *Dancing on Ice*, even after two bad falls left me in severe pain, but I knew in the end I couldn't do the routines. I made it to the semi final though!

I can't believe that's me spinning round in the air! My partner Stuart looks like I'm light as a feather (bless him!)

The best day of my life with the man who saved my life.

Bernie, me, Maureen and Linda singing – yes, you've guessed it –
'I'm in the Mood for Dancing' at my wedding to Ray.

his eyes out. 'I want to go back to my old school,' he told me. 'I want to go and live with Dad.'

He was so upset I couldn't bear it. It felt as if someone had stabbed me through the heart, and I just wanted him to be happy. 'If that's what you want to do then we can do that,' I told him, even though it was killing me. So I phoned his new school and explained and they kindly said they'd keep his place open for a month.

Of course Shane was thrilled to have his son living with him and offered to drive up to collect him. But in my heart I knew Shane Jnr would last three or four weeks and then want to come home. It wasn't that he didn't love his dad, but I knew he'd find living with Shane very different to living with me. It was one of the hardest things I've ever done, packing his suit-case, and my family thought I was nuts. But I never wanted to have a row with Shane Jnr, and for him to turn round and claim I forced him to go to a different school. So I had to let him go and find out what he really wanted for himself. But when his dad came and picked him up and I carried his suitcase out it nearly broke my heart.

At first Shane Jnr was loving it, and I wondered what I'd done. But after two weeks I got a phone call from him, sob-bing. 'Mum, I want to come home, I want to come back to you,' he said. He loved being at school but when he got home he missed having me around.

Shane came on the phone and said, 'He needs to come back, he wants his mum.' I can't tell you – it was the happiest day of my life.

So Shane Jnr came back and thankfully had only missed two weeks of his senior school in Blackpool. 'You know you can't ask to move back to Dad's now, don't you, Shane?' I explained to him. I wanted him to realize he had to stay, but he never ever asked me again. He settled in, and thankfully Jake loved his school too.

Shane was really good at coming up to Blackpool to see them, so they still got to spend time with their dad almost every weekend.

In the meantime I'd found a house I loved opposite Stanley Park. It was a ninety-year-old detached four-bedroom house with a little front garden and a back yard and we were moving in on 11 September.

Luckily I'd sold the old house for a decent sum, so I could buy the new one outright and put the rest of the money into a savings account.

Ray had already met Shane Jnr and Jake with Shane a year before, but when I moved into my new house I told him he had to come round and meet them properly.

I said to them, 'I've got a friend coming round who's bringing fish and chips.'

'Mum, he's not your friend,' Shane Jnr laughed. 'He's your boyfriend!'

'You really like him, Mum!' Jake joined in.

'OK, yeah, he is,' I agreed.

Ray was really nervous about meeting the boys. 'They're going to hate me!' he kept saying. But actually they both really took to him straight away.

Then later that month I found out I was pregnant. I was upstairs at home in Blackpool when I did the test. The line turned blue and I was so shocked, but also thrilled – I just couldn't wait to tell Ray. The fear set in later of course, especially at the thought of telling other people – most of my friends and family nearly had heart attacks! But I just felt really sorted about it. Once I'd embarked on life without Shane I'd become a lot more independent. I had a home, money in the bank and *Loose Women* liked me. I was very much my own person and I didn't rely on anyone else to tell me what to do. I'd been a single mum once and I knew I could cope if it happened again.

I phoned Ray to tell him the news while he was heading back from Leeds. He'd lost his dad the same year as me and went home every Friday to see his mum. On the Saturday he was driving back when I broke it to him and he missed his turn-off!

From the moment we found out I was pregnant Ray was so into it, which was fabulous because I'd never had that before. He was just so thrilled and emotional.

'You have to come with me to tell Linda and Brian,' I told him.

So we went round the next morning and walked into their kitchen. 'We've got something to tell you,' I said. Ray is the biggest giggler on the planet and immediately started laughing.

'What?' Linda said.

'Guess,' I said.

'You're moving in together?'

'Not yet!'

'You're pregnant?'

The grins immediately confirmed it. Linda put her head in her hands for what felt like twenty minutes but was probably only about five. Her shoulders were shaking and I couldn't work out if she was laughing or crying. She took her hands away.

'Why are you laughing?'

'Oh, I can't wait for you to tell the others!' she said.

It was incredibly exciting but incredibly scary too, telling people. The worst moment was one night when we were sitting round the table having dinner, me, Ray, Shane and Jake. That day I'd had a phone call from the *Sun* newspaper saying that they'd heard rumours I was pregnant. I denied it, but realized I had to tell the boys.

I'd already told Shane Jnr I was pregnant earlier that day and he'd thrown his arms round me with delight, but I hadn't told Jake yet. Jake was my baby boy and quite possessive of me. I didn't know how he'd react. So while we were sitting down at dinner we were asking Jake lots of questions. Then I said, 'What would you think if we had another baby?'

'If you had a baby I would run away and I'd never come back and never see you again,' Jake replied, pouting.

Ray and Shane Jnr just looked at each other and got up and walked away. I thought, *God, I'm not telling him now!* But the next morning when he got up for school I knew I'd have to tell him. So as I was helping him lace up his shoes I said, 'Jake, you know you say you'd run away if I was pregnant?'

'Why, are you?' he said.

I looked down and said through gritted teeth, 'Err, yep!'

'Oh, Mum!' he cried and then he threw his arms around me. 'Do you know what it's going to be?' Then he ran out into the street and said, 'Guess what, my mum is having another baby!' to a complete stranger. He was so thrilled.

After that he was like a little mother hen. He was always telling me not to lift things. He was worse than a husband. So not only did it feel so right for me and Ray, but the boys were into it too.

All I had to do now was tell Shane, and I was dreading it. He'd only just got over the fact that I'd met someone! But I didn't want Shane to read it in the paper, so I called him. 'I've got something to tell you. I'm pregnant!' I blurted out.

He just went really quiet and said, 'Oh congratulations, thanks for telling me.' It was actually quite sad.

If my family had any doubts they mostly kept them to themselves. Like Linda, Amy and Julia screamed at the news, they were thrilled and so excited for us. Maureen was really worried though. 'Oh Jesus, what have you done?' she said. I think she was more shocked that we'd actually been trying!

Mum had already met Ray and loved him straight away. And this time she didn't mention getting married, she just said, 'Oh great, another grandchild!' Whether she was secretly worried I don't know, but she knew how happy I was so she never said anything.

Towards the end of October Ray moved in and it was perfect. We seemed to be perfectly suited. He was somewhere in the middle of the exuberant Shane and the oh-so-quiet Dave and it just worked. He wasn't always vying to be the centre of attention, but we could chat for hours, and when I needed him to, he'd take control and sort things out. Ray was also a devoted family man. When he moved in and we knew the baby was on the way, the first thing he said was, 'I need to get my mum nearer.' So we found her a great sheltered flat. I just knew from the way Ray looked after his mum that he was a keeper.

Ray's mum, Irene, was lovely, and absolutely thrilled that she was finally going to be blessed with a grandchild. Seeing as Ray was forty-three and his older brother was yet to have children, she must have thought it would never happen!

As my pregnancy progressed, Ray came to every test and scan with me, as well as attending all my antenatal classes, and he was reading every baby book on the planet. 'Did you know our baby is now the size of a kidney bean?' he told me after two months. 'Did you know the baby now has fingerprints?' he told me at three. He loved it!

At our second scan we asked about the sex. 'It's a girl!' we were told.

Initially, when I first got pregnant, I think Ray had wanted a boy to carry on the Fensome surname, especially as his brother wasn't going to have any children. So after the scan I thought: *Oh God, I hope he's not disappointed. Is he just pretending he's glad?* But I needn't have worried – he really was delighted. He was doing lots of boy stuff with my boys anyway, and this really was a new beginning for all of us, as I'd never had a girl. It was a double-whammy of excitement. We blew up the scan picture to 10 by 8 and made everyone look at it.

Keen to get some inspiration, we bought a book of baby names and boy did we have a laugh. There were all these ridiculous names like Clytie, which as far as we could tell was actually pronounced clitty!

'Oh, we have to call her that!' I joked to Ray, while he pulled faces.

One day we were standing in our kitchen having a cuppa with Amy and one of her friends who'd called in, and talking about baby names. This girl said, 'I like Ciara.'

'Oh, that's it!' Ray immediately said. 'I love it.'

It took me a few hours but Ray was one hundred per cent sure. 'It's got to be Ciara,' he insisted, and after a while I knew he was right.

Generally I had a brilliant pregnancy. As with the boys, I didn't have morning sickness but there were periods when I'd be very tired. And unlike most celebs, I grew to the size of a detached house. I was enormous.

We were such a happy household. Jake talked to his sister through my belly and Ray was busy decorating the nursery. It was lovely to be with someone so excited from start to end. Every time she kicked he'd be there, he was so into it. But much as everything seemed rosy, those first two years of our relationship were testing and how we stayed together I don't know. Every obstacle that could be thrown at us just was!

It was a lot of change for the kids to take in: a new house, their mum pregnant, and the realization that Ray was going to be their step-dad full-time. Jake was nine and would say things like, 'Well, you're not my dad, you can't tell me what to do.' It was an adjustment for Ray too. He had to find the line between being their friend and being a parent, and he was very different from me. I'd say, 'Don't do that, if you do it again I'll ground you,' but I'd say it ten times before doing it. But with Ray you only got one warning and that took a long time for the boys to get used to. In that respect I think he changed their lives. He was a good father figure and a very fair disciplinarian.

For a long time I felt guilty about them being from a broken home, so I spoilt them. Ray made me realize I really wasn't doing them any favours. If he grounded them for a week he'd stick to it. He'd tell them, 'Sorry mate, it has to be a week otherwise you won't believe me next time.' The discipline was good for them but I was also very much in the middle. If they did have a row I couldn't turn to Ray and say, 'You can't tell them what to do,' but it was also hard for me not to say, 'Don't shout at them.' I'd end up being the one everyone wasn't speaking to! We did have a couple of very bad patches with the boys, and after the baby was born there were some serious battles. But thankfully it didn't happen often. Occasionally things would flare up, but the rest of the time we were a proper family and Shane Jnr, Jake and Ray are best friends now.

The boys knew immediately that they could rely on Ray,

whether it was going to footie matches with them or doing their homework. He'd sit with Jake for hours, discussing things and going on to the internet to explain things to him, and Shane Jnr always says he wouldn't have got half of his GCSEs if it hadn't been for Ray being so strict with him.

Ten

As well as getting to grips with Shane's and my children, Ray had another daunting task ahead – getting to know the Nolan clan and extended family. So when I was six months pregnant, in March 2001, the two of us and the boys joined a mass family holiday to Orlando in Florida to celebrate the fact that Anne had completed all her treatment for breast cancer. There was Mum and Aunty Theresa, Tommy and his wife Jackie and their kids Tommy Jnr and Laura, Anne and Brian and their daughters Amy and Alex, Denise and her boyfriend Tom, Maureen and Ritchie and their son Danny, Brian and his girlfriend Annie, and Bernie and Steve and their daughter Erin.

On top of that, Shane and Claire came and joined us for a few days (my Aunty Theresa just couldn't grasp how I didn't want to drown Claire in the pool), and one of Anne's best friends from school came out with her daughter. It was just chaos, and I have to say, never again!

It was a stressful holiday in so many ways. Not least because I'd noticed that Mum was getting very, very absentminded. She'd ask me a question and I'd think: *Christ, I just told you that!* She was constantly looking for her handbag when it would be at her feet and I began to wonder if it was a bit more than just old age. But if any of us broached the subject of her being a bit dippy she'd get irritated.

'I'm seventy-five,' she'd snap. 'I'm entitled to be a bit forgetful.'

But nothing held Mum or Aunty Theresa back from coming everywhere with us, even though Aunty Theresa had to have an electric scooter because she had terrible arthritis.

We'd arrange to meet at 9 a.m. every morning, as all the nieces and nephews wanted to be together at all the theme parks. But it was an organizational nightmare. Ritchie and Anne's husband Brian would take control, but you could never please everyone all of the time so we'd always end up having big debates.

'The kids want to go to Magic Kingdom.'

'No, we've got to go to Sea World.'

One day, while the debate was still raging in the hotel reception, I said, 'Hang on five minutes, while I change some money,' but when I got back they'd gone, leaving me, Ray and the boys behind. I was really angry, as Shane was twelve and loved hanging out with Danny and Tommy Jnr. 'They could have waited,' I raged to Ray.

That wasn't the only tension on that holiday. Ray found it difficult to be accepted by all the men in my family. I suppose the problem arose because, while all my brothers-in-law are great, they are real manly men. They go to the pub while their women cook dinner. Ray has his moments. He will get trolleyed, but he won't do it every day and the most important thing to him is being at home with his family. All the men were acting very cliquey and Ray was not part of their gang. It made him feel like an outsider and it made me cross. In the evenings, when we'd all meet in the bar, all the men would sit together getting pissed and the women and kids would be in the corner.

Well, Ray would come and sit with us and because he wasn't propping up the bar he felt he wasn't part of the group. Their attitude was that he could have come over, but he was never invited to. I just thought they could have been a bit more welcoming. All those men had known each other for years, and it wouldn't have taken much effort to make Ray feel at home.

Ray got on wonderfully with all the kids during that holiday, though. On one of the days there was a 6 a.m. rocket launch from the Kennedy Center. Ray and the kids wanted to see it, so they all went on a 3 a.m. coach trip. None of the rest of the adults could be bothered, so Ray took all the children with him. I just loved the fact that he was so family-orientated. The children were always the most important thing to him.

There were a few good moments on that holiday, but generally it was absolute hell. I couldn't wait to get home, and Ray and I both breathed a big sigh of relief the moment we walked in the door.

There must just have been bad feeling in the air for everyone that holiday, as when we got back we were all saddened to hear that Anne and Brian were splitting up after twenty-five years of marriage.

Although my pregnancy was pretty straightforward, I was quite uncomfortable towards the end. The last month I could hardly walk, but I was working right up to two weeks before I was due. By then I was doing three days a week. At 8 a.m. I'd do a show called *Live Talk* – it was like *Loose Women* and filmed in Manchester. Then I was doing another programme in the evening for the Wellbeing Channel on Sky called *Girl Talk*, which was to do with health issues.

On my very last *Live Talk* show the producers sweetly presented me with a teddy bear and a bunch of flowers. And we also had Marti Pellow on the show. He patted my stomach and said, 'I'm singing this for you two,' before launching into 'Close to You'.

Ray was watching it at home and actually cried. He was more emotional through my pregnancy than I was – I think he must have got all my hormones!

Just before the birth we'd decided to have work done on the house, knocking a wall down to combine the kitchen and dining room. The builders had promised it would be finished before Ciara's birth, but it wasn't, so we had to move in with Maureen for a week after the baby was born, which she absolutely loved.

Like the boys Ciara wasn't exactly in a hurry to make an appearance, so once again I was induced and she arrived ten days late. I was admitted to Blackpool's Victoria Hospital to give birth – it wasn't until about midnight that I felt the first twinge, and by 2 a.m. the contractions were getting much stronger. They immediately called Ray, who nearly fell out of bed! Normally nothing wakes him, but he had been sleeping with the phone next to his ear. Meanwhile I couldn't sleep at all, it was so painful.

Ray was there in ten minutes and sat with me while I did breathing exercises in the bath, trying to get to grips with it all. Then I got out again and they took me to the labour ward.

By 6 a.m. the contractions were so bad that I was on the gas and air. As I panted and groaned, Ray was having a fit, saying, 'Do something, she's dying!' So I took my mask off and growled, 'Calm down, I'm not dying.'

I didn't want an epidural despite the pain, I'm too scared of needles. But the baby was trying to come out and it wasn't working. I wasn't dilated enough – only seven centimetres instead of ten. So I finally agreed to the epidural, which worked like a bloody miracle! Within ten minutes the pain just went and I was chatting away as if nothing was happening. I even went to sleep for an hour and a half. Then the midwife woke me up and said, 'Sorry to wake you, but you need to start pushing!'

In the end it was pain-free and beautiful. Ciara was born at 11.15 a.m. on 19 June 2001 and Ray actually delivered her, helping to pull her out and cut the cord – we both cried of course.

Oh my God, she was massive – 9lb 4oz! She looked like a proper baby straight away, a little chubby thing. And thankfully I was fine; I didn't have to have any stitches or anything and because of the epidural I wasn't in any pain.

While I sat and had a lovely cup of tea, Ray held her. He was so smitten and couldn't take his eyes off her. 'It's her, isn't it?' he said. 'Little Fensome Face!'

I suppose there was a little bit of me that was fearful that once Ciara was born Ray might not be as devoted to the boys, but I have to say I landed on my feet and that has never been the case. He has never left the boys out. He's devoted to all three equally. And the day Ciara was born he was so overjoyed that he couldn't wait to go home to pick the boys up and bring them back to the hospital. They ran in all excited and gazed in wonder at their new little sister. Watching them with her was amazing. They were just so in awe of her.

After I'd been in hospital for forty-eight hours, we took baby Ciara home to Maureen's. She loved looking after us all and it was brilliant that she could get Ray and the boys their dinner while I got used to everything and tried to breastfeed.

During that week Ray also brought all his family round. It was so emotional for Ray to see his mum hold his daughter. I think we all welled up a bit.

Although I'd bottle-fed Shane Jnr and Jake, proud new dad

Ray had been convinced that breast was best for his little Fen-some Face. Bernie kind of persuaded me too, as she'd done it for eight months with her daughter Erin and had loved it. So knowing it would be my last baby, I gave it a try for six weeks.

I have to say I didn't have one day of it that I enjoyed. Ciara kept feeding really well on one boob and not the other, and it got to the point where I was actually sitting there crying from the pain of it. It turned out I had mastitis, a common and painful condition where the breasts get inflamed and the milk ducts blocked.

I eventually gave up, and from the moment I put Ciara on a bottle she was like a different child. She'd seemed constantly hungry and grouchy while I was breastfeeding, but now after her bottle she was very contented. It was such a relief, as I'm not one of these women who can just whip them out in front of people anyway. I hated the way it tied me down, and I wasn't keen on expressing with an electric pump either. *Just call me Daisy*, I thought!

But as soon as she was on the bottle Ciara fed beautifully and slept all night. We were just getting to grips with our little routine when ITV called up to request a meeting with me down in London.

They'd originally called just before Ciara arrived, when I was five days late, and I'd had an interesting chat with the assistant to Maureen Duffy, the controller of ITV daytime, who said she'd like to see me. 'I'd love to,' I'd replied at the time. 'But to be honest I'm nine months pregnant and literally about to drop!'

So it was agreed that she'd call me back to reschedule a meeting. When Ciara was ten days old she called again and I agreed to travel down to London. At the time there was wild excitement, as Richard and Judy were leaving *This Morning* and every TV personality in the land seemed to be itching to get that presenting job, but I never for one second thought it could be that.

When I arrived I was taken straight to Duffy's office. She was a very elegant, glamorous woman, tall and dark and very well groomed. She had that real Hollywood film star glamour about her. I'd seen her before but never met her, and I found her to be warm and lovely. We just chatted for ages and she asked me how I liked working on *Loose Women*.

'I really enjoy it,' I said.

'Well, I think you're really good,' she said. 'Have you heard about Richard and Judy leaving?'

'Yes,' I replied, absolutely astonished by the way the conversation was leading. 'It's such a shock, isn't it, after all these years? They'll be hard boots to fill.'

'Well, how would you feel about it?' she asked. At which point I nearly fell off my chair.

'We're screen-testing a lot of people,' Maureen continued. 'But we want someone homely and fun.'

I sat there gobsmacked but just about managed to keep a professional composure. I just wanted to pick up the phone to Ray, but instead I stayed very calm and said, 'Thank you, I'd love to have a go.'

Then I agreed a date for a screen test with Maureen's assistant and left the building to call Ray, closely followed by everyone I knew!

Back home that night I couldn't stop smiling, but I also couldn't really believe I was being asked. 'I've never anchored a show,' I said to Ray. 'How on earth am I going to do that if I get it?'

'You'd get used to it,' he grinned. 'I have a really good feeling about this.'

The following week I arrived in London for my screen test. They sat me on the sofa in front of an autocue and then brought in Johnny McCune, who was the editor of *This Morning*, to pretend to be a guest. He was an attractive man, medium build and very slim with short hair. I got on with him straight away. We just clicked. We had the same sarky humour and he immediately put me at ease, and afterwards Johnny actually became a very good friend. The whole thing was really good fun. We had to go through flower-arranging segments and a few other things and I really enjoyed it. Afterwards Johnny said they'd be in touch soon and they called me a car to take me to the train station.

When I got back to Blackpool I immediately sneaked into the bedroom to kiss my little sleeping cherub, then I sat down to tell Ray all about my day. I could tell he was trying to be excited for me, but I noticed he was also a bit quiet. I imagine he was probably thinking about how much our lives would have to change if we had to move to London.

It would be such an upheaval, but at that point I don't think either of us truly believed I'd bag the job.

But then suddenly Maureen's assistant was on the phone offering the role to me. They wanted me to do three months of Monday to Friday, and then once Fern Britton came back from maternity leave I'd do the show every Friday, as well as having other responsibilities on the show. It was an amazing job opportunity. I put the phone down, instantly dizzy from the head rush of it all. It was a massive decision, and all so immediate. They wanted me to start the show that September, in about eight weeks' time.

There was no way I would go down to London without Ray and my children, so sitting them all down we talked through the news.

'You have to take it,' Ray said. 'It's the opportunity of a life-time and I'm more than happy to be a full-time dad to Ciara.'

By now Ray had started up his own production company, which he'd been running from home, so moving to London wasn't a problem. He was also willing to take a back seat for a while, as he knew how much it meant to me, and he loved being with Ciara.

That's the thing about Ray. Being a father was always so important to him. He'd been so broody when I met him and he was a very, very hands-on dad from day one. When Ciara was born I didn't change her nappy for ten days, as he wanted to do it; he wanted to develop the sort of bond I was developing through breastfeeding. I was very lucky.

Thankfully Shane Jnr, now twelve, and Jake, nine, were also very happy about the prospect of having their mum back on the telly. 'It's exciting, Mum!' Shane Jnr trilled. 'Do you think you'll get to meet Kylie?'

So next I called John Conway, Shane's agent. I'd used him for years to book our summer seasons, so he immediately got on the case for me. The money was very good, much more than I'd been earning before.

Suddenly there were all these decisions to make, about where to live and schools for the boys. We decided not to put the Blackpool house up for sale, as Ray wanted to come home every week to see his mum. We were also aware that my contract was only for three months.

It was such a manic time already with a new baby, and we had no idea where we would live. So the day I accepted the job I called Shane to tell him I was moving to London with the boys.

'We've got to move down in two weeks,' I told him.

'Well, come and live with us,' he said. 'You can stay here until you get sorted.'

'Really?' I replied hesitantly. The thought of moving in with Shane and Claire freaked me out, but when I put the phone down the more I thought about it the more I realized it was the perfect solution.

Then when I discussed it with Ray he thought it was a great idea. We were all quite friendly because of the boys, and quite honestly I don't know what we would have done without Shane and Claire's help. I suppose we would have had to rent somewhere, and finding a place for a family of five before you have any wage coming in is not an easy thing to do. So that was that.

Bedlam broke out and we literally left Blackpool within a fortnight, when Ciara was just eight weeks old. It was weird pulling up in the car at the old house I'd shared with Shane and moving my things into the spare room. But Shane and Claire were an oasis of calm as we flapped, making suggestions about schools and helping with the kids.

Because it was almost September we quickly found schools for the boys, but they were literally starting the following week. Their new headteachers had told us not to worry about uniforms, but I knew standing out so much on their first day would make the boys uneasy, so Ray stayed at home looking after Ciara while Claire and I raced to the shops to get both of them everything they needed. It was literally, 'You go this way and I'll go that . . .'

Then suddenly days later I was gearing up for my training for *This Morning*. I was scared to death! The programme had won so many awards and was so highly acclaimed. *How on earth am I going to cope with taking over a two-hour live show?* I wondered. I was presenting the show with the iconic Sixties model Twiggy, which seemed a bit odd. There had always been a man and a woman before, and I wasn't sure about the dynamics of having two women. But what did I know? So instead I concentrated on signing up for all the help I could get to help me prepare for the show. Suddenly my days were filled with presenting workshops, going out with stylists and filming pilots, before I'd rush home to spend blissful evenings with my beautiful baby daughter.

Living with Shane and Claire was fairly chaotic, but I have to say Claire was so brilliant with Ciara and was always helping Ray out when I wasn't there. Likewise if I couldn't make it to pick up the boys she'd do it, and she regularly took them to school. She really was an angel. I'm not denying there were times when I'd find it really bizarre sitting in my old kitchen, where I'd first met Claire, and asking, 'Is it all right if I put the kettle on?' But most of the time our domestic situation – albeit weird – really worked.

Bless Ray, he was an absolute saint during that period. It must have been completely stressful for him, as Monday to Friday I was out of the house while he'd be stuck at home looking after a tiny baby and making small talk with Shane and Claire – mainly Claire actually, as Shane was out of the house a lot working on his film *Shoreditch*. But it was all very civil, bordering on cosy. Shane often did weekend performances at Butlin's and Ray would go with him to play guitar. Meanwhile Claire and I would sit in having long girly chats. By now I really liked her and was beginning to think she was far too good for Shane.

Before I knew it, the big day of my *This Morning* debut arrived and I didn't feel ready for it at all. Thankfully it was a nice atmosphere to work in and I felt like everyone was rooting for me. I got on really well with the crew, the women in the phone room and the hair and make-up girls, and everyone made me feel very welcome and at home.

But what made it particularly difficult was that I didn't actually get to meet Twiggy until literally a few days before we went on air. I'd done loads of one-on-one coaching, but we hadn't practised working together.

When I was introduced to her for the first time she was lovely. But I couldn't really grasp why, while I was shaking in my boots, she wasn't at all fazed. 'I've been in this business thirty-odd years,' she reminded me.

'Yes, but not as a live TV presenter!' I wanted to scream.

So actually we only got to sit on the sofa together for the first time the day before we went live, which looking back now seems utterly ridiculous. Immediately there were problems. Twiggy wore glasses but didn't want to wear them on screen, so they had to make the autocue really big for her. But that made it really difficult for me, as I could only see about two words at once!

And there wasn't exactly an instant rapport between us either. In fact it soon transpired that our sense of humour couldn't have been more different, which made me nervous for the show. Maureen Duffy had been convinced that having two women presenting would make a nice change, but I wasn't so sure. There was just something about Twiggy and me that was feeling quite forced, and I wasn't sure the general public would buy it.

That first morning we went live, oh my God, you have no idea how frightening it was! Before the show began Johnny had come to me and told me I would be driving the show. 'Twiggy's not hitting it right on time for the breaks,' he explained. 'So if we give you the countdown to the lunchtime news you have to hit it on time.'

Well, Jesus, Mary and Joseph! Talk about adding to my pressure. Suddenly I felt as if I was teetering on the edge of a cliff in a gale force hurricane! Twiggy and I taking over on *This Morning* had sparked a massive interest in the press – it had even made *News at Ten*. I knew that the world and his wife would be tuning in to see how we fared compared to TV stalwarts Richard and Judy. And as the thirty-second countdown began I actually felt nauseous. *My entrance on screen will be me vomiting on this coffee table*, I thought. But then the adrenalin kicked in and somehow we made it through the opening and into the first ad break. Phew!

One of our first guests that day was Joan Collins. She was obviously quite a special guest to have, and she and Twiggy clearly knew each other, as before the interview there was lots of air kissing. Yet she didn't overly impress me. She kind of had the air of being a diva, almost as if she'd ask you to curtsey if she could.

For some reason during the interviews they'd get the guest to sit in the middle of me and Twiggy, which meant that they would naturally have their back to one of us – and during this interview that was me. While Twiggy was taking the lead with the interview, there was only one thing on my mind – hitting the lunchtime news on time. All I could think was: *The news is coming, the news is coming! I have to hit the news!* Meanwhile Twiggy and Joan were chatting away, leaving me looking like a spare part at a wedding. Then suddenly in my ear the countdown to the news had begun, but Joan had only just started a story. *I need to shut her up!* I thought. So I literally butted in halfway through her sentence with, 'I'm terribly sorry to interrupt you. Anyway, coming up after the news . . .'

Afterwards all the crew were laughing, saying, 'Oh my God, you actually interrupted Joan Collins!'

'I had to!' I gulped.

'It wouldn't have mattered that much if you were a few seconds out!' Johnny laughed.

'Oh great!' I huffed. 'Now you tell me!'

Of course if I'd been a seasoned anchorwoman it would have been a lot more seamless than it was; it was just a bit clumsy, but not as bad as I initially thought.

For the next few weeks hitting the news on time was always my big fear. When I watch back the tape of those shows now I can actually tell when the news is coming up – I start rubbing my hands together because my palms are sweating!

Altogether that first ever show was the longest of my life. And when it finished I felt as if the sigh of relief I let out was the first breath I'd taken in two hours. I did feel really exhilarated, though, as it was such an achievement for me. And when I walked in the door I was greeted with rapturous applause from Ray, Shane and Claire. They'd bought me helium balloons and flowers, which was really thoughtful.

But no sooner had I settled down on the sofa for a nice cuddle with Ciara than I thought: *Oh God, I've got to do it all over again tomorrow.*

The next morning I arrived at the studio to the daunting news that we'd been slated all over the newspapers and the *This Morning* forum was going bananas. As I'd feared, after thirteen years of Richard and Judy people weren't particularly keen on change. And our critics were having a field day. The general consensus seemed to be that Twiggy and I didn't gel, but initially they weren't being too hard on me. 'Hopefully Coleen Nolan will get better with experience,' one write-up said, but Twiggy was described as wooden. *Oh, give us a break,* I thought. *We've only done one show.*

I don't think I've ever been under as much stress as I was at that time. Every morning I had to leave the house at 4.30 a.m., and having a newborn baby meant the little sleep I snatched was disturbed a lot. Eventually Ciara started sleeping five or six hours a night, so we did get into a little routine where I'd do a feed at 10 p.m. and then Ray would be up at 3 or 4 a.m. to do another. Then when I clambered out of bed at 4.30, Ray would be close behind, up with Ciara again. We were both constantly knackered. Sometimes I'd lie in the bath wondering why on earth I was putting us through it all.

There's no doubt *This Morning* couldn't have come at a worse time, but it was also a once in a lifetime opportunity. And to be honest, by the end of the first week I absolutely loved it. I began to feel less nervous and was really getting into the swing of things.

In fact everything was just beginning to settle down when I got a Friday night phone call from Charlie Bunce, the lovely, laid-back executive producer of the show. 'We don't want you to worry, but we've decided that things with Twiggy aren't working out,' he said, to my utter shock. 'She won't be in on Monday, but we want you to know that you're doing a great job.'

'Oh,' I said, tongue-tied. 'So who *will* I be doing the show with?'

'We've lined up John Leslie,' he confirmed.

I put down the phone feeling a bit weird. *Poor Twiggy*, I thought. *This business really is cut-throat. I hope my job is more secure.*

I was pleased to hear I'd be working with John Leslie, though. I'd met him when I was still with Shane at various showbiz dos and I'd always liked him. On the Monday I discovered that hosting the show with John was actually a lot easier than with Twiggy. We gelled from the first day and immediately struck up a rapport. He was also a safe pair of hands who could take over from me anchoring the show. John had been presenting for years, and it was now nice to be the co-pilot. *He can worry about hitting the news while I enjoy myself,* I thought.

After that I had a great time on the show. The programme started to do much better with the mix of male and female presenter and I felt I could be more myself. More of my personality was coming out and I could have a laugh. I was much more relaxed. Before John came in I was doing all the big interviews, which had been quite daunting.

The first week I was on the show we had Anne Marie West, the daughter of Fred and Rose, on the sofa and I'd had to interview her on my own. I'd never really interviewed anyone before, so suddenly grilling someone about such a harrowing tale was quite a challenge.

But having John there made it a lot easier. If he ever saw me falter or felt my nerves during an interview, he would very calmly and seamlessly take over. There was a great spark between us, and we would flirt and giggle and generally have fun together.

It went on like that for a while and I felt that everything was finally slotting into place. The boys were doing really great at school and I was finding my feet on *This Morning*.

But Ray was knackered getting up with Ciara all the time, and I was craving some home life with my partner and little girl, so it was with some relief that I heard Fern Britton was coming back from her maternity leave. Of course the newspapers had a field day, saying Fern had been brought in to save the show, while I was being dropped. But I didn't really care. I knew that had always been the plan, and after three months' hard graft I was pleased to be doing my Friday slot with John.

It meant the best of both worlds and more time at home with the kids.

My original contract was coming to an end, though, so I did ask about it. I just wanted the security of knowing I would be in work for a while so that Ray and I could justify looking for a place of our own. Living with Shane and Claire had been great, but it did get to the point where we needed to move out. It was just too bizarre. Just like before, I'd morphed back into their agony aunt, and whenever they had a row, Shane would come and tell me his side then Claire would come and tell me hers.

Oh my God, this is weird, I thought. *I am so glad I'm with Ray*. It also made me sad. At times it reminded me too much of the hard times I'd been through with Shane.

Keen to give them some space, often after my Friday show we'd pile into the car and drive up to Blackpool to stay in our old house. Ray would regularly take Ciara up to see his mum on his own as well. She was still a newborn and, God love her, he took her up and down that motorway. It was such a change from Shane. Ray used to look after her all weekend, doing everything, feeding her and sterilizing her bottles. He was a sensitive new age man and I loved it!

Over the next few weeks there was little improvement in relations between Claire and Shane. He was always off doing his own thing and I could tell she was becoming very unhappy. For ages she just seemed at a really low ebb, and it was as if all the life had drained out of her. I actually told her, 'You need to leave.' She was like a zombie, just miserable all the time.

It was clear that having Ray and me there as they sounded the death knell of their relationship was also not at all helpful or fair, but still I didn't know whether to buy a house or rent one, so I asked Johnny again.

'Look, as far as we're concerned you can buy two houses,' Johnny laughed. 'You're definitely going to be staying.'

So of course we went house-hunting then! As it happened, our timing couldn't have been more perfect and we totally fell on our feet, as Maureen's ex, Pete Suddaby, told us that he wanted to sell his home in Ickenham, Middlesex. It was a beautiful mock Tudor detached house in a cul-de-sac, five minutes away from Shane's. We moved in November and it worked out perfectly.

Everything was rosy apart from some of the neighbours, who were snobby gits. They seemed to take exception to the boys and their friends playing football in the street, and one day a neighbour told them, 'Would you mind stopping playing football. You're turning the close into a council estate.'

When the boys told me I was livid. 'Right, if you want council, I'm not mowing the lawn front or back,' I decided.

Not long after we moved into our new house Claire turned up one day looking terribly forlorn. 'I've come round to tell you I'm leaving Shane,' she said. 'My dad's coming tomorrow with a van.' Poor Claire, after five years of being messed around by Shane, she too had finally had enough.

Life had been hectic, but once we got into the new house it was fabulous and I felt much more settled. I was doing my Fridays and other odd reports on top of that. If it were a Christmas show we'd all be on – me, Fern, John and all the resident experts. Fern Britton was always absolutely lovely to me. She'd always greet me really warmly and say, 'Hello darling!' and give me a kiss.

It was nice doing such a high-profile show. I was getting recognized all the time and I was apparently getting a fair bit of mail, although there's a lot of weird stuff they don't give you.

I'd been told that there was some sexy mail and a few nasty letters, but I didn't want to see them. As far as I was concerned ignorance was bliss, and I'd rather that than be frightened to go out of the front door. But despite the oddballs, I was assured that there were really good reports back about the ratings for the Friday show, and the ladies in the phone room were always telling me I was getting a lot of calls and fan mail. It was a good time and I began to feel more relaxed. I felt that I'd found my feet and had started to earn my stripes.

Meanwhile Shane had been really upset about Claire leaving, and phoned me up crying the day she moved out.

'Shane, this is a good opportunity for you,' I told him. 'Go out and have fun, and be young, free and single.'

But it didn't surprise me at all when he got a new girlfriend within weeks. Shane never could cope with being on his own for very long. This new girl was a dancer called Christie Goddard, and he'd met her through mutual theatre friends. Immediately Shane was raving on about her.

'You'll love her, Co,' he told me. 'She really reminds me of you, you've got the same sense of humour.'

I first met Christie at a Christmas party John Leslie threw, and I have to say she was quite shy. She was very young – fifteen years younger than Shane – but very pretty and clearly very into him. It was nice to see him happy again.

That Christmas we went back to Blackpool to our old house and spent Christmas up there with all the family. It was lovely to have a break, as I hadn't seen a lot of Mum and my brothers and sisters since Ciara had arrived.

The new year started positively for us. As far as I was concerned the show was doing well, and I was still being told that Fridays were popular and everything was great. Then a new editor called Helen Warner replaced Johnny, who'd moved on to a different show. When I met her I really liked her. She was a couple of years older than me and was quite slim with long dark hair, and always had a positive attitude.

Around February time I was told by my new agent, Alex McLean-Williams, that Helen wanted me to do a holiday piece from the Maldives. It was odd, as they already had a presenter called Mark Simpkin who did outside broadcasts from abroad. I wasn't actually that keen. It would mean six days out there, as there was only one flight in and out a week. I didn't want to be away from home, with just a cameraman and soundman. I wanted to be with my family. But they were going on and on about it, and Alex kept calling and saying, 'Helen really wants you to do it. She thinks it'll be brilliant for you.' It was a nice compliment, but I did think: *I don't remember Richard and Judy or Fern ever doing this*. And it also meant I'd be off the show for a week, with Jane Moore filling in for me on my Friday slot.

I didn't want to do it but they kept upping the money, until I couldn't really turn it down. So I went and it was beautiful, just fabulous, although I didn't appreciate it as much as I should have because I really missed the kids and Ray.

When I came back the following week, John Leslie immediately took me to one side before the show. 'I don't know what's going on but you need to keep an eye on things,' he said.

Concerned, I took the opportunity to chat to the day producer of Friday's show, who was called Mark, who told me not to worry. If something was up, he clearly didn't know about it so I put it out of my mind. Then literally two weeks later I got a phone call from Alex, telling me that Helen and Charlie wanted to have a meeting with me on a Thursday in about three weeks' time.

'What is it about?' I asked.

She didn't really know but thought it could be to discuss my new contract. It made sense, since my current contract ended in April, which was the following month. 'They've told me they're sending a car and want to speak to you about how things are,' she added.

Well, immediately I feared the worst, so I called John. 'John, they've called me in,' I said. 'Do you think they're going to kick me off the show?'

He tried to reassure me that this wasn't likely. 'Hmm, I've got a funny feeling,' I replied.

As the next couple of weeks passed I was nervous. I was going over the scenarios in my mind and trying to think positive, but the whole thing left me feeling very uneasy. Alex had said she'd come with me, so when the Thursday finally came we got into the car ITV had sent for me. When we walked in Helen seemed her usual self and offered us tea. But although Charlie smiled, he seemed subdued. As we sat down to business I just knew from his reaction that it wasn't good news.

'We're really pleased with everything you've done so far,' Helen said. 'Everyone really likes you, *but* we're not renewing your contract.'

'Oh,' I said, stunned. 'Can I ask why?'

'Well, Friday ratings aren't that good,' she replied. 'We get letters in saying people are not happy with you.'

I was taken aback, as I'd thought the Friday show was doing well.

'But all the women in the phone room, they said I get lots of fan mail . . .' I stammered.

'Coleen,' Helen interrupted. 'It's not personal. *I love you.* I don't want you to think I'm firing you, we're just not producing any more shows with you.'

'So will I go at the end of April?' I asked.

'No,' she replied. 'I think it's better you go from today.'

I looked at her, completely winded. Charlie, who I'd been very close to, couldn't even make eye contact with me. He just sat there staring at the wall. *Don't you dare cry*, I told myself.

'Your piece in the Maldives was so brilliant,' she continued. 'We'd still like to use you for outside broadcasts.'

I nodded, but as she tried to make small talk I could feel a burning lump in my throat that was nearly choking me. I knew I needed to get out of there before the tears came. Suddenly I remembered my dressing room, which was full of personal artefacts, family pictures and good luck cards. 'Can I go back to the studio?' I asked. 'I want to pick up my stuff and say good-bye.'

'No, we'll send it on,' Helen said firmly.

I was floored. So I couldn't even say goodbye to all those people I'd worked with for seven months.

'We could have told Alex over the phone but we felt we owed it to you to bring you in,' said Helen. I'm sure many people would prefer to be given such news face to face but not me.

'No, you're wrong,' I replied. 'You should have said it over the phone.'

After the meeting all I wanted to do was go home and cry, but Alex had lined up another meeting afterwards with the producers of a programme called *Celebrity Fit Club*.

Like me, Alex was upset and very angry, but we both took a deep breath and headed off to our next meeting. *Celebrity Fit Club* was a new show where eight overweight stars had to go on a boot camp to lose weight for charity. Seeing as I was still carrying all my baby weight it appealed to me a lot, and I decided that I really wanted to take part. But as we sat there listening, one of the well-meaning producers chirped up with, 'It'll be great because you can talk about it on *This Morning!*'

Oh my God, I've just been fired, I thought. I thought once they knew they wouldn't want me, but they did and we started filming a couple of weeks later.

On my way home from that meeting I called Ray and I cried a lot. All the way home on the train in fact. Ray was so angry on my behalf.

'You need to meet me at the station,' I told him sadly. 'We need to put the house on the market.'

When I arrived at the station, Ray was there waiting for me and he was livid. He wasn't cross because they'd decided to change things, but he was upset by the manner in which it had been done.

The next morning I sat at home watching Jane Moore, who'd taken my role on the show, and trying not to cry. The thing about Jane is she's a really good journalist and good at doing a hard-hitting documentary, but I don't think she gives out the warmth you need to make people relate to you on a daytime show like *This Morning*.

As it turned out, she was replaced by Fern, who soon ended up doing the show five days a week. In the meantime I stopped watching.

Of course the minute I was out on my ear the press got wind of it. 'Coleen axed from *This Morning*,' the headlines read. A Sunday paper offered me a fortune to spill the beans but I turned them down. I knew that if I did it would be career suicide, so I sensibly stayed quiet.

After that I was really quite depressed. It wasn't just about losing the job. It was also the worry. I felt terribly guilty that I'd uprooted my entire family to a different part of the country for no reason. And it frustrated me that I'd given up those first few months with Ciara for something that hadn't been so life-changing after all.

It was just a relief that we hadn't sold the house in Blackpool. Although we wanted to move back there, we decided we'd wait until the boys had finished their full school year – that way it would cause them minimum disruption.

The day I was sacked I phoned John Leslie and left him a message. He called me back and told me that apparently Helen had approached him after Thursday's show. 'What's the plan for tomorrow?' he'd asked and that's when she told him. He was absolutely livid, and totally devastated.

John was always fabulous to me, but that same year he absolutely went through the mill. Just six months after I lost my job, it all went downhill for him too after rumours went flying around that he was the unnamed celebrity Ulrika Jonsson claimed had raped her in her autobiography. The siuation got worse when Matthew Wright blurted John's name out on live television. Ulrika never made any comment on whether the allegation in her book referred to John or not and once the rumours had started they went on for ages. During that whole period I was shocked and horrified by the situation – it was so unfair. Poor John was then charged with two counts of indecent assault, after a complaint made by a different woman. He always maintained his innocence and I was so pleased for him when he was cleared of these charges.

I'd always got on well with John who was good fun to be around. I also knew his ex-girlfriend Abi Titmuss back then and thought she was awfully quiet, just very normal and quite plain. I could tell she was mad about him, but I didn't feel he was so mad about her. I always thought it very strange when Abi came out as this sex kitten afterwards, as the Abi that was with John and the one that emerged were so far removed. The Abi I knew was easily shocked and always covered up.

When it all kicked off, I left messages on his answerphone offering support but he didn't call me back. Probably at that point he didn't know who his friends were. I felt terribly sorry for him.

I met him at a function nine months after and I was so embarrassed, as I didn't know what to say. So in the end I went up to him and said, 'John Leslie, I sat for seven months on that couch and you didn't try it on. I'm so insulted.'

He laughed, but I've not seen him since.

After a few weeks I got cracking with *Celebrity Fit Club* but it didn't earn me anything. The idea of the show was that they paid your expenses, but the money for each pound you lost went to charity. I'd chosen the Rhys Daniels Trust, a charity that offered free home-from-home accommodation near hospitals for the parents of critically ill children.

The other contestants included Rick Waller, a former *Pop Idol* contestant, who moaned a lot and was so obese that he really ought to have been losing the most, but he didn't have the willpower and the only month he actually lost a stone was when he was ill.

Ann Widdecombe, the Conservative MP, was a nice enough lady but she could be eccentric. She'd have a go at the experts, in particular Harvey Walden, who was an ex-marine and did the punishing physical training with us. 'No, I'm not doing that,' she'd say, if he told her to do something gruelling. 'I don't want to be a marine!' And she'd tell Dr Adam Carey, our nutritionist, that he was talking crap too.

Sometimes I wondered why on earth they had agreed to do the show.

Nicola Duffett, from the soap *Family Affairs*, made me

laugh, and I got on great with Tommy Walsh, the builder from *Ground Force*, as with Jono Coleman, the radio DJ. Ian McCaskill, the weatherman, was so eccentric but really lovely, and *Emmerdale* actress Kay Purcell and I got on brilliantly and even stayed in contact for a while after the show ended.

When I went on the show I was pretty big at 12 stone 13 pounds, but I got down to 11 stone by the end of it. I actually got really into it. I suppose it helps when you know your weigh-in is going to be filmed on national television. I did the best of all the women, and I lost the highest percentage of body fat. I remember feeling really proud when Harvey said in a newspaper interview afterwards that I was his little marine! He used to scream at you, but he didn't care if you were slow as long as you gave it one hundred per cent and I always did.

Doing that show was a good distraction, and something different for me to focus on. It was filmed over six months, and I ended up making £11,000 for my charity.

After that, *This Morning* did use me for a few outside broadcasts. I did a Paris holiday slot and got a five-minute interview with Britney Spears at some do or other. But after that I hardly worked at all. I could not get a job with ITV. It was almost as if they'd disowned me.

Then I found out that *Loose Women* was coming back, but they were filming it from Norwich. I was really chuffed to receive a call saying they were considering me for it, but found it odd that they wanted me to do a screen test. 'But I've done *Loose Women* loads of times,' I questioned. 'Is it really necessary for me to go for a screen test?'

'We're changing the format,' the researcher said. 'Everyone has to test for it. Even the regulars.'

So reluctantly I traipsed to Norwich, arriving well before my allocated time of 11.30 a.m. It was a long journey, and when I arrived I was ushered to a makeshift green room in a Portakabin. I sat there for ages, but my name wasn't called. Yet every celeb woman on the planet seemed to be coming and going. There was Paul Daniels's wife Debbie McGee, the former *Big Brother* contestant Alison Hammond, TV presenter Fiona Phillips and loads of others going in and out, but I didn't spy one single regular girl there.

Each of the auditionees I knew just looked at me, confused. 'Why have you got a screen test?' they asked.

So I shrugged, saying I didn't know.

Eventually one of the researchers came in. 'Sorry for the delay,' she said. 'The producer will be down to see you in a bit.'

'Who *is* the producer?' I asked, curious.

'Helen Warner,' she replied. Well, my heart just sank. *I don't want to be here and I don't want to do this*, I thought.

I sat there getting more and more despondent, and I can remember phoning Ray and telling him it was her, at which point I thought he'd spontaneously combust. 'I want to get in the car and come home,' I said.

'Don't cut your nose off to spite your face,' he told me, clearly gritting his teeth. 'You may as well just do it now.'

So finally at 5 p.m. – almost six hours after I'd arrived – I was called in. There was a quick 'Hello, how are you?' from Helen, and then I went on and they trotted out exactly the same formula we'd always used on *Loose Women*.

Then, knackered and miserable, I drove the 140 miles home to Ickenham.

A couple of days later I received a call from a researcher. 'Sorry,' she said. 'Helen doesn't think you're right for the show.'

Thankfully the series in Norwich didn't last. It was terrible.

They had a different panel on every day and the audience never really got to know any of them. I have to say there was a part of me that was thrilled it wasn't working out.

Eleven

When we headed back to Blackpool almost a year after I'd left to do *This Morning*, I was embarrassed. My pride was battered and my spirits were low, but it also made me think that every-thing happens for a reason. It turned out that just at that time I was needed back in Blackpool to help with Mum.

She'd gone downhill ever since our family holiday to Florida before Ciara was born, and over the past few months while I'd been away she'd deteriorated dramatically. Ever since my dad died Mum had lived in sheltered accommodation, but now we were beginning to wonder if she was really up to coping on her own. Although it had started off with her being very absent-minded and constantly asking questions that we'd already answered, now she was too dippy for words.

In the months after I moved back to Blackpool I couldn't believe how muddled she was getting. Once I called her at 4 p.m. and she asked, 'Why are you calling me at this time?' She thought it was the middle of the night. Then one morn-ing the phone rang at 5 a.m., startling me, and it was Mum on the other end. 'What time are you picking me up for Mass?' she asked.

'It's only five o'clock, Mum,' I said.

'Oh, have I missed it?' she replied.

'No, Mum,' I said wearily. 'You need to go back to sleep, Mass isn't until eleven.'

Then on a third occasion she knocked on the door at 6 a.m. and exclaimed, 'Are you still in bed? You lazy devil!'

There was clearly something seriously wrong. Whereas Mum had always been easy-going, now she seemed to be frustrated and cross all the time, and nothing made her angrier than being told she wasn't very well.

It took us an age to actually get her to the doctor, but eventually she allowed Anne, Brian and me to take her. 'I'm doing it for you,' she barked. 'But I'm not very happy about it.'

It was that day that the GP confirmed the thing we feared the most – that she had Alzheimer's.

'Maureen, you're not very well,' the doctor told her very gently. 'I'm afraid your memory is not very good.'

She just went nuts. She started crying, telling the doctor, 'I'm not mad.'

Then she turned to us.

'I can't believe you've brought me here,' she said, glaring at the three of us and folding her arms protectively across her chest. 'I hate you. You've all turned against me.'

I glanced sideways at Anne and swallowed hard. There were going to be some very difficult times up ahead.

Although we all feared she was ill and took her to the doctor mainly to confirm it to her, it was still very upsetting.

Meanwhile, Ray, Shane Jnr, Jake, Ciara and me had quickly settled back into life in Blackpool. Ray was pleased to be living near his mum once more. Little Ciara, now walking and beginning to pick up words, loved the attention her aunties lavished on her, and the boys had settled back into their old schools. But while I was happy to be back up north, I was really worried about work. It was hardly fair, but all the publicity about my sacking from *This Morning* seemed to have tainted my professional reputation and I was barely being offered anything.

After sending out a few feelers I eventually managed to get a regional TV job doing the odd broadcast for the BBC's *Inside Out*. They sent me to Liverpool to explore the history of the Beatles and to visit the house where John Lennon grew up. And following on from that I did sporadic reports for the programme, but it was more monthly than weekly and I never knew when my next pay cheque would be arriving.

Local television reporting could be a fairly thankless task as well. It was clear that there was a big difference between how regional and national reporters were treated, and I was amazed by how rude some people could be.

At one stage *Inside Out* sent me to interview a girl band but it seemed that they viewed a chat with the local TV channel as rather beneath them. To my disbelief, that day they kept me waiting outside their trailer for two hours. I could hear them inside giggling and laughing, but every time I asked the press officer from their record label how long they'd be I was told they weren't ready yet. Then when they finally surfaced they weren't in the least bit apologetic. I just thought it was thoroughly unprofessional and ill-mannered.

Throughout all the years the Nolans were riding high in the charts, I would never have dreamt of treating anyone like that. It was just one of those moments when I really wanted to let rip and tell them exactly what I thought. But instead I had to swallow my pride and do my job.

Despite my lack of regular work, thankfully we were able to survive for a while. Luckily we had no mortgage on our place in Blackpool, and we were also able to live on our savings and the profit we'd made from selling the house in London. Ray was doing the odd gig, playing guitar with the

Legends here and there, but we were both aware that neither of us was raking it in. And as more and more time passed me by I started to panic. I really needed to try to get back into TV.

That was when I'd emailed Dianne Nelmes to ask if she knew of any suitable jobs coming up at ITV. When I read her reply telling me *Loose Women* was coming back and that she'd ask someone to contact me, I immediately got butterflies in my stomach. I hardly dared dream but I had a good feeling about this.

Then, as luck would have it, within days I got a call from Johnny McCune, my old *This Morning* editor. It turned out he was the new editor of *Loose Women* and had thought to get in touch, not even knowing about my email to Dianne.

As we chatted, it was clear that he was one of the few people who still rated me and he was willing to take a risk. 'I'm doing *Loose Women* and I've persuaded them to give you another chance,' he said.

But I didn't do anything wrong, I thought to myself, although I was hardly about to make that point.

Johnny was clearly looking out for me when he had no obligation to. He's one of those rare people in TV who is steadfastly loyal. 'So we'll film a couple of shows with you and take it from there,' he said.

'That's brilliant,' I replied. 'Thank you so much.'

When I put the phone down I literally jumped for joy. Although I'd done *Loose Women* many times before and was ironically a much more skilled presenter after my stint on *This Morning*, I was very, very anxious before my first show.

'I really need the job,' I told Ray. 'I'm so nervous.'

'You'll be fine,' he told me. 'Just be yourself.'

So I went down to London to film my first show an absolute bundle of nerves. It just felt like my last chance saloon. By now it was 2003, and two years had passed since I'd had regular TV work. I knew this one show could make or break me.

But as soon as I got to the studio my fear subsided. There was Johnny with a big grin on his face, and then in walked Kaye Adams, who seemed positively delighted to see me. I knew then that I was really among friends.

Joining us on the panel were Carol McGiffin, a feisty, straight-talking ladette and former producer of *The Big Breakfast*, and Jenny Trent Hughes, an American psychologist with a wicked sense of humour.

So just like old times we all filed out in front of the studio audience to talk about the day's news stories and gossip. It was so exciting to be back, and as we got into the swing of it I could feel myself relaxing and I really started to enjoy it. It was just fabulous, as if I hadn't been away at all.

I did a couple more shows and then Johnny called to say that everyone really liked me. 'We're going to give you a regular slot,' he said. I was back on the map!

Again it was the same scenario – we'd do a six- or eight-week run and then have four or five months off. We never knew if we'd be recommissioned, but with each series the show seemed to grow in popularity. Being back on *Loose Women* had a knock-on effect for my career too. Having previously been a leper of the TV world, it seemed I was now deemed fit and healthy once more and was consequently invited on shows like *It's Only TV But I Like It* and *Never Mind the Buzzcocks*.

As a family we also did an experiment for the *Tonight with Trevor McDonald Show*, in which they filmed us for two weeks attempting to teach Shane Jnr and Jake the value of money. Basically we had to write down every single thing we paid for or they asked for in one week and then work out how much

we spent individually on them in four weeks. It included everything – takeaways, magazines, clothes and football stickers.
Then we had to give them their monthly allowance in cash and
trust them to make it last the whole month. At the time Shane
was fourteen and Jake was ten and it was an amazing transformation for both of them. I don't think they ever bought
another football sticker, and whereas Shane had always wanted
designer tops he suddenly learnt the value of money and went
looking for bargains instead. They had so much enjoyment
from it and really learnt to budget.

It was something we continued with them for many years
afterwards, pretty much until they left home.

Meanwhile I was now doing *Loose Women* once a week and
really liking the fact that the pool of presenters was a lot
smaller. There were now only about eight to ten of us, and a
really nice bunch at that. Even if *Loose Women* finished tomorrow we'd still text each other to catch up. Everyone genuinely
gets on.

I think having that familiarity of working with the same
girls week in and week out has also done wonders for the show.
It has ensured that we all gel better and means the whole thing
is a slicker operation. And it's actually a bit like therapy for us!
In the morning meetings before the show we quite often devi-
ate to discuss personal things, and everyone pipes up to give
their advice. And quite often we all find ourselves revealing
more than we expected during the show too. The format is
so chatty and informal that suddenly I realize I'm telling the
nation that I'm dying for Ray to propose or we're congratu-
lating Carol on going out with a twenty-six-year-old!

It's funny, as a lot of people who have joined the show, like
Jackie Brambles, a former Radio One DJ and showbiz reporter,
GMTV weathergirl Andrea McLean and Jane McDonald, who

shot to fame on reality TV show *The Cruise*, all intended to hold back on the personal stuff. But they all broke eventually. You just get so wrapped up in the show that you can't help it.

Kaye was always my closest friend on *Loose Women*, and it was hard for me when she left in 2006 to have her daughter, Bonnie. I thought I'd never be able to accept the new anchors, as it almost felt a bit disloyal, but actually Jackie Brambles is fabulous and so is Andrea McLean. And strangely, even though we're poles apart, I've forged a very unlikely friendship with Carol McGiffin. In theory we have nothing in common: she's a party animal who likes going out and getting pissed (it only takes two glasses of wine) and is not at all into kids, while I'm most content at home with my family and a nice cup of tea. We shouldn't get on but we really do, and I love everything about her.

Carol sometimes ends up pie-eyed in the corner at celeb parties and award ceremonies, so the rest of us are always dead protective of her, formulating a plan to get her out and home avoiding the paps. It's like being out with a naughty child sometimes. She's a bugger for making me laugh, though. We sit on stools behind the desks, and often although we're very glam from the waist up we're actually wearing trackies, scruffy jeans or trainers and will have our shoes off. But Carol is a little more risqué and will often sit there in a micro-mini with her legs wide open! I can tell you, if that desk fell away the audience would get a right eyeful.

I'd be lying if I didn't admit that some days the girls irritate the hell out of me, but I think that's fairly normal when you work with the same people week in and week out, and is probably more to do with me occasionally being in an irritable mood or tired from getting on the train at 5.40 a.m. to travel down to London.

You also get the odd guest who rubs you up the wrong way. One actor kicked up a complete storm about a car we sent for him for *Loose Women*, complaining that the driver hadn't met him on the platform with a name board. Then he walked round with a bloody attitude. Yet he's an example of someone who can just switch on the charisma when the cameras start rolling.

It's funny, as most guests are terrified of stepping out to be grilled by four women, but we're very nice and more often than not it's just hilarious being there. Sometimes it gets really silly, and there was one show recently when Jackie and me were just completely giddy. We couldn't look at each other without laughing. It got to the point where we had tears dripping off our chins, and thankfully Jane McDonald was there to hold it together. I love those moments.

Another time we were talking about how different parts of the country have different colloquialisms to greet people: for example in Scotland they call you Hen, in Liverpool they call you La and in Birmingham they say Bab. The discussion was in mid-flow when I heard the voice of Carl, one of our editors, filtering into my earpiece.

'I dare you to say Cock,' he challenged.

'I quite like Cock,' I immediately piped up deadpan, and the whole panel collapsed into shocked laughter.

Apparently my sister-in-law Annie was tuned in that day and told me later that she'd just taken a bite of her sandwich and a swig of tea. So when I said it she ended up spitting it all over her lounge. It's good to have the jokes though, otherwise it can feel like *Groundhog Day*.

As 2004 began we were all getting increasingly worried about Mum, and over recent months we'd all upped the amount of time we spent with her. But now it seemed that even her memories were getting muddled. You could walk past a random building with Mum and she would say, 'I was born there,' or 'That's my old school.' And as the illness really kicked in over the next few months she'd talk about my father like he was a different person and she was constantly rewriting their history together.

My dad was not the type of man who would have ever indulged in public displays of affection, but Mum now saw things very differently. 'I remember when your dad and me used to walk in the park hand-in-hand,' she'd say. Or she'd announce, 'He was a great man, your dad, so kind. He looked after us all so well.'

I used to think: *Hmmm, he had his moments.*

But gradually Mum's illness took on another dimension as we began to realize that Mum was becoming a danger to herself. One day Anne went round to the flat and found it full of foul-smelling smoke because Mum had put her electric kettle on the hob. God knows what would have happened if Anne hadn't arrived. There was no escaping it – Mum now needed twenty-four-hour supervision.

So it was agreed that I'd look after her during the day and Anne would have her at night, with everyone else helping out too whenever they could. It was hard work, but after all she'd done for us throughout our lives it was ultimately a small sacrifice to make.

By the beginning of 2005 Ray and I had been together for five years and I was beginning to wonder if he'd ever propose. In fact it was growing to be a running joke on *Loose Women*.

'Come on, Ray,' the other girls would nag on camera, winding him up. 'You need to make an honest woman of her.'

Every time we neared Valentine's or Christmas I'd wonder whether he might pop the question.

Although Shane had stalled when I'd first filed for divorce in 1999, by now I'd had my decree absolute for a couple of years. Yet Ray never took the plunge. I knew it was shyness holding him back. The thought of being the centre of attention and giving a speech at our wedding terrified him. But then Ray told me he was planning to arrange a party for my fortieth birthday. He was throwing a big black-tie do and that's all I knew. I didn't know where it was or who was coming. It was very exciting and it took him months to organize.

When I woke up on the morning of my fortieth, Ray brought me a cup of tea in bed and handed me my presents. As I surveyed the brightly coloured packages I thought: *I wonder if there's a ring in there*. But as I ripped off the paper it was clear there wasn't. Although he'd been very thoughtful, there was a part of me that felt really disappointed. Not that I could feel like that for long. I had a party to go to!

I'd bought a long vibrant blue evening dress and had my hair done especially, wearing it loose. Once I'd finished getting ready, Ray bundled me into a taxi and we pulled up outside the De Vere Hotel in Blackpool. When I walked in I was just flab-bergasted: there were about 250 people, including lots of folk I hadn't seen for years – all my family from Ireland, my friends from London, the *Loose Women* girls. Ray didn't leave anyone out.

When I walked through the bar they threw open these big double doors and suddenly there was a fifteen-piece orchestra blasting out 'Happy Birthday'. There was all this fantastic food, and a cake of the *Loose Women* set with us four sitting behind the desk. I was just made up.

It was proving to be a fantastic party, and then halfway

through the evening a big projector screen started up and everyone turned to watch it. Playing on it was a montage of film, with all these things from my childhood, messages from all my family, the boys and Ciara. Then right at the end Ray came on. He was sitting in his office. 'Well, that's it, darling,' he said. 'I hope you're having a brilliant night and I hope you like everything I've done for you. Now there's only one thing left to say . . .'

Well, I assumed he would say, 'Happy Birthday,' but then suddenly he added: 'So I need to get down on one knee. Coleen, will you marry me?'

This massive roar went up and I looked from the screen to Ray completely gobsmacked, my hands in front of my mouth. He hadn't told anyone, and at that moment appeared in front of me grinning and holding out a gorgeous sparkler – a lovely gold band with a solitaire diamond. To be honest, I was so happy I would have loved it if it had been a plain metal band!

It was so brilliant. Bless Ray, he knew he couldn't get up in front of everyone so he'd videoed it. He'd sweetly asked Shane Jnr's and Jake's permission and had confided in Maureen in order to get my ring size. It was so perfect and unexpected – he should have just got the priest in and we could have done the whole thing at once!

After I'd accepted Ray, Shane Jnr and Jake got up with the orchestra and sang McFly's 'It's All About You' and I cried with happiness. It could not have been more perfect at that moment.

So the following week I headed back to work to relive the story all over again on *Loose Women*.

However, after the excitement of my engagement had worn off I suddenly found myself at the centre of a media storm of the sort I'd not encountered since I'd been axed from *This*

Morning. It all started with a throwaway comment on *Loose Women* about how I'd told Shane Jnr, who was now fifteen, that as an incentive for him to revise for his GCSEs I'd pay for him and a friend to go away for the weekend.

'He told me he wants to go to Amsterdam!' I told the *Loose Women* panel.

'Why did he pick Amsterdam?' someone else commented.

To which I replied, 'Well, he's not going there to smell the tulips!'

'What if he's going to a prostitute?' they questioned.

'Well, I'd rather he did that, and used a condom, than shag four girls in Ibiza with no protection,' I said, giving my honest opinion. Then I joked that I'd have to send Ray with him to supervise.

After my upbringing, when sex was never talked about and I'd naively fallen pregnant at sixteen, I was determined to speak openly about sex to my children. So when I'd noticed Shane taking a healthy interest in girls I'd sat him down and discussed the birds and the bees. I emphasized the importance of taking precautions and using a condom, and I also told him I'd like to know when he did it. A few months later he announced that he'd lost his virginity the night before.

I had my back to him in the kitchen and it did make me tearful. Here was my first-born growing up. But before I could even say a word, he said, 'And yes, I did use a condom.'

He went on to say it was with a girl from school and that it had happened at a party.

When it came to going to Amsterdam, I was pretty sure Shane Jnr would do no more than gawp at the prostitutes in the red light district before realizing it was actually a bit icky, just like any teenage boy would. But the point I was trying to make was that seeing as I already knew Shane Jnr was sexually active, I wasn't going to bury my head in the sand. I was going to talk to him about it responsibly.

Well, oh my God, the next day you would not believe the furore in the papers. When I saw the *Daily Mirror* I was horrified. Dr Miriam Stoppard had really gone to town and appeared to have got the facts all wrong. The way the story read it was as if I'd said to Shane Jnr, 'If you get five GCSEs, I'll send you to Amsterdam to sleep with a prostitute,' and she accused me of irresponsible parenting.

Then Shane, his father, kindly waded into the storm, saying he was 'disgusted and appalled' by my comments. 'I can only think she said this for shock value,' he added. 'And I hope and assume it was said in total jest. No responsible parent would even think of such a thing – let alone state it.' He was on the phone to me before long too, screaming blue murder.

For the next few days every single paper went bananas for the story and the magazine I'd just started doing a problem page for even sacked me. Yet women were coming up to me in the street and saying, 'I totally agree with you,' and blokes were even shouting, 'I wish you were my mum!'

Thank goodness *Loose Women* were fantastic throughout the whole sorry debacle. They knew the context in which I'd made the comments and totally stood by me. When a couple of Shane's calls really upset me and got me panicking that I'd be sacked from the show, Dianne Nelmes, creator of *Loose Women* and Director of Daytime Programmes, helped calm me down. 'I'm not worried by all this, Coleen,' she said. 'I think it's quite funny. The more you let Shane get to you, the worse this seems. And your job is not under threat.'

Shane seemed to feel I deserved to lose my job.

'Oh my God!' I said to him. 'What is wrong with you? How

on earth do you think I will continue to support our children without my job?'

'No son of Shane Richie is paying for sex,' he ranted at me. Then he revealed that he was planning to pay for Shane Jnr to go on holiday to Magaluf!

'Oh, so he can shag a load of slappers as long as he doesn't pay for it?' I retorted.

There was no reasoning with him, but it was one of the few times I'd actually stood up to him.

To my relief, Shane Jnr stuck up for me the whole time, and when his father told him I was out of order, he remarked, 'This is from the man who had seven in the bed and says he's slept with over a thousand women.'

Well, that shut him up!

Ironically, two months after I was taken to the cleaners for my lack of mothering morals I actually landed a weekly parenting column in the *Daily Mirror* and was applauded for my modern approach to bringing up children.

For months now Anne, myself and my other sisters had been looking after Mum full-time at our homes, but it was becoming increasingly difficult. We were all supporting each other but it was incredibly hard, especially for Anne, who was also trying to cope with the breakdown of her marriage. Meanwhile, slowly but surely, our mother was lapsing into being like a child. You had to go to the toilet with her and she had tantrums like a kid. Anne and Denise would tell her off as if she was a child, but I couldn't bear it and I hated myself if I had to do the same. When she used to stay with me I found I couldn't wipe her when she went to the loo or help her in the bath either. It was just too much. Emotionally I just couldn't cope. I'd never seen my mother naked. She'd been so very private when it came to nudity, but now suddenly she was like a kid with no inhibitions. She had to be forced into the bath and you'd have to undress her and put cream on her. The few times I had no choice but to do it, it broke my heart.

But my other sisters, to their credit, did most of that stuff and I'll always be grateful to them for that.

It got to the point where you had to watch Mum every second. I remember once I told her I needed her to get ready for a party and she just stood up in the lounge and proceeded to strip off in front of everyone. Ray legged it into another room and the boys were saying, 'Gran! What are you doing?' while I tried to get her into a bedroom.

When you dressed her she'd stand there fidgeting like a little girl while you pulled up her tights.

It was hard for the kids, as they were young – she would literally ask the same question over and over and sometimes they'd snap at her. I'd instinctively tell them off and say, 'Don't speak to her like that, she's ill,' but then later I'd feel guilty that I'd been too hard on them.

The one good thing was that Ciara, being so small, used to play with her like another kid. They'd be playing nicely and then Mum would suddenly snatch a toy off Ciara, who would snatch it back. It was actually very funny to watch them playing and squabbling like a pair of four-year-olds. Those were the moments of hilarity that brought us rare glimpses of sunshine during that time. Ciara and Mum just adored each other.

But it got to the point where Mum was becoming not only a danger to herself but also to Ciara. A few times when I popped upstairs she escaped out of the front door, which was bad enough. But for me the turning point was when she handed Ciara some pills and told her they were sweets. Thankfully Ciara showed them to me before she put them in her mouth, but it was a real wake-up call. Reluctantly we all agreed it was time for Mum to go into a home.

We must have taken her to loads, but she just hated them all. Each time we visited one she'd have a tantrum and say, 'I'm not staying here. I want to stay on my own.' Whenever we said, 'No, Mum, you're not capable of looking after yourself,' she'd go mad. She never once accepted that she was ill.

Putting her into a home was the hardest thing I've ever done. We eventually found one she liked, but once we moved her in she went berserk. One minute she would be screaming and shouting and calling us bitches, and the next she would be begging and sobbing like a child. 'Please don't leave me,' she'd say. 'I'll be really good. I'll sleep in the pantry.'

Every time I visited it was the same. 'Coleen, I could be your baby-sitter, I'll look after Ciara,' or 'Can I come and live with you? I'll clean your house.'

She'd sometimes say, 'Can you call my dad and ask him to pick me up?'

I just used to walk out to the car and sob. Each time it was like someone twisting a knife in my heart.

We'd tried to make her room all nice for her, with lots of pictures of the family and her own television, but then one day we went in and the room was empty. 'I'm really sorry,' the nurse explained. 'She pulled all the pictures off the wall and smashed them and pulled the telly over, so we had to remove everything for her own safety.'

It was awful. I'd go into her room and find shoes stuffed under her pillow or clothes under her bed.

'They've stolen my clothes,' she'd tell me angrily.

Other times she'd call me up claiming the nurses were trying to poison her.

In an attempt to get her out and about, Denise organized

for her to have her hair washed and set at a hairdresser's once a week. It started off as a weekly treat, but after a while it was just proving too difficult. You couldn't predict how she'd be, and she'd often lash out if the water went in her eyes. Alzheimer's is such a cruel disease and I wouldn't wish it on my worst enemy.

That December, in 2005, we picked her up from the home on Christmas Eve and she spent a few days with us all. Mum had always loved Christmas, but now she was barely aware of what was going on. Still, it was nice to have her at home with us all.

If we'd hoped to start 2006 with some happy news, it was sadly lacking.

A few weeks earlier Linda had confided in me that she had a lump in her breast and, alarmed because of Anne's history, I'd been nagging her ever since to go to the doctor. She'd been busy doing *Blood Brothers* and then a panto in Northern Ireland, so she kept putting it off. So when I called a few times and she still hadn't been, I was cross.

'I will,' she said. 'Please don't tell anyone.'

'OK,' I sighed. 'But I'm putting this phone down and giving you an hour to make an appointment. 'If you haven't when I call you back, I'm telling the whole family.'

My threat seemed to work, as immediately she booked to see a doctor. It wasn't good news. Brian called to say Linda had a massive tumour in her left breast and needed a mastectomy. Linda was too upset to call herself.

Poor Linda, the night before the operation Ray and I joined her and Brian for what she'd dubbed her 'Farewell to my boob' dinner.

In recent years the four of us had become very close. Linda

and I had always been thick as thieves, and Ray and Brian got on from the moment they met. They were like our best friends really. So as usual we found some dark humour to make light of it all, and Linda indulged us by smiling and laughing despite everything she was going through. I was really impressed by her strength, but I knew if I was too sympathetic she'd start crying, so instead I made reference to the fact that like me she'd always been a complete coward as a child when it came to visits to the dentist and doctor. Then I tilted my head to one side and said, 'You're very brave,' in a singsong voice.

'Oh, shut it,' she laughed.

The next day, the day before her forty-seventh birthday, she went in for surgery. When I went in to visit her on the afternoon of her operation she looked surprisingly upbeat.

'Look at you, with your make-up on, sitting up looking all fantastic,' I commented. 'It's very disappointing. I wanted to come in and see you with lots of tubes and moaning. If I can't be Nurse Nightingale I'm taking the grapes home!'

The way she was handling it all was just incredible. By the time they got to the lump it was grade three, and they'd discovered tumours in her lymph nodes as well, which they'd also removed. She needed an aggressive form of chemo in the hope that she'd make a full recovery. It was very gruelling and resulted in her losing her hair.

I know she had her moments when she sobbed. As well as feeling terrible, Linda had to cope with such a dramatic change in her physical appearance. Out of all of us Linda was always the one people remembered because of her breasts and hair.

'Who's your sister with the long blonde hair and big boobs?' people would ask. To lose those two major parts of your identity in just a matter of weeks would be traumatic for any woman, not least Linda.

Since they'd been back on tour with *Blood Brothers* Linda and Brian were no longer renting their house in Blackpool, so when her treatment began they moved in with their friends Sue and Graham. But it was clear as Linda went through the full-blown sickness and fatigue of chemotherapy that they needed a place of their own. So Ray and I offered them a two-bed place that we'd just bought to let. Financially we couldn't afford for them just to have it, but we gave them a knockdown rent and did it up especially with a new kitchen and carpets. They loved it and I think it helped Linda to remain upbeat.

Thankfully her bone marrow and CT scans had come back clear, leaving her consultant optimistic that the cancer hadn't spread, although she'd have to wait a full five years before they could say that for certain.

I was amazed when Linda, just like Anne, proved to have such fighting spirit that she'd just got on with her treatment and then got straight back to work. Sadly I do think with both of them there was that element of fear that they couldn't afford not to get back to work. That made me sad, that they couldn't just get on with recovering without worrying about the financial side of things.

Because things were a bit tight at the start of 2006, Anne offered to come and work for us. I was flat out doing a good eight-week stint on *Loose Women*, doing four to five shows a week. It often meant leaving home on Sunday and not getting back until Thursday. Ray was working too, so it was a struggle for him looking after Ciara and the boys as well as getting on with all his stuff, and I'd asked my niece Amy if she had any friends who might be interested in a job as a nanny.

But then Anne called up. 'What about me?' she asked. 'I'd love to look after Ciara and I could use the cash.'

'Oh my God, that would be perfect!' I replied.

It worked out brilliantly for ages. Ciara loved her Aunty Anne, and I'd come home on a Thursday to find Ciara and Ray sitting on the floor doing a puzzle while Anne was preparing us all dinner.

The thing was, Ray and Anne had always had this fiery relationship, which the rest of us would laugh at. They got on brilliantly but they didn't half rub each other up the wrong way at times. But it was never serious, just the pair of them winding each other up. 'Oh, shut up, Ray,' Anne would say.

'No, you shut up,' he'd immediately throw back.

But then one day I got a call from Anne. 'Look,' she said. 'I don't want you to get involved, but Ray and me have had a fight and he doesn't want me to come back. But I just wanted to let you know that I can still have Ciara round at mine if you want.'

'Oh, don't be silly,' I replied, assuming it was all very trivial as usual. 'I'm sure it'll all blow over. I'll give you a call tomorrow.'

When I got home Ray immediately greeted me sheepishly. 'Anne and me had a big row today,' he said.

'I know,' I said, rolling my eyes. 'What are you two like? What was it about?'

When he filled me in I have to say it just sounded silly. Apparently Ray had annoyed Anne by telling her that it made him sad that her daughters Amy and Alex were not making more of their singing talents. Then she'd gone on the defensive. When she'd got really wound up he'd stupidly laughed because he found it funny, but Anne went ballistic and made some comment about the pair of us being backstabbers.

It all struck me as ridiculous, and to be honest Ray and Anne sounded as bad as each other. I assumed that everyone just needed a bit of space and it would all be fine.

The following evening Ray and I went to the *Loose Women* wrap party in London and had a brilliant time. But as we were sitting on the train travelling back I received a text from Denise inviting me to a girls' night at her house – just me, Anne, Aunty Theresa and Alex.

Anne and I hadn't spoken yet, and I wanted her to cool off a bit before we did, so knowing that I wouldn't be back until quite a bit later anyway, I replied, declining. 'Thanks so much for the invite but think I'll give it a miss because of situation. But have a brilliant night and see you soon.'

I didn't mean anything by it but suddenly I got a barrage of texts from Denise, all highly critical of Ray. She accused him of treating Anne badly even though she'd lost her husband and was broke.

'Den,' I replied. 'No one understands the heartbreak of a marriage break-up more than me.'

It was different for me, she replied, because I had money.

I just sat there thinking: *I don't understand. This is nothing to do with Denise. Why is she being so hostile?* I was really hurt by Denise's reaction and I also felt very defensive of Ray, as it seemed really unfair.

I was so fuming, but I decided to ignore her. Then when we stepped in the door the phone rang. It was Aunty Theresa. 'I'm phoning as I know Ray and Anne have had a row,' she said. 'I don't want to get involved, but if what Anne has said is true then Ray is so out of order.'

'So you are involved,' I said.

'No.'

'Yes you are,' I replied. 'But you've only heard one side.'

Well, it started off as this stupid argument between Ray and Anne and then it just escalated and escalated until lots of other people were involved. There was name-calling, accusations – all this stuff dredged up from the past. It got totally ridiculous.

It was awful for Ray, as he felt like a condemned man on death row. He wrote a letter to Anne offering to talk to her but got no reply. Then suddenly we were rowing too. Just recently Ray had finally agreed we could start organizing our wedding for the following year, after I'd joked, 'If you don't hurry up I'll put my engagement ring on eBay!' But now he was getting cold feet.

'I love you but I don't know if I can go through with it,' he told me. 'I can't see how I can marry into this family.'

I could understand why he felt that way. He'd always felt like an outsider, and now Anne and Denise had confirmed that his suspicions were right. The thought of getting married in front of members of my family who didn't really like him was mortifying for him. He was really upset, but filled with such anger as well – to the point that I thought he might have a nervous breakdown.

'Right, the thing is, Ray,' I told him, as we sat at home one night. 'You're not marrying them, you're marrying me. I don't want them at the wedding either.'

'But if we don't invite them the rest of your family will hate us,' he said sadly. The whole situation was a complete mess.

Eventually Anne phoned and asked to meet for dinner. 'OK,' I agreed. 'But I'm not ready to meet Denise. I don't really know what to say to her.'

So Ray, Ciara and me met up with Anne and Alex for something to eat. We didn't touch much on the row but it kind of broke the ice a bit.

Meanwhile, I faced every mother's nightmare – one of my beloved sons was leaving home. Ever since the age of two, when Jake had bopped on my knee watching his dad in *Grease*, I'd known that my baby boy would end up singing, dancing and acting. Shane Jnr was still crazy about his football, but Jake was my little performer. So when he was old enough he'd joined Tiptoes Theatre School in Blackpool. At one time his singing coach was actually Jodie Prenger, who later won the BBC show *I'd Do Anything* and landed the role of Nancy in *Oliver!*

At school Jake auditioned for every play, and Ray taught him guitar. Most kids give up, but once he started learning he never put it down. And he and Ray were always writing songs together. Then, when he was fourteen, Jake saw an advert in *The Stage* for the Sylvia Young Theatre School in Marylebone, London.

'Mum, please can I audition?' he begged me, so I called up the school and they agreed to see him.

So one Monday morning the pair of us got the train down to London and I sat in a coffee shop for a couple of hours while Jake did his audition. After a while he came bursting out, grinning, 'I've got a recall for Thursday!'

It was exciting, but we knew he was up against at least thirty other kids for just one place. Then, just as we started to make our way to the train station, I received a call from the school saying, 'We'd like to see Jake now for his recall.' When he went back they offered him a place right there and then.

When we got outside the two of us were just screaming, running up and down the street. I was absolutely thrilled for about twenty-four hours, but then reality started to set in. *Oh my God, he's going to have to live in London*, I thought.

So it was decided that during the week Jake would move in with his dad.

Really, it wasn't the end of the world. I often travelled down to London at the crack of dawn on a Monday to film *Loose Women*, so that meant Jake and I could make that journey together. Plus he could stay with me on the nights ITV put me up in a hotel for the shows. But it was just weird not to have him around all the time. How I sobbed. Ray cried too. The pair of us were heartbroken. In fact, when I bid Jake farewell at the station the first time he travelled down on his own, I was blubbing so much that the train steward asked me if I was OK.

'Yeah, but he's going away,' I sobbed.

'Don't worry,' he said. 'I'll look after him.'

As soon as Jake arrived in London he called me up. 'Mum,' he said. 'When I go back every week, can you always cry? They put me in first class!'

By now my own mother was pretty much wheelchair-bound, as she was getting weaker and weaker and couldn't walk very far. And once Linda had recovered from the chemo she came with me to try to get Mum out of the care home for the day. It was easier said than done. The minute you walked in you'd know straight away what mood she was in, and the happy, placid days were proving much less frequent than the aggressive ones. There were times when you had to laugh, otherwise you'd cry.

I can remember once when Linda and I took her into town to try to get her some new clothes. Mum was being fairly unresponsive, but suddenly straightened up in her wheelchair, all alert. 'Linda,' she whispered, grabbing her hand. 'Don't look now, but there's a woman in here who is the spit of you! She's like your twin!'

When we both looked over we realized Mum was looking at Linda in the mirror. God, that creased us up. After that we'd often catch her talking to her reflection in the mirror, thinking it was someone else.

But before long the comedy moments ebbed away for good. Back at the home she started attacking the nurses if they went near her. That was one of the hardest things to handle, seeing her becoming so aggressive. It just hadn't been in her nature before she got ill.

It was also depressing to see the way the disease ravaged her appearance. While she was only five foot tall, Mum had always been a cuddly size 20, but gradually she disintegrated into a frail little doll. And as she deteriorated she had no strength left for tantrums. Bit by bit she grew less aware of our visits, and I could tell she wasn't even sure which daughter I was. She stopped speaking altogether and became bedridden. And even on a warm day we'd have to wrap her up in loads of blankets, as she'd always be cold.

Sometimes when I turned up the nurses would be playing her videos of the Nolans in the hope that it would spark something in her mind, but she'd lie in bed completely unresponsive. Eventually the only things she could move were her mouth and eyes, and because she had terrible bedsores, they had to turn her every hour. At first I tried to help the nurses, but I couldn't bear to listen to her screams of pain so I'd have to leave the room.

'We're sorry, Maureen,' the nurses would soothe her afterwards, stroking her forehead. It never failed to move me how compassionate and kind those nurses were. I will be eternally grateful to them; they were just lovely. They always made such an effort with Mum, even when she was being incredibly nasty and swearing like a trooper – something she'd never done before the Alzheimer's.

After a while she didn't scream any more, which was almost worse. You could stand in front of her and there'd be no expression in her eyes. 'She's gone,' I thought.

She'd be like that for months, then suddenly her eyes would follow you round the room and it would give you a little bit of hope.

In December 2006 Shane Jnr turned eighteen and we had a big birthday party for him at a hotel in Blackpool. But I was really hurt when right at the last minute Anne didn't come. I'd thought we'd smoothed things over, so it was a real kick in the teeth. I also thought it was unfair on Shane Jnr, but because we'd made up I didn't make a fuss. Instead I did the Nolan thing and swept it under the carpet.

By now Mum was bed-bound and didn't seem to know us any more, so for the very first time the Nolans' family Christmas went ahead without her. I took Ciara to visit her in the home on Christmas Eve, but Mum was out for the count. Still, we took her presents and she had a nice tree and decorations up in her room.

The family spent Christmas Day together in Blackpool at ours. Although I still hadn't said a word to Denise, Anne and Aunty Theresa came and it was nice. We were all smiling, trying to enjoy ourselves, but underneath it all there was such sadness about Mum. It was like that until the day she died actually – there was so much guilt, sorrow and anger racing through our minds.

Throughout everything the Alzheimer's Society were unbelievable. They really supported us. There were so many things we were racked with guilt about, but the charity is run by people who have been through exactly the same thing. Guaranteed if you called them up, a kindly soul on the other end of the phone would always say, 'But you don't have to feel guilty.' They were so supportive and caring.

I'd pretty much given up on seeing Mum interact with me ever again, but then one day, in early 2007, I was sitting stroking her face while she slept when she suddenly opened her eyes and stared at me.

'I love you,' she murmured in a barely audible voice.

I was so thrilled to hear it but at the same time utterly heart-broken. It immediately reminded me of the warm, affection-ate mum I'd lost. I went home and cried.

It was the last time I ever heard Mum speak.

Twelve

After a sad Christmas with Mum absent, I started 2007 desperate for some light relief. So I set about trying to plan my wedding.

My *Loose Women* colleague Jane McDonald had suggested that Ray and I could get married on the cruise ship she was performing on that Christmas and we liked the idea. 'If you got a magazine to cover it they'd probably do you a deal in return for the publicity,' she suggested. But although we set the wheels in motion it all began to go pear-shaped. It was just the logistics of flying everyone out – it was becoming more of a hassle than it was worth. So after that we were kind of stalling.

Funnily enough, 2007 was the year Shane married Christie. They'd had a son called Mackenzie Blue the year before and went on to have a daughter called Lolita Bell in 2008. Although I was invited to Shane and Christie's wedding I decided not to go. I thought it might be a bit weird for me to be there. I also didn't think it was very fair on Christie – surely the last person you want at your wedding is your husband's ex-wife.

Meanwhile the whole idea of planning our nuptials seemed like such a pain in the arse – it was impossible to find the time to do it all. What I really needed was for someone to take charge and organize it for me!

Towards the end of 2006 I'd parted company with my agent Alex and briefly joined another agency for a trial but soon began to get itchy feet again, which is when my co-presenter Denise Welch mentioned that she knew a celebrity agent called Neil Howarth who really wanted to work with me. 'Can I give him your number?' she asked. I agreed, and the next thing I knew there was this very enthusiastic man on the phone talking ten to the dozen.

He told me he had loads of ideas that could work for me, and was full of exuberance and excitement. 'There's this fashion shoot that would be perfect for you,' he said.

'Me, do a fashion shoot?' I laughed. I just thought he must be a bit of a nutter, so I said I'd have a think about it all and call him back.

Meanwhile Ray and I were jetting out to Egypt to embark on the biggest challenge of our lives – a 400-kilometre five-day bike ride along the River Nile to raise money for the Alzheimer's Society. For weeks leading up to the event Ray had been going out on his bike every day, but I felt very unprepared. Although I'd lost weight on *Celebrity Fit Club* in 2002, during the years that followed I'd soon piled the pounds back on thanks to my penchant for toast and butter, chocolate, chips and crisps! So for the past three months I'd been concentrating on losing 3 stone by doing the LighterLife weight-loss programme. I was going to the gym whenever I could, but I hadn't had a lot of time to cycle. To be honest, the longest bike ride I'd done prior to the event was twelve kilometres, which had nearly killed me! Not surprisingly, by the time we got to Egypt I was bricking it.

When we arrived in Cairo we met the forty-five other cyclists taking part. Many of them had first-hand experience of relatives with Alzheimer's, and others were carers. I was amazed that some people taking part were even in their sixties.

I'd been teasing Ray all week, saying, 'I'm just the token celeb. I'll just have a picture taken at the start and then at the end but I'm not doing the bits in between.' I was convinced I couldn't do it because of my lack of training, but as soon as I met all the other cyclists I was overwhelmed by the camaraderie. Suddenly I thought: *Even if it kills me I've got to give it my best shot.*

We set off at 7 a.m. on the first day. I'd planned to do a little bit just to see how I got on, but I managed to do the full fifty-two kilometres! Ray was up the front most of the time, while I was right at the back. I had this sweet lady called Linda and this lovely guy who stayed with me the whole time and they were just willing me on.

The next day we went on an amazing journey off the beaten track through little villages. You would not believe how poverty-stricken they were. There were kids running down the street next to the bikes who had nothing, but yet they had these lovely big smiles on their faces. Then we'd turn a corner and go down dead straight roads for miles, then all of a sudden pass gardens with camels in!

It was absolute agony that day but I forced myself to keep pedalling. Whenever I felt my resolve wavering I'd imagine my mum. I thought about all the things she'd done for me over the years, how she'd forced herself up at the crack of dawn each morning to light the fires for us at Waterloo Road, how she'd nearly broken her back squeezing damp clothes belonging to eight children through the mangle in the back yard, and how she'd pawned her engagement and wedding rings just to see us smile on Christmas Day. She'd devoted her whole life to her family – a lifetime of sweat and toil – so five days of cycling was little enough effort to make for her in return.

On the third day we went through a desert for hours and I actually thought I was going to die from heat or boredom – and I also acquired a substantial war wound to my backside. No one had told me that I shouldn't bother wearing knickers under my two pairs of padded cycling shorts, and now I had an open wound thanks to the chafing from my knicker elastic. I applied bucketloads of Sudocrem to my arse and screamed every time I got on and off my saddle.

On the penultimate day I'd got about forty kilometres into the trek when I just hit a wall. The temperature had soared to thirty degrees and my legs were like jelly. I was wobbling all over the place. My mind was willing but my body couldn't carry on. I was ordered to stop by the doctor and he helped me into his van to rest. I was completely devastated and cried my eyes out. As the other cyclists hurtled on past I felt so disappointed in myself. Getting out my phone, I texted Shane Jnr and Jake.

'I failed today,' I wrote.

'What do you mean you failed?' Jake quickly typed back. 'I'm very proud of you.'

'It's great having a marine for a mum,' Shane Jnr added. Well, that made me cry even more!

After I'd recovered that night there was no way I wasn't getting on my bike to do the fifth and final day. So, summoning up my willpower, I got back on and did the final leg. I've never felt so jubilant as when we crossed that finishing line. Remarkably, between the whole team we'd raised £150,000 for the Alzheimer's Society.

Ray and I returned from that trip triumphant and humbled, but within weeks we were left very distracted – Anne had released a tell-all book about Dad abusing her and the phone was going crazy. Every time I answered, it seemed to be a reporter asking me what I thought and whether it had happened to me too. 'No,' I said.

'Do you believe her?' they'd insist.

'Yes, I do,' I replied. 'That's all I've got to say.'

When I got hold of a copy I did flick through and read the abuse bits, which wasn't easy. Anne had told me the gruesome facts before, but seeing it in print was hard to handle.

I know a lot of family members were angry when Anne first started to write the book, but I was always behind her. She never told anyone what Dad did for years and she'd never faced him before he died, so I hoped putting it down on paper would prove cathartic for her. But even reading it in black and white couldn't make it sink into my brain. It's just weird for me, as I get so angry whenever I hear stories of child abuse on TV. I'll even say things like, 'They should just get a lethal injection.' And Jesus Christ, the thought of anyone touching my kids – well, I'd bloody kill them. But yet I still can't think that way about my dad. Perhaps that shows how unconditional a child's love is. I hate him for what he did to Anne, but I also love him because he was a great dad.

In a way I often think it was just as well that he had died by the time I'd met Ray and had Ciara, as it would have caused so many problems. Ray says things like, 'There's no way that man would be in the house anywhere near my daughter.' We've had many heated discussions about it. To this day, when I talk about what he did, it's as if I'm talking about someone else – I can't connect that abuse with my dad. I know he did it but I can't feel emotion about it. It just won't sink in.

Once the media storm had subsided, Ray and I quickly had other things to think about – we were both worried sick about

Linda's Brian. In early 2007 he had a fit and was rushed to hospital. Prior to Linda having breast cancer he'd suffered from a terrible ulcer, but he'd recovered from that after an operation.

When Brian had his turn Linda immediately called me, so I dashed out of the house to meet her at the hospital. When I arrived at A&E, Brian was being questioned by a doctor who seemed to be asking him about every aspect of his health. Another doctor came flying down the ward with some test results from Brian's liver.

'How much do you drink, Brian?' he asked.

'A bit,' he replied.

'He does drink quite a lot,' Linda added softly.

Well, it turned out that because Brian had been ill for a couple of days, and hadn't been boozing as normal, his body had had an adverse reaction to the lack of alcohol. They thought he'd be OK but advised him to cut down.

'You can have the odd drink,' the doctor told him. 'But keep off the spirits and try beer instead.'

After Brian's health scare had subsided I received another call from Neil.

'The photoshoot I asked you about is going ahead,' he said. 'I'd still love you to do it. So what do you think?'

I was really surprised that he was still serious. And it's really hard to turn down someone brimming with such enthusiasm, so before I knew it I'd agreed.

When I arrived at the shoot, which was for a fashion range, Neil was there to meet me. I liked him immediately. He was younger than I'd expected, in his late twenties, but clearly knew his stuff. We just hit it off straight away. And I was impressed with how much interest he took in everything to do with the shoot. He also didn't mince his words.

'I'm never normally this forthright with someone I don't know,' he said bluntly. 'But you could be doing so much more.'

'And you think you could do that for me, do you?' I asked, raising my eyebrows.

'I absolutely do,' he said, dead serious.

I didn't know quite what to make of him, or whether to believe he could deliver what he promised.

'Okay,' I said. 'If you can get stuff for me, then phone me.'

I really didn't expect him to put his money where his mouth was, but within days he was back on the phone. He asked me to tell him all the things I'd like to achieve, so I gave him a list of about five things off the top of my head and never expected to hear from him again. But within weeks every single thing I'd asked for he had delivered. I loved his enthusiasm for everything, his obsessive professionalism and his work ethic, so I decided to go to his agency. Neil was absolutely thrilled, and continued to be like a little whirlwind. He'd call me every day with good news, 'I've got this, I've got that, don't forget this . . .'

At first I'd wondered why on earth he wanted me. I didn't think I was very marketable, but then he got me a column in *Woman* magazine, a fashion deal with Debenhams and my first magazine front cover – all within a month! I also won a contract for Iceland, the food manufacturer, who wanted me to work with Kerry Katona. *Should be interesting,* I thought.

I actually liked Kerry a lot, and there is something very endearing about her. Although she's married with four kids, she reminds me of a naive little girl who desperately wants to be loved. She trusts everyone who comes into contact with her, even though she shouldn't. Over the years I've worked with her there have been times when I've felt fiercely protective and wanted to tell the world to leave her alone. Other times I'm like a frustrated mother who just wants to slap her and tell her not to be so stupid.

Behind all the bad press she gets there's a really nice girl. She's great with her kids and adores them.

In a nutshell, from the time I met Neil my life changed. He was a complete blessing. After everything I'd gone through self-esteem-wise with Shane, and facing some hard times in the industry, it was like someone was looking down on me, saying, 'We need to send her a guardian angel.' Because all of a sudden there was this man who totally believed in me.

When I told him about everything that had been going on with my family, he wasn't at all fazed. He immediately said, 'We need to get your wedding sorted now.' So he got on the phone and secured a deal with *Woman* magazine, who agreed to cover my nuptials.

Unfortunately, even after the LighterLife diet and the bike ride in Egypt, I was already beginning to pile the weight back on. Yo-yo dieting was just pretty much part of who I was, and for years I'd made jokes about being fat before anyone else could. The previous year I'd even had a little mention on *Corrie* when Vera Duckworth had said, 'Is *Loose Women* on today? . . . I like that chubby Nolan.' I laughed along with everyone else, but deep down I was ashamed of myself. Above all I wanted to be slim for my wedding day.

But seeing as I weighed 13 stone 3 pounds and wore a size 20, I didn't hold out much hope. When I looked for wedding dresses it was so depressing. I just didn't like anything larger than a size 14. *I can either turn up on my wedding day looking like a big meringue or I can do something about it*, I thought to myself.

So I confided in Neil and he immediately lined up a great incentive. 'Rosemary Conley wants you to follow her plan,' he said. 'You're going to try it for the next few months and record a fitness DVD.'

Well, bloody Nora it was hard work. Immediately I started to do aerobic workouts three times a week at home, and I did sit-ups to tone my tummy and used water bottles as weights. I also cut down on the packets of biscuits I'd been scoffing with my tea and opted for low-fat versions of foods. Every time I fancied a sugary treat I imagined myself looking like a fat bride until the urge passed.

We'd planned to get married in November, but it was proving really difficult to find a venue for the wedding and we actually didn't get it sorted until later that summer. In the end Neil went on the computer and looked up all these venues and kept sending them to me. We weren't one hundred per cent sure about any of them, but then Neil called, sounding triumphant. 'Found it!' he whooped.

He'd discovered this beautiful place called Hazlewood Castle in Leeds and instantly I knew he was right – it was just perfect.

By then the family argument was kind of blowing over a bit, and although I still hadn't spoken to Denise, the invitations to the wedding had gone out and I had invited Anne and Aunty Theresa. I'd asked Amy and Alex to be my bridesmaids, and one night when they were round discussing their dresses I asked them if their mum was looking forward to coming. Their faces immediately fell.

'Has Mum not called you?' Amy said. 'She's not coming, you know.' I just went quiet.

'Please let's not discuss it,' Alex added. 'We don't want to get involved, but she says she's not coming because she feels disloyal to Denise.'

A week later I still hadn't heard a thing from Anne, and I

was down in London doing photoshoots for various things when I received a text from one of the girls from *Woman*. 'We need to know pretty soon who's coming,' she said.

So I quickly texted everyone who hadn't replied yet, including Anne and Theresa, asking could they just confirm for me if they could make it. Lots of people texted me back to say they could, but then I got a message from Theresa who was cross that I was, in her eyes, putting pressure on her. She told me she wasn't coming.

At that point if I hadn't been surrounded by people on a shoot I would have just sobbed. I couldn't bear it. I just felt like I'd been kicked in the teeth again. I was hurt and angry and shaking. As soon as I had a break I called Ray, trying my hardest not to cry.

'I don't believe it,' he seethed. But then I had to get back to the shoot. About an hour later I got a text from him saying, 'As soon as you're done, please phone me.'

When I called, Ray revealed that no sooner had he put the phone down from consoling me than Theresa had walked in the door.

'How are you? I just thought I'd pop in for a cup of tea,' she'd said, like nothing was up at all. Unfortunately, unlike our family, Ray doesn't sweep things under the carpet, so he remarked, 'I'm not too good actually. I've just heard you're not coming to our wedding.' To which my aunty replied, 'It's nothing to do with you.' And yet another big row ensued.

Of course all this got parroted back to Anne, and the last I heard from her was a message she left on the answerphone saying, 'I totally blame both of you for all of this. You split this family up.'

Now any excitement I had about the wedding completely evaporated. I phoned up Neil, crying and asking him to call it off. But thankfully he didn't and I later changed my mind. I was sitting in the hairdresser's when I received one final text message from Denise pointing out that Anne was being loyal to her.

I just texted her back and said, 'Yeah, whatever, Den, you're all right and I'm wrong. Now please, please leave me alone.'

I realized I could never beat them or make them understand my point of view and that was it. Even now Ray and I think it's so tragic. I no longer speak to two of my sisters and my aunty because of something that started off so small. The sad thing is that if Denise and Theresa hadn't got involved it could have all been sorted out in a week. But you can only take that kind of upset for so long – just because we're family and blood it doesn't mean you can forgive everything. It just seemed that no matter how hard I tried to make the peace there was just too much simmering resentment going on there and we couldn't get past it.

Despite the family rift, when my brother Brian married his long-term girlfriend Annie in August 2007 and asked all us sisters to sing we all did! It was about Brian and Annie, not us, so we all went round to Maureen's every day, learnt the song and ignored the problem and got on with it. The wedding was fantastic actually – Ray and I stayed at one end of the hall in the hotel where the reception was held and Anne, Denise and Theresa at the other!

I was a bit worried about Linda's Brian though. He couldn't really walk properly and said his legs felt swollen and sore. I think then he knew it was something serious, not that he let on. But a few weeks later Linda called to say that Brian had been admitted to hospital in Aberdeen while she'd been doing *Blood Brothers*.

He'd stayed in overnight because the pain was so bad in one

of his legs. They'd wanted him to stay longer, but he discharged himself and drove them all the way home to Blackpool. Brian was due to see a specialist at the local hospital in a few days, but before that the pain got so bad that he needed to be admitted to A&E again. He was quite a big man, but both his legs were swelling up and one was about four sizes bigger than it should be.

In a cruel twist of fate, the day after Brian was admitted Linda got sick herself. She had cellulitis, a bacterial infection in the wound where she'd had her mastectomy. It was really painful, and the doctors said she shouldn't visit in case she infected Brian. Meanwhile Ray went up to visit Brian and came back looking pale.

'I don't want to be negative, but I don't think he'll come out,' he told me. 'I honestly think Brian might die in there.'

But when Linda called she seemed to be very unaware about how ill Brian actually was. She told me she was just upset because she couldn't visit him and said she'd spoken to her breast care nurse, who had told her to go into the hospital the following day but to come and see her first. 'Will you come with me?' she asked.

The next day we went in and sat down. 'Do you understand how ill Brian is?' the nurse asked her.

'I know he's ill, but he's not going to die, is he?' Linda remarked.

'Yes, Linda, he is,' the nurse replied softly.

Well, at that moment I thought my heart was going to break. Just seeing the pain on Linda's face killed me. I held her in my arms as she sobbed, but there was nothing I could say to take the agony away.

Then we went to see Brian. He looked dreadful and was slipping in and out of consciousness. But he managed to tell her he loved her before drifting off again. The doctors explained that he had liver failure and he was all bloated from the toxins in his body.

I stayed at the hospital with Linda and Brian's other relatives all night, but the next day a doctor explained that he was bleeding internally. They wanted to do an operation to put an elastic band in his tummy to slow the bleeding.

'He will die, but this will make it less painful,' the doctor explained.

While Brian went off for the operation we all went up to the canteen. But then Linda got a call on her mobile telling her to go back to the ward. Sadly by the time she got to Brian's bedside he'd already slipped away. He was only sixty years old.

Those next few weeks were awful. Poor Linda was inconsolable, and Ray and I were utterly bereft too. The whole family had adored Brian, including Ciara, who'd always called him 'Silly Brian'. There was a massive void in our lives without him.

His funeral was just packed, and even in those dark times we found some humour for Brian. He'd loved the business, not least going on tour, so his coffin was done like a flight case. It came complete with handles and stickers that said 'Fragile' and 'This Way Up'. And the pallbearers had tops with 'Crew' written on them.

I think the saddest thing for Ray and I was knowing that Brian wouldn't be at our wedding two months later. He had been so excited about it all, as we'd asked both him and Linda to be our witnesses.

As the date of our wedding, 3 November, neared, I was very worried about Linda. I'd asked her to be my chief bridesmaid, but it concerned me that it could all be too sad for her. 'I won't be offended if it's too hard for you,' I told her.

'Don't be ridiculous,' she replied, waving her hand dismissively. 'I wouldn't miss it for the world.'

The night before our big day Ray and I both stayed at hotels near Hazlewood Castle. He was staying with Shane Jnr and Jake, and I was with Ciara and Linda. It was very emotional for her. Brian and Ray had been such good mates, but in some ways I think the wedding helped to distract her a little from her grief. It gave her a sense of purpose. For days she'd been frantically organizing, racing around sorting everything out, but every so often it would just hit her. She'd have a moment, but then take a deep breath and carry on. She was just fantastic, and I don't know how I would have done it without her.

The night before the wedding we had such a laugh. I'd bought loads of presents for people, and she sat up with me wrapping all the gifts and sorting them out into bags so they wouldn't get mixed up. Then she woke me the nest morning singing 'Here Comes the Bride', which she continued to sing for about three hours. I felt really calm but also really excited.

On the day we had the castle to ourselves, and as we drove up this impressive drive to the house all the staff were there to greet us. As they immediately dished out teas and coffees, Linda and I were so impressed. We'd had to get there early, because although Hazlewood Castle had a twelfth-century chapel it didn't have a licence for weddings, so we were actually getting married at 10.30 a.m. in one of the rooms at the castle before having a service in front of all our guests in the chapel.

I hadn't been that fussed about the civil ceremony at first. We were just going to do it in front of the kids, Linda, and Ray's mum Irene. I'd thought: *Oh, we'll get it out of the way and it'll only be ten minutes*, but actually it turned out to be one of the nicest parts of the day for me.

I hadn't bothered putting full make-up on or getting all done up for the ceremony, that would come later. So I just put on the outfit I'd worn to my brother's wedding two months before – a beige dress with black and cream around the neckline and a matching coat. Ray was wearing a pinstriped suit and everyone else was pretty casual.

I hadn't expected them to do the room up for us, but when I walked in it was beautiful. They'd covered the chairs with cream and bows and the table had a big spray of stunning flowers. The atmosphere was wonderfully relaxed and intimate, and as Ray and I stood in front of the registrar grinning at each other, beams of sunlight were streaming through the windows. In the distance you could see horses galloping across the fields in front of the castle. I felt that the moment couldn't be more perfect.

Linda was saying, 'Don't do it!' and we all had a laugh.

Then in a really quiet moment I looked out of the window at the beautiful Yorkshire countryside and thought to myself: *I just want to remember every single part of this day.*

Just before the civil ceremony began I looked at Ray and saw that he had tears in his eyes. I couldn't stop smiling with sheer happiness, but as the emotion of the occasion hit me I started to cry too and we both had to stop for tissues. It just occurred to me that this was so far removed from my ceremony with Shane all those years beforehand, when everything had seemed a bit surreal. Now this was the real deal and it felt amazing. It was all over within minutes and suddenly we were man and wife!

Everyone clapped and Ciara jumped up and down in excitement, although she groaned at the kissing bit, which she'd been dreading.

Next we sat down and signed the register. Linda was a

witness, along with Ray's mum. It was a sad moment, as obviously it was meant to be Brian. But Linda was incredible that day. She never once made me feel uncomfortable about being happy and she was genuinely excited for us. Whatever I've gone through in my life is nothing compared to what she did in those two years, having breast cancer and losing her husband. She was so strong and brave.

After we'd signed the register Linda handed me my present to give to Ray, gold cufflinks with our initials intertwined in diamonds. I'd also got him a card with 'To my husband on our wedding day' written on it. After I'd presented it to him Linda handed Ray a bag for me. In it, to my absolute surprise, was a beautiful necklace with a teardrop-shaped jade stone in the middle surrounded by little diamonds. I recognized it as a necklace I'd admired when I'd bought Ray's cufflinks. So Linda had taken Ray back to the jeweller's and showed him and he'd bought it for me! It was just all so emotional. Then reluctantly we had to part company to go and get ready for the main event!

'So are you excited that I just married your dad, then?' I asked Ciara, as she skipped along holding my hand.

'Yeah,' she said. 'Is Erin coming now?'

I laughed. Ciara was more excited about seeing Bernie's eight-year-old daughter, who was also going to be a flower girl, than anything else!

I'd always wondered about letting a magazine cover my wedding, as you always hear stories about the stress of it – guests not being allowed to take photos or having to sign confidentiality agreements and the day not really being your own any more. But I have to say, organizing the wedding with *Woman* was the best thing we ever did. It was the first celebrity wedding they'd ever covered but they did a sterling job. Everything was so relaxed and perfect, it just went like clockwork.

When Linda, Ciara and I walked into the suite we were amazed. There were all these clothes laid out, people steaming dresses and suits, a team of three make-up artists, and Lee Din, who does my hair on *Loose Women*.

I'd asked Linda to be my chief bridesmaid, and I also had Amy and Alex, and Tommy's daughter, Laura, as bridesmaids. And of course Ciara and Erin as flower girls. When Erin turned up I didn't think Ciara could have got any more excited, until the make-up artist brought out some glitter for her eyes! 'Do you want some on too?' she asked Erin.

'I can't wear make-up,' Erin replied dejectedly. 'Mum and Dad will go mad.'

'Well, just have a little bit of glitter,' I told her, knowing Bernie wouldn't mind really. 'And if your mum says anything, you just say, "Aunty Coleen says I have to."'

So we all sat there getting our hair and make-up done, ridiculously excited. Meanwhile Ray was elsewhere with Shane Jnr, who was going to be his best man, and Jake, who was going to give me away. Having the boys take on those roles was really important to us. It meant that it wasn't just a wedding for Ray and me, it was a confirmation of us all as a family.

The other groomsmen were my nephews Danny and Tommy, who were Shane's best mates. They were like the comedy act the Three Stooges and they all looked gorgeous.

It was quite funny, as while you'd expect all the girls to be in a complete lather about their appearance it was actually the boys who were flapping. Someone kept saying: 'The boys need Lee upstairs!' The Three Stooges were driving him nuts! Their suits even had to be re-steamed because someone had knocked them into a crumpled heap on the floor.

Meanwhile poor old Ray was in a right old state. His initial thing about getting married had always been that he was too shy to stand up in front of people and do a speech, so he was getting very nervous.

After they'd had their hair and make-up done, my nieces and Linda went to meet Bernie and Maureen to practise 'Let It Be Me' by the Everly Brothers, which they were singing in the church. It was an incredibly poignant song, as Linda's Brian had picked it. And it was only much later when I watched the wedding DVD that I saw Linda had burst into tears during the rehearsal. Just as the song ended she'd started sobbing, and there was a flurry of activity as her sisters and nieces swooped in to throw their arms around her. They were all crying too. I must admit I cried buckets when I saw that.

But on the day Linda bravely wiped her eyes and came back smiling, so I had no idea. She was just so selfless in that way.

With all the girls back, it was time to get changed and it didn't go without drama. I was in one of the rooms with Linda when we heard this almighty kerfuffle. She ran out, then returned saying, 'I don't want you to panic, but I need you to know that Laura has just spilt a pint of orange juice down her dress.'

'Oh well,' I shrugged. 'It's not my dress!'

'I have to say you are the calmest bride I've ever known,' Linda laughed.

So poor Fiona, the fashion editor from *Woman*, spent ages pouring water on Laura's dress then trying to dry it with a hairdryer.

When it came to me putting my dress on they all went off to the other room, as I wanted to get the full effect of their reactions. I'd chosen a £300 dress from Debenhams and just added some crystals to the bodice. It was a satin strapless bodice dress in ivory with a really fitted, long skirt with a train at the back. I also had a veil with diamanté crystals sewn through and a tiara. When I put it on I was just thrilled. I stood there feeling a million dollars. The dress was a size 12, and I was so pleased with myself for losing the weight. I'd reached my target dress size about a month earlier, and had lost over 3 stone. I felt as if I'd got my confidence and spark back, and I also felt incredibly sexy. I no longer dashed into the bathroom to change at night, or quickly turned out the lights and dived under the covers to hide my body from Ray.

I couldn't look better than I do today, I thought proudly, as I studied my reflection.

And when I stepped into the other room the reaction was fabulous.

'Oh my God, I've never seen anything like it,' Amy cooed. 'You look gorgeous.' Bless Amy, if I'd walked in dressed in a vest and pants she would have given me that same reaction.

Then it was suddenly time to go to the chapel, where we had 120 guests waiting. As we walked over, for a split second thoughts of my mum flickered into my mind. 'She'd love to be here,' I thought sadly. But then I let my mind wander some-where else. I didn't want anything to make me feel sad. Out-side the church I was met by a very proud Jake, looking very dapper in a midnight blue suit.

I'd decided against a traditional wedding march, and instead I opted for Shania Twain's 'From This Moment'. For the first bit of the song I had Erin walk down the aisle followed by Alex and Laura at big intervals and then Amy. Then Linda walked in on the instrumental break, with a lovely big smile, and everyone immediately started crying. Next it was Ciara's turn to walk down, throwing rose petals. Then when the key changed again, Jake and I appeared.

Suddenly I heard all these gasps from people who hadn't seen me since I'd lost weight, and then the whole chapel applauded and took my breath away. But best of all, there stood Ray and Shane Jnr, smiling and looking handsome in their midnight blue suits and lovely silver waistcoats. I thought immediately: *I'm so lucky. I met Ray and he is just wonderful and then he met my boys and they all love each other! And now we're here and it's my wedding day and I couldn't be happier!*

I could just tell Ray was so made up too. I think it would have been a massive regret in his life if we hadn't done it and his mum hadn't got to see him – Irene was eighty-three when we got married and she just cried buckets at seeing one of her children finally get wed. She was thrilled.

As we stood there in front of the vicar it was just magical and perfect. The sun was blazing, it was a beautiful setting and there was not one person that we didn't want to be there. On top of all of that, the vicar was fantastic. When we got to the top of the aisle he asked Shane, Jake and Ciara to step forward. 'Is it OK if I marry your mum and Ray?' he asked. It just felt like a wedding for five.

Everyone was convinced Ray was going to pass out, but he made it through, just about. He was crying again and so was I, and then when the girls sang 'Let It Be Me' there wasn't a dry eye in the place. Jake did a reading from *Captain Corelli's Mandolin*, and then my brother Brian read a beautiful piece he'd found about love as a surprise.

Coming out of the church we played Leona Lewis's 'A Moment Like This', and the icing on the cake was when Carol McGiffin cried. 'Oh Tubsy, you look so beautiful,' she gushed, her eyes welling.

'Well, I never thought I'd see the day *you* shed a tear,' I exclaimed. 'The whole wedding is worth it just to see that.'

'Oh, I've just got something in my eye,' she insisted.

The wedding breakfast was held in a banqueting hall, and opposite the top table were floor to ceiling windows overlooking just miles of green fields. All the chairs were cream with beautiful big bows and each table had a stunning mirrored centrepiece which a friend of Ray's had organized as a wedding present. Everything just took your breath away. There was a really jovial feeling in the room and at one point everyone started singing.

My family started it off by singing songs from *The Sound of Music*, and then all Ray's friends started singing Yorkshire ditties. What we hadn't told them was that we'd secretly organized two singing waiters. They were walking around serving everyone when suddenly this man and woman launched into an amazing opera number. They were fantastic and got a standing ovation at the end.

When the speeches came I felt very nervous for Ray, as I knew it was the biggest dread of his life. But I have to say that if he was nervous you couldn't tell. He did a brilliant speech, it was really funny and lovely, and in the end he just had verbal diarrhoea, to the extent that his mum actually said, 'That's enough now, Raymond, sit down!'

Shane and Jake both made speeches, which were fantastic and brought a tear to many an eye. Shane's was so funny. He said, 'To be honest with you it's just as well I liked Ray when I met him, because about two weeks later my mum was pregnant!' Everyone just fell about. Then he told us both that he loved us and said other lovely things as well.

Then Jake got up and said what an inspiration Ray had been to him and what a happy day it had been for all of us. 'I love my step-dad,' he finished.

I did a speech too, saying, 'I never thought after all I've been through that I'd be standing here on my wedding day with someone I love as much as Ray. As long as I have Ray and the kids by my side nothing else matters.' Then I said how I missed the fact that my mum and Brian couldn't be there. Beside me Linda started crying and I could feel myself welling up too, so I quickly moved on, thanking everyone for coming and telling them that it was the best day of my life.

Then Ray and I got to cut the cake, which was a gorgeous chocolate extravaganza with an outside of white chocolate and about three or four tiers.

When the music began we moved into another beautiful room and our first dance was to Bryan Adams's 'I'll Always Be Right There'. Of course Ray immediately thought he was John Travolta and took his jacket off, to reveal a sign that said, 'See what I did for her!' Yet another Rayism!

I was fairly sober throughout the day, although I did have the odd glass of champagne. I just didn't want to get to that really drunk stage where I'd miss anything. And what I loved was that although Ray was having a drink, he didn't get blotto. I've never seen him so happy, and he was fabulous with me. Sometimes bride and groom are so busy they don't spend a lot of time together, but he kept hugging and kissing me and joking, 'Have you met the wife?'

Next the Drifters came on to perform. We hadn't told anyone we'd booked them and they absolutely stormed the place. They were just brilliant and the whole place was up dancing. When they went off stage, Ray got up with the band and he and Jake did an acoustic version of 'It's My Life' by Bon Jovi, with them both singing and playing guitar. They were followed by Shane Jnr, who sang 'Crazy Little Thing Called Love' by Queen.

Then I got up and sang, 'You're Still the One' by Shania

Twain, while Ray played guitar. That song was so poignant to me, as when I looked back at the seven years we'd been together, we'd both been through so much. Yet he was still the One. In the beginning no one had thought it would last between us, and although it sounds like we had an easy time, we really didn't. Every obstacle that could be thrown at us to test our relationship was. Yet Ray helped me find my confidence again and made me realize I don't have to simply put up with things. He pushed me to speak up and made me express how I really feel. I never thought I'd meet anyone and have another child, let alone a little girl. But now I just look at Ciara and think, 'She's our little gift from God.'

So on our wedding day it just hit me. We'd passed the test and here we were proving so many people wrong.

After I'd serenaded Ray there were a ridiculous amount of drunken requests for one particular Nolans classic – so my sisters and I got up and sang 'I'm in the Mood for Dancing'. It was very bizarre singing and doing the routine in my wedding dress! And when I looked over at the dance floor, everyone was going mental. Meanwhile Ciara was playing chase with Erin and another little girl called Meg, having a whale of a time.

After all the singing we had a DJ and I danced all night, to the point that Linda actually asked me if I was on drugs! 'You haven't been drinking and you've been dancing all day and night and smiling. I'm worried you might have taken something,' she said quite seriously.

'Well if there's a drug that makes me feel like this, I need to bottle it and sell it!' I laughed. In fact I danced so much that I forgot to throw the bouquet!

My only other sadness was that Anne and Aunty Theresa weren't there. It was a fabulous day and they would have had a great time.

The day after the wedding everyone came back to our house in Blackpool and saw Ray and me off on our honeymoon. It was the icing on the cake to be going away, and we spent five glorious days in Cyprus. We were still on such a high. And now that I'd lost lots of weight I was able to wear my bikini with pride. We spent our time chilling out by the hotel pool and going out for lovely meals in the evening. I even went to the pub with Ray to watch a Leeds United match.

'You wait until Monday on *Loose Women*,' I teased him. 'You are going to be so slagged off for making me sit here and do this.'

Before we knew it we were back home and settling into life as Mr and Mrs Fensome. Christmas was coming round again, so Linda and I put a tree and lights up in Mum's room as usual and sent her cards. Then on 23 December I arranged to meet Maureen and Linda at the home and we all stood there and sang Christmas carols to her.

We knew Mum was coming to the end. We were getting phone calls all the time saying that she had deteriorated and had stopped eating. But then the home would call again the next morning and say she'd had some porridge. She was 5 stone now and like a tiny sparrow, but she still had this real will to live and such a strong heart. In those last few weeks I often used to stroke her face and say, 'Mum, you can go.' But when it got nearer to Christmas, I changed my mind, thinking: *Please don't let it be now*. Christmas was always her favourite time of the year and it would just be too heartbreaking.

Christmas Day came and went without any news, then I took Ciara to see her. She was fast asleep, tucked up in bed, and looked very peaceful. I touched her hair and kissed her goodbye. It was the last time I saw her. She died in her sleep two days later, on 30 December.

I thought it was very apt that she slipped away just before the New Year. She always hated it. She wasn't a drinker and saw New Year as an excuse for everyone to get sloshed.

I joined Tommy, Anne, Brian, Linda and various nieces and nephews at the care home to say goodbye to her. She was just lying on her side with both hands under her head. She looked so peaceful, as if she was fast asleep. Brian was sobbing and so were all my nieces and nephews. The people who owned the care home and some of the nurses were crying too. They always made us feel that they loved her as much as we did, which was touching.

I couldn't cry, because in a way I felt happy that she was finally out of her misery and had died so peacefully. She hated hospitals and I'd always prayed that she'd just slip off in her sleep. After three or four years of hell it was the least she deserved.

After Mum's death the first bouquet and cards I got were from *Loose Women*, and they told me not to come back until I was ready. I think because we are all women there's that understanding that ultimately family are more important, and we do all cover for each other.

As the days passed I kept expecting the tears to hit me, but they never did. 'She hasn't cried,' I overheard Ray telling Linda. 'And she's just doing normal things with the kids.'

I know this sounds dramatic but I honestly think I do a lot of crying on the inside. When the day of the funeral arrived, my biggest wobble was when they played the song 'You Raise Me Up'. I just knew if I started crying I was never going to stop, so I pulled back and suppressed it for another time. But there was no doubting that the lyrics were just so perfect for her. She wasn't a great talker, Mum, but she was so selfless, she just gave up so much and did such a lot for everyone around her.

After the funeral I took a week off, but then I decided I had to get back to work. Mum loved *Loose Women*. When she got really ill she kept saying to me, 'Can I come to *Loose Women* with you next week?' Sadly I knew I couldn't take her, but I really wish I'd been able to. So I headed back to the studio and dealt with all my emotions in my head, on my own.

To this day I still feel a sense of relief that she's at peace, but the devastation I also feel is shocking. I still miss her all the time. I miss her when I'm ill, as you always want your mum when you're poorly, and I miss her when exciting things happen.

In April 2008 Ray and I moved to a beautiful house in Cheshire and I would have loved for Mum to have seen it. We moved because the area where we were living in Blackpool had become quite rough. It seemed as though hardly a week would pass without a car window being smashed, and I just longed to wake up and see fields.

All Ciara wanted was a trampoline, and our garden wasn't big enough, but then we found this amazing house and it was perfect. It was a lovely double-fronted place with four bed-rooms, a gorgeous cosy lounge with a real fireplace and a mas-sive kitchen and family area. But best of all, when we looked in the garden there was a trampoline! It was like a sign. So we put in an offer and moved to Cheshire.

I often wish that both my parents could see that I'm all right and I've done well on my own. They were always proud of me, I think, but when my marriage split up and I didn't have a career they were worried about me. They never saw me on the cover of magazines or losing all my weight. But at the same time they didn't have to go through the terrible worry of things like Linda's breast cancer and heartache over losing Brian, which is a real blessing.

Sadly just after Mum died it was time for another little bird to fly the nest – Shane Jnr. He had been worrying me for a while, as despite being a very talented footballer from a young age, it was clear that life as a professional footballer was not his destiny. He had lots of trials for clubs like Blackpool, Chelsea and Arsenal, but in the end he wasn't enjoying it much. Ability-wise he could have done it, but mentally he was not right for it. So once he left college he just got a part-time job in a bar. He'd get up at 2 p.m. to go to work and would spend his wages on going out, but that was it. He just seemed so lifeless and bored.

The thing about Shane Jnr is that, like Jake, he is a talented performer. In his last year at school he'd auditioned for their production of *Grease*. I thought he might get a role as a T-Bird, but he actually landed the part of Danny Zuko! (We laughed at that!) And my God he was as brilliant as his dad! With the footballing dreams now behind him, I felt that he needed to go off somewhere and do something that would give him that same passion. And at my mum's wake I spoke to his father about it.

'I'm worried about Shane Jnr, he's doing nothing with his life,' I told Shane. 'He needs to do something he really enjoys. I think he'd make a great rep.'

'What about a bluecoat?' Shane asked.

And that was it! We decided between us and went over and told Shane Jnr. I was gobsmacked when he immediately said, 'Oh yeah, I'd love to do that!' So Shane arranged for him to go for an audition at Pontin's and he went off, wowed them and got offered a job! Sadly it meant him moving 200 miles away, to Brean Sands in Somerset, and once again I tearfully waved a son off at the train station. But when I went down to visit I have to say I was so pleased to see Shane Jnr having the time of his life. Some evenings he was doing two shows a night and I was just spellbound watching him. I've always said Shane has a lovely voice, but I didn't know he could dance! There he was doing proper routines and taking the lead in songs. I was so shocked, as I had had no idea how talented he was. And everyone kept coming up to me and saying, 'We love Shane!'

He's been there for almost a year now and he still loves his football and has even set up a five-aside team. But he's also passionate about being a bluecoat. He loves singing and dancing. I do miss him and Jake terribly though. When the boys were living at home I used to look at the state of their rooms and think: *I can't stand this mess!* They were going through their teens and were so lazy and untidy, but now I can't bear that they're not here. I walk into their bedrooms, which are clean and tidy with the beds made, and I want to trash them and put dirty boxers, smelly socks and wet towels all over the floor! I just have that empty nest feeling and I'm dreading it happening with Ciara, even though she's only seven. (Ray says Ciara's not leaving until she's at least thirty-five.)

But after Shane Jnr left I didn't actually get to mope for long. Thanks to Neil the work was piling in, and 2008 was proving to be my busiest year yet! As well as doing *Loose Women* and my *Woman* and *Mirror* columns, I had more Iceland adverts and another fitness DVD to record. On top of that I had great fun appearing on *All Star Family Fortunes*, *Al Murray's Happy Hour* and *Alan Carr's Celebrity Ding Dong*. I even got my best compliment to date – another mention on *Corrie*. And this time it was from a young character called Grahame Procter, declaring, 'That Coleen Nolan's fit.'

'You're joking, she's old enough to be your mum,' his friend David Platt replied.

'Exactly, knows what she's doing,' Grahame leered.

I nearly fell off my chair! 'My life's complete!' I laughed to Ray.

Then I got a call from Neil. 'Time to get your skating boots on, love!' he said triumphantly. 'I've got you *Dancing on Ice!*'

Oh, my dear Lord.

Thirteen

It was a cold day in October when I found myself zig-zagging unsteadily across the ice towards a couple of living legends – Jayne Torville and Christopher Dean. The pair of them grinned in unison as I tried desperately not to fall on my arse. Suddenly I realized the enormity of what I was doing. I was actually going to attempt to dance on ice – how bloody ridiculous.

When my agent first told me he'd bagged me the hit ITV show I just laughed. 'Please tell me you're joking!' I scoffed. It took him a good five minutes to convince me he wasn't. I thought it was a crazy idea to be honest. But then I made the mistake of telling Ciara and the boys.

'Mum you'd be so good!' Ciara announced with wide eyes. And Shane Jnr and Jake seemed to think it was pretty cool too. Somehow I found myself being swept up in their enthusiasm. When Neil called again, I sighed.

'So will you do it?' he asked tentatively.

'OK!' I blurted out before I had the chance to change my mind.

But from the moment I put the phone down the fear started to creep in. *I won't be able to do it*, I thought to myself. *I've got big boobs, a back that doesn't move and my knees and hips are knack-*

ered! That night I lay in bed finding it hard to drift off. *Dancing on Ice* was still a good three months away but already a feeling of foreboding and dread was beginning to kick in. I remembered back to the previous year when I'd watched the show from the comfort of my front room gasping at the death-defying stunts of contestants like Suzanne Shaw.

'That's definitely one show I couldn't do,' I'd told Ray. 'I wouldn't have the bottle.'

Famous last words or what!

So I just kind of tried to file it away in the back of my mind. *I'll worry about it later,* I told myself. But when, a few weeks later, I told the rest of my family and was met by a sea of gobsmacked faces I really began to brick it. While Ciara and the boys were still wildly excited, Linda, Bernie and Maureen just stared at me with worry etched across their brows.

'God Coleen, I'm dead scared for you!' Linda blurted out. And Bernie and Maureen just looked at each other mouthing, 'Oh my God!'

'It'll be fine,' I told them, trying to convince myself at the same time. 'How hard can it be?' Yeah right.

Then a week later I found myself in the surreal setting of Lea Valley ice rink in London teetering about on the ice in front of Jayne and Chris. *Oh my God*, I thought, as I attempted to glide across the rink with an air of nonchalance. *I'm actually on the ice with Torville and Dean!* I was so in awe that by the time I reached them I was shaking and a bit choked with emotion.

Jayne, who was just tiny, instantly greeted me with a warm smile. She's got a real air of calmness about her that immediately puts you at ease. Chris was smiling too but there's no messing about with him. As I stood there dumbstruck and grinning like a loon he picked me up and spun me round until

I thought I was going to vomit. Then all wobbly and star-struck I skated off again!

That afternoon I was excited to meet a few of the other contestants taking part. There was Roxanne Pallett, a former *Emmerdale* actress, Jessica Taylor, who was in pop group Liberty X, Ray Quinn, who came second in *X Factor* a few years ago, TV presenter Michael Underwood and former *Hollyoaks* actor Jeremy Edwards.

Rather annoyingly the competition was already looking pretty stiff. First I sat watching in disbelief as Ray skated out and did a triple spin and then all these little jumps! *Oh God, he's so young and brilliant, there's really not much point!* I sighed to myself. Then Jessica skated out looking like a graceful swan. 'Bloody Nora,' I muttered under my breath. In contrast to them, just standing on the ice was a task in itself for me.

After the meet and greet I was given the number for a skating coach who would teach me the basics at an ice rink near my home in Cheshire. At that point it was all shrouded in secrecy. Even the coaches don't know who is going to call them. Realizing I didn't have a minute to lose in terms of practise, I dialled the number as soon as I got home and introduced myself to my new mentor Donna.

When I first met Donna a few days later I really liked her, which is saying something considering I had to get up at 5 a.m. to meet her at a sports centre in Manchester. The truth be known when I arrived, sleepy and apprehensive, the last thing I felt like doing was attempting to skate around a freezing cold rink. But Donna was lovely. She was about the same age as me, blonde, slim, very bubbly and extremely patient. We instantly bonded and had such a laugh together. 'Don't worry, you'll soon pick it up,' she laughed as I stumbled around.

But there was no denying she'd got a complete novice on her hands. Over the next few weeks just trying to master the basics like skating forward using the proper technique or doing backwards crossovers was a nightmare. Despite training three times a week it felt like even this simple stuff wasn't computing. *Never mind,* I told myself. *If I can't do it I can always pull out.*

During my initial training in Manchester I often bumped into another contestant from the show – Rugby League legend Ellery Hanley. I took to Ellery straight away. He is one of the nicest men I've ever met. A real gentle giant and I never thought I'd meet a rugby player who doesn't drink, smoke or swear!

Although I never really got used to the 5 a.m. starts, I persevered and Donna painstakingly taught me the basics. Before long I was thrilled to actually be skating properly. I'd zoom across the ice thinking, *Yay! This is so bizarre! I can skate forward! I can keep my balance!* Then after four weeks I was told it was time to meet my skating partner for the show. 'I hope he's dishy,' I joked to Ray and my niece Amy the night before.

'I wonder if it's my friend Stuart,' Amy replied. 'He's one of the professional skaters.'

When I arrived at the rink in Manchester the following day, bursting with nervous excitement, I was greeted by the *Dancing on Ice* camera crew and head coach Steve Pickavance, who's married to judge Karen Barber. They ushered me towards a tall, friendly-faced young man. 'This is Stuart Widdall,' Steve grinned.

'You know my niece Amy, don't you!' I laughed. I was thrilled, as having Amy in common immediately put us both at ease.

But as the camera crew filmed us making small talk it suddenly seemed very real. *Jeez, I'm actually doing this,* I thought.

Then the next thing I knew Stuart was picking me up and spinning me round – fast! I closed my eyes as everything swam out of focus and felt my tummy churning rather unpleasantly. It was such a relief once it ended and Stuart placed me back on the ice, at which point I almost keeled over. I was so dizzy I couldn't focus on a thing.

'My brain is still moving, I can't see,' I wailed. 'There's no way I'll ever be able to skate after that!'

'Yes you will,' Stuart laughed.

After I'd forgiven him for taking me by surprise like that, Stuart and I got on like a house on fire. He is the biggest giggler I've met in my life and we soon developed a great rapport.

As if preparing for *Dancing on Ice* wasn't enough I also had my fitness DVD *Discoburn* to work on. I'd come home from training every day aching and wanting to crawl into bed. But no sooner had I sat down for a cup of tea and a biccie than a dance instructor would be banging on the door. 'You're not coming in, until you promise to treat me gently,' I'd tell him, scowling on the doorstep.

After devising an hour long workout – including core exercises to build up my muscles, abs and lifting weights for my bingo wings – I'd be almost crying with exhaustion. And with the never-ending demands of being a full-time mum, filming *Loose Women* and finding the time to do my weekly columns, I was pretty sure a full nervous breakdown could be imminent. But having so much on was also a welcome distraction.

Four days before I met Stuart for the first time, on a Sunday evening in November, I was having a bath to ease the aches and pains of training (and warm myself up!) when I discovered a lump in my breast. Because of Anne and Linda's history of breast cancer I always check myself. But it was one hell of a shock to actually find something.

I was running my hand over my right breast when I noticed it – a lump the size of a fifty-pence piece on the right hand side, just off centre. Immediately panic seared through my veins. *Maybe it's the way I'm lying?* I tried to reason. But when I quickly climbed out the bath it was still there. Grabbing a towel I hurried downstairs to find Ray, leaving soggy footprints on the carpet in my haste.

'Ray, I've got a lump,' I blurted out, when I found him reading the newspaper in the kitchen.

His face immediately paled. 'Shut up. What do you mean?' he asked.

'Exactly what I've just said,' I replied.

'Are you sure,' he insisted. 'Can you still feel it?'

'Here,' I said, attempting to guide his hand.

'No, I can't,' he said looking queasy. 'Promise me you'll go to the doctor tomorrow.'

But the next day at the crack of dawn I was on a train heading to London to do *Loose Women*. Between filming I got a call from Ray. 'I've got you a doctor's appointment for Wednesday,' he said. 'I don't want you putting this off, not even for a few days.'

So two days later I sat in the doctor's surgery trying desperately to quell my nerves. *He probably won't be able to find it*, I told myself. *He'll tell me it's ok*. I lay on the examination table staring at the ceiling and wishing it would all go away as my GP began to poke around. 'OK, here it is,' he finally said. 'There's definitely a mass here.'

I swallowed hard and sat up trying not to shake as I put my bra and top back on. Then I sat next to him as he started to key details into his computer. 'I'm not extremely worried,' he told me. 'But I want you to go and see a consultant.' I took some comfort in the fact he wasn't putting me down as a priority case.

'I'm going to refer you,' he told me, handing me a piece of paper. 'You just need to call this number to make an appointment.'

Back home I didn't hesitate in calling up the hospital. But I was dismayed to hear it would take six weeks for my appointment. It seemed like a very long time.

'I don't think I can wait that long,' I told Ray. 'I'm calm now but in six weeks I'll be cacking myself.'

So after a short discussion we agreed I'd go private instead – but even then it was still a two week wait! An agonizing fortnight passed until the day of my appointment finally arrived. Poignantly, my consultant at the Alexandra Hospital in Cheadle, Cheshire, was the same breast cancer specialist who had seen Linda. She was booked in the following month to have reconstructive surgery with him.

He was a nice man with a warm manner but as he examined me I struggled to relax. *Please God don't let it be cancer*, I prayed silently in my head. Having watched two of my sisters go through it I knew only too well how hellish it could be. Finally the consultant spoke. 'I'm pretty confident it's nothing serious Coleen. But I want to put a needle into your breast to take a biopsy. We won't know for sure until the results come back.'

Next he sent me for a mammogram and ultrasound scan. Once they were done I headed back into the waiting room, where I was met by an anxious looking Ray.

'What did he say?' he asked me, his eyes filled with worry.

Repeating the consultant's words I felt myself relaxing a little. I was relieved but at the same time the cautious side of me wanted to wait for my results. Thankfully I didn't have to wait too long. The consultant's secretary called the following evening to say my mammogram was fine. Then a few weeks later I was told I had very dense breast tissue and an infected gland that had swollen up. The relief was immense and with my mind at rest, I turned up at training the following day with a real spring in my step. I felt ready to conquer the world.

Stuart and I were beginning to make some real progress and by now I felt completely at ease with him. It was just as well really, considering how intimately we were going to have to get to know each other! Something I'd never given any thought to was where exactly the male skaters have to put their hands when they lift you. I can tell you right now that no part of you is sacred. And as the weeks went by Stuart appeared to be touching me in places that even Ray hadn't found yet!

'It's just as well you've met Stuart,' I said to Ray one evening, as he spotted handprints all over the inside of my thighs. 'Otherwise you might have kicked me out by now.'

But where Stuart's hands wandered was actually the least of my worries. The daily doses of nasty looking bruises and aches and pains were coming thick and fast. At first I went quite a long time without coming a cropper, merely because the fear of falling was holding me back. 'You're gonna have to fall so you can get over it,' Stuart warned me, until inevitably I experienced my first tumble. *Oh God that hurt,* I thought as I lay there stunned. *I hope everything is still attached when I get up.* 'Come on, stop milking it!' Stuart commanded, dragging me up, and that was that! Then for the rest of the week I trained with bruised ribs, wincing every time Stuart lifted me.

The next few falls really hurt – as they do when you land on bloody rock hard ice. And there's nothing worse than landing on your hip – that kills! Generally my legs, my hips and my knees were really suffering as I'm just not that flexible. All I can say is thank God for the physio!

After four weeks training with Stuart I was summoned down to Hertfordshire to meet the rest of the contestants. The producers were hosting a kind of 'show and tell' at the studio in Elstree to introduce the crew, the other contestants and their partners. But worst of all they expected us all to perform our first routine for the show in front of everyone.

Predictably, the day before I started to panic. 'You have got to get me out of "show and tell",' I pleaded with Neil on the phone. 'I can't do it!'

'Yes, you can,' he pacified me. 'You'll be fine!'

So the next day I waited heart-in-mouth and fidgeting in an uncomfortable plastic seat, as couple after couple dazzled us with their routines in a small training rink next to the main *Dancing on Ice* studio. When it was Stuart and my turn it was horrifyingly embarrassing with everyone watching but once we'd finished to whoops and a round of applause I was actually quite pleased with myself.

There was a real sense of camaraderie because we were all going through the same thing. It was also quite exciting meeting all the other contestants. As well as the six I'd met previously there was actress Gemma Bissix, TV presenter Donal MacIntyre, former *Blue Peter* presenter Zoe Salmon, model Melinda Messenger and footballer Graeme Le Saux. The only people who couldn't make it were Ray, who I'd met already, and Todd Carty, who I also knew.

During the skating displays I sat with Gemma, who I got along great with. 'What on earth are we doing?' I whispered to her. And the pair of us kept sneaking outside for a fag.

Up until that point I thought I was the only one who was

scared but I soon realized it was the same for everyone. And actually the worst ordeal of the day turned out to be squeezing into various lycra costumes to film the opening credits. I gasped in horror as I was handed two skimpy numbers in blue and red which were cast-offs from previous contestants Gaynor Faye and Emily Symons.

'Oh God, I'm going to look like mutton dressed as lamb,' I whined to Melinda, who I'd also clicked with instantly.

Back in Cheshire the following week I juggled my training and spending time with Linda. She'd just had reconstructive surgery and had caught a terrible infection. She was in hospital for two weeks and I felt so bad for her. *Christ almighty can nothing go right for this girl?* I wondered, dismayed at the injustice of it all. But in typical Linda fashion she never uttered a word of complaint and soon she was out of hospital with a new lease of life. And, selfless as ever, she was supporting me all the way.

As Christmas approached I was really beginning to panic. I'd walk in from training and pace the kitchen. 'I've got to get out of this,' I'd tell Ray. 'I can't do it.' I'd often wake in the morning to find Ray looking at me, his forehead wrinkled with concern. 'You were crying and screaming in your sleep,' he told me on more than one occasion. 'If it's too much for you, love, then don't do it.'

But somehow I could never quite make that call to quit. I think it was the thought of letting people like Stuart, Steve and Donna down that did it. And there was also the fact that I wanted to prove people wrong. The amount of times my friends would scoff and say, 'You skating! Surely you're too old?' Or, 'I'd better get tickets early as you won't be in it for long!' *Oh for God's sake I'm killing myself here!* I'd think. *You're probably right but now I want to prove you wrong.*

It was our first Christmas at home in the new house – just me, Ray, Jake, Ciara and Ray's mum Irene. Sadly it was the first Christmas Shane Jnr was away from home working at Pontins. I was so sad at the thought of spending it without him. But he called me at 7 a.m. on Christmas Day to say he was having a great time.

January arrived in a flurry of rehearsals. By now Stuart and I had carefully put together our first routine to 'Dream a Little Dream of Me' by The Mamas and the Papas and were trying to polish it. Then suddenly 11 January arrived and it was the day of the first show. Thankfully at this stage it was just the boys skating. But as much as I appreciated having that extra week, even just coming out on to the ice that night to be introduced had my stomach knotted with anxiety. I kept thinking, *If I'm dying with my nerves this week what will I be like next week when I actually have to perform?* I've never known fear like it and it didn't subside!

Don't get me wrong. I've had times before when I've felt nervous. But even on *This Morning* when I felt totally out of my depth I could keep it under control. I'm used to feeling nerves in my stomach, a churning feeling – but for some reason skating in front of an audience affected me so badly that my legs were physically shaking. I just couldn't stop them. And there's nothing worst than skating with shaky limbs. But before I knew it the show was over and poor Graeme Le Saux had been voted off.

For the next week I hardly slept a wink. I remember saying to Ray, 'I can't believe I've said yes to this. What am I going to do?' I was such a wreck. Then suddenly I was waking up on Sunday morning after barely two hours of feverish sleep. I headed to the studio early in the afternoon for a last practice. Then about an hour before the show went live I sat in the green room shaking.

Roxanne, Jessica and Zoe were all in there giggling with nervous excitement and eating McDonalds! I'd hoped their eagerness would rub off on me but I just felt suffocated, like the walls were closing in on me. For the next hour I tried to ease my nerves with Rescue Remedy and fags but it was no good. I just felt sick.

Then suddenly I could hear the warm-up man egging the crowd on. The countdown began and presenters Phillip Scofield and Holly Willoughby introduced the show. Within minutes all us girls were skating on to the ice with our partners to be introduced. Then it was time for our individual routines. Roxanne went first, followed by Melinda. I watched in horror on the big screen backstage. 'Oh Jesus they're so good!' I whispered to Stuart. Then after the ad break we were up.

How can I explain that feeling of skating on to the ice once your name is called? For me it was almost like slow motion, like I was in some sort of weird, fuzzy trance. I held Stuart's hand tight as we skated through the tunnel then suddenly we were hit by the bright studio lights and a sea of faces. My stomach lurched and then there was a roar from the crowd making everything very exhilarating. The judges – Karen Barber, Nicky Slater, Jason Gardiner, Ruthie Henshall and Robin Cousins – were sat to our left as we skated round.

I could almost feel the heat of their stares boring into me. Not that I looked at them. Week in week out I never really looked at anyone apart from my family.

Seeing Ciara waving her little banners, Ray and the boys – or my sisters Bernie, Linda and Maureen in later weeks –

cheering me on was the only thing that ever got me through that thoroughly terrifying experience.

Our routine actually passed in a blur, I had no idea whether I'd got it right or not but at the end I have never felt such relief in all my life. I couldn't believe I'd actually gone out and done it and I let out a little sob, which I then had to suppress as I stood with Phil, Jayne and Christopher to hear our score. We scored 12.5 out of 30, which quite frankly I was thrilled with!

Next up were Zoe, Gemma and finally Jessica. Then after an agonizing hour long wait they revealed who was in the skate-off – Gemma and Melinda. In the end it was poor Gemma who lost the judges' vote.

It was with a weird mix of feelings that I started training the following week. Half of me felt proud as punch that I had made it through to the next round while the other was horrified that I'd have to do it all again!

Now that the show was in full flow I was really getting to know the other contestants. Melinda was the one who took me most by surprise. She's this stunning bubbly blonde, with massive boobs and a pearly white smile. She looks so sweet, like an angel, but she can sound like a docker when she opens her gob. She can even burp the alphabet.

Zoe, a former Miss Ireland and *Blue Peter* presenter, was very sweet. She's this stunning Amazonian blonde with the sort of willowy figure the rest of us would die for. She immediately struck me as lovely but very loud. Zoe never stopped talking for the whole time she was in *Dancing on Ice*. 'Zoe shut up!' I'd beg wearily when our chairs were by each other in make-up. She soon cottoned on to my nickname 'Nolan Face' so I called her 'Salmon Face' in reply.

Donal MacIntyre was a gutsy investigative reporter and

was a doll. He was so encouraging. He and Zoe were always the most obsessed with the ice.

I never got to know Jessica that well. She was really nice though and another fresh-faced willowy beauty. She struck me as quiet but lovely and was thick as thieves with Roxanne. I really liked Roxanne's partner Daniel, and found myself spending a lot of time talking to him.

For week three of the competition Stuart and I had put together a routine to 'Islands In The Stream' by Kenny Rogers and Dolly Parton. Beforehand Ray found me outside the back of the studio chain-smoking. I could hardly speak for nerves. That week I was fourth up and to my utter amazement we scored 17 out of 30 and I actually got a nice comment from Jason Gardiner! 'What you lack with technique you make up for with your performance,' he told me. 'I couldn't help but smile and enjoy what you were doing.' Blimey.

That week it was Jeremy who bit the dust after a skate-off with Ellery.

Despite getting through again and Jason's kind words, the following week I was still struggling with my nerves. The nightmares about skating were coming thick and fast. Over and over I'd feverishly dream about falling or skating out and the music starting only for me to look at Stuart and say, 'I don't know it'.

That week we'd chosen to skate to 'I'm in the Mood for Dancing' which I'd hoped would be a bit of a lucky charm but on the Saturday night Neil called. 'I don't want to panic you,' he said. 'But you need to know Anne has a story in the *People* tomorrow.'

I put the phone down trying not to cry. 'I can't deal with this tomorrow, not on top of everything else,' I told Ray.

The next morning I rose with a heavy heart to look at the

paper. 'Dancing on Ice's Coleen Nolan at war with older sister' the headline read. Inside Anne talked about my fall-out with her and Denise, and claimed that she wanted to heal the rift. But reading between the lines she still seemed to blame Ray for everything, which meant he was every bit as worked up as me when he saw it.

Walking into the studio that day I was really embarrassed. I'd never discussed the row with my sisters, but all the newspapers and magazines are laid out in the green room so all my fellow contestants would have seen it. They were all very good though and no one said anything. The saddest thing about the article was that it made the rift seem much more trivial than it was. It sounded really petty and stupid and like I was just being stubborn. *Everyone's going to think I'm such a bitch*, I thought. *They won't know it runs much deeper.* And the tragic thing was that if Anne and Denise could just swallow their pride and call me up to apologize we could all make up.

That night, a nervous wreck, I managed to score 16 out of 30 and Karen Barber said I had a new confidence, which was nice, even if I wasn't feeling it!

In the skate-off the judges chose to save Melinda and we all said a fond farewell to Michael Underwood who I felt very sorry for. He'd been in *Dancing on Ice* the previous year but was forced to leave after he broke his leg. Despite everything he came back and was so fired up – so for him to get voted out in week four was such a shame.

Although I felt euphoria at having survived, it also worried me that by now all the other celebs appeared to be loving it – yet I'd get out of bed every morning thinking *I don't want to go.* I knew I was nearer the end and it's an incredible feeling to know you are making your kids proud. But my feeling of being the underdog never really dispersed. It didn't help that every week I'd miss a whole day of training because of *Loose Women*. Every Monday I'd leave the hotel in Elstree at 6 a.m. to head to the ITV studios in Southbank to film the show. After the exhilaration and tension of the night before I was always completely knackered, practically nodding off in our morning meeting.

Bless Jane McDonald who was always beside herself with enthusiasm about my performance the night before. 'I'm so proud of you!' she constantly told me, jumping up to give me a hug. Then the others would bombard me with questions, but most weeks I was almost too tired to talk. A couple of times I actually fell asleep in make-up.

After a busy Monday filming two lots of *Loose Women*, there was usually no time for any training. So each week the panic would set in at 8.30 a.m. on Tuesday morning with the realization that I was already a day down. Everyone else would know the basics of their new routines yet I was just beginning.

That week Stuart and I were skating to 'Can't Fight The Moonlight' by LeAnn Rimes. It was really raising the bar and I had only four days to learn it. I just couldn't get the routine in my head. After training on the Tuesday I was doing some filming for an ITV documentary called *Eternal Youth* examining why people are so obsessed with trying to stay young. By the time I headed home to Cheshire late that night I'd worked myself into a frenzy. 'I can't do it,' I cried to Ray, when he met me off the train. 'I'm going to look like a fool.'

On Wednesday morning Stuart and I ploughed on with the routine at the rink in Manchester. But after three hours I just didn't feel like I was making any progress. We were supposed to be putting it to the music but I was still nowhere near that stage. 'I can't even think about the music yet,' I told Steve Pickavance, who was helping us to train.

By Thursday afternoon I still hadn't mastered it and as time ticked by I just felt more panicked. I knew I was being really negative but I couldn't help it. 'Give me a minute,' I told Stuart and Steve.

Skating away from them I could feel the tears coming. I hate crying in public but suddenly I couldn't stop myself and the sobs came out in a flood. I'd forgotten I had a mike on so everyone could hear. Thankfully Ray was there watching and was on hand to give me a cuddle. 'Come on, you can do it!' he told me.

'You'll get it!' Steve added.

'But I haven't got it,' I told them. 'I'll never get it!'

Then my phoned bleeped with a sweet text from Melinda asking me how I was getting on, so I blew my nose with a tissue and tried to pull myself together. But for the rest of the afternoon I was in a terrible state. I dried my eyes but then whenever anyone asked me how I was, it would set me off again.

'How's it gone today?' the camera crew would ask. 'You seem a bit upset.' Then that was it! I'd be off again and crying for the rest of the day.

That night as I left Ray and the kids and caught the train down to London I felt completely deflated. So I tried to get a good night's sleep and was up early the next morning to go through my routine with Chris and Jayne. 'Please don't talk to me,' I told Chris. 'I'm feeling rather unstable.' It was weird as I've never had a meltdown like that before.

'Try not to worry,' Jayne assured me kindly. 'You get to a halfway point and most people have a meltdown.'

'Maybe I could have a glass of wine on Sunday to settle my nerves?' I suggested. 'Just one glass would make me feel great! It relaxes me.'

But Chris and Jayne shook their heads firmly. Apparently drinking alcohol before you skate is an immediate sacking offence so that bright idea went out the window!

Towards the end of Friday I finally began to get to grips with the routine and I spent the weekend necking Rescue Remedy. I literally drank bottles of the stuff! Then typically on the Sunday I was absolutely fine. I actually felt like it was one of the best routines I'd done so far.

On the night I had a ridiculous ponytail hairpiece. Before-hand I amused everyone by tapping my foot like a horse and shaking my hair about. We scored 15.5.

Todd, an appalling skater who'd been cracking everyone up with his raring enthusiasm and comical mishaps on the ice, became the latest person to leave after appearing in the skate-off with Ellery.

After my meltdown I started rehearsals for week six actually feeling quite optimistic. The fact I was being kept in week after week, and people were voting for me, was giving me such a boost. I was beginning to believe in myself and was even get-ting annoyed about being compared to Todd or John Sergeant who'd been a terrible dancer on *Strictly*. 'I *can* skate!' I told Ray. 'And I'm really trying my best.'

Not that Ray was going to let me off that easily – at times it felt like I was actually living with Jason Gardiner. Ray never held back in telling me what he thought I was doing wrong. 'You're great,' he'd tell me. 'You've just got to bend those legs, get more speed and sometimes you look really scared.'

'Ray, I *am* scared,' I'd reply. 'I can't bend my knees because my knees are knackered and I can't get more speed because I might fall and I don't want to!'

He was right of course. He'd see me having such a laugh in training but once I got to the live show I'd go to pieces. But that's because it's the hardest thing I've ever done. Up until that point cycling by the Nile seemed like the biggest endurance challenge I'd ever been through. It had been many, many years since I'd stepped so far out of my comfort zone. But week after week it was Ray and the kids that got me through it. 'You're really good,' they'd constantly tell me. 'This is the proudest we've ever been!'

That Sunday I hoped to distract everyone from my lack of technique by hamming it up to 'Lady In Red' by Chris de Burgh. But when the routine was over I knew I'd been a lot slower than in rehearsals. I feared I was skating on thin ice. I held my breath as our final score – 14.5 – was read out and Nicky told me, 'I've seen you skate faster earlier in the com- petition so I hope you can get that back.'

In comparison Ray Quinn was just bloody brilliant skating to 'Nothing's Gonna Stop Us Now' by Starship. It earnt him sixes from all the judges, gaining full marks of 30.

That week I was in the bottom three and this time it was poor Ellery who lost out in the skate-off to Melinda. Although I felt thrilled to have survived, it's hard to celebrate when you've lost someone as lovely as Ellery.

I began week seven in a state of shock and awe that somehow I'd found myself in the last six. It was also mortifying to know that everyone else was technically better than me. I do think it is quite unfortunate that the year I did *Dancing on Ice* there were superstars like Ray and Jessica to contend with. With Ray in par- ticular there was nothing they gave him that he couldn't do. I'd even heard Chris saying, 'Christ I'm running out of things to challenge him!' But despite sickening me with his talent I was very fond of Ray. He's like my son really. He's the same age as

Shane Jnr and was always playing up spraying ice at me with his skates. 'Oi you,' I'd shout. 'Don't make me ground you!'

But if we'd all been as good as Ray Quinn the competition would have been very boring. I know in my heart I could not have tried harder. I really did do the best I could. And every week I'd have to pinch myself thinking, *Oh My God, I've just danced on ice!*

That Sunday I was skating to 'The Shoop Shoop Song' by Cher. To my utter horror I was on straight after Ray who was as good as ever, skipping around the ice making it look like child's play. Afterwards I told the judges, 'May I just say thank you for making me go after Ray Quinn!'

We scored 16.5, but that week the judges weren't holding back. Karen told me, 'Coleen you are so much fun until you put your skates on.' When it was Jason's turn to comment I gritted my teeth and waited for the onslaught.

'My dear Coleen, it was much better, especially the choreography,' he said to my utter shock. But it seemed he hadn't quite finished. 'At the beginning when you go into the cartwheel it was like a gingerbread man,' he added to a mixture of laughs and jeers. Ouch!

As usual as they gathered us up on the ice to reveal who was in the skate-off my legs turned to jelly. To my utter astonishment it was Jessica and Melinda and once again I'd made it through! As Melinda skated around to 'Let's Hear It For The Boy' by Deniece Williams I was filled with sadness. There was no way the judges would vote star skater Jessica off. I knew that night I'd be bidding Melinda goodbye. I was gutted. She was my closest friend on the show. When I saw her afterwards in the bar she came up to me and kissed both my boobs. 'You're just weird,' I told her.

★

Another week and another routine – this time to 'I Just Wanna Make Love To You' by Etta James. Our performance had to incorporate a prop and Stuart and I had decided to camp it up with feather boa. On reflection I looked a bit like Big Bird from *Sesame Street*. We scored 16.5 and I braced myself for an onslaught from the judges.

'Coleen that was particularly painful,' Jason simmered.

For once I didn't bite my tongue. 'It's not always about being the best,' I responded. 'It's about trying your best and I do that every week.'

I was sure it was time for me to bow out, but low and behold it was Roxanne who lost out to Zoe in the skate-off. I felt choked with emotion and disbelief that I'd survived. Maybe my words had struck a chord with the viewers? They knew I wasn't as good as the others but perhaps they were keeping me in because I was giving it all I'd got?

I started week nine with a new determination. 'If people are voting to keep me in then I can't let them down,' I told Stuart. 'We have to do something special this week.'

I'm not normally a competitive person but I have to say I started that week feeling fired up and actually a little bit angry! I love Chris, Jayne and Karen but as we met up on the Tuesday to talk about my routine I could sense their disbelief that I was still in the contest. That week the required element was an unassisted jump and it was almost like they were thinking, 'What on earth can we do with her? She's totally out of her depth.' 'Come on let's show them,' I whispered in Stuart's ear and we skated out to show them a move we'd been practising in secret – a terrifying spin where I was suspended from Stuart's neck by my ankles. Afterwards they all looked suitably impressed. Ha!

As the week went on I was doing really well with my

unassisted jumps. But ironically, after feeling the most fired up I'd ever been, suddenly disaster struck. Stuart and I were in the middle of rehearsing our routine on the Thursday night at the rink at Elstree when one of our moves went wrong. We were going through the whole routine when my foot slipped from under me. I could see I was going to land badly so put out my left arm in the hope of cushioning the blow but instead I landed heavily on my left hand. I knew I'd done something bad the moment I hit the ice – the pain was excruciating.

Stuart immediately helped me up and a member of the crew drove me to Barnet Hospital. I sat in A&E feeling thoroughly fed up. *I've been trying so hard to push myself for the viewers and to stop the judges from giving me a hard time*, I thought. *Why now?*

After a little while the nurse ushered me off for an X-ray. Then I sat in the doctor's office awaiting my fate. 'You may have a small fracture in your thumb,' he told me.

'Will I be able to skate on Sunday?' I asked, biting my lip.

'I don't know,' he told me. 'You need to be assessed again in 24 hours.'

I left the hospital with my arm in a sling feeling like the walking wounded. Suddenly I couldn't give a stuff whether skating would hurt me, instead the thought of pulling out of the show so close to the final was devastating. 'Ciara will just sob her little heart out,' I told Stuart. 'And I think I might too!'

I decided to spare Ciara's tears by not telling her anything until the producers had made up their mind. The next day I waited on tenterhooks as the show's physio, Sharon, gave me the once over. 'I think you may have fractured it,' she told me. 'But I'm prepared to strap it up so you can skate on Sunday.' Well, I nearly kissed her!

That Sunday I felt unstoppable. In a weird way I think getting injured spurred me on. Plus I was now just two weeks away from the final. 'I really want this now,' I told Stuart.

'Me too,' he smiled.

That week I was wearing a black diamante outfit that I felt really reflected my mood of meaning business. We pulled off a dramatic routine to 'Diamonds are Forever' by Shirley Bassey complete with our ankle spin. The crowd went wild and I was ecstatic to score 18.5, our highest score yet.

Jason even raved: 'Good girl Coleen, you came out and gave a performance I've been waiting for. I applaud you for doing the lifts you were doing tonight.'

I must have done something right as to my utter joy I escaped the skate-off for the eighth time. This time poor Zoe lost out to Jessica. 'Oh my God, Oh my God,' I screamed to Ray in the bar afterwards. 'We're in the semi-final! I just can't believe it!' I went to bed that night smiling from ear-to ear. *Maybe I can actually do this!* I thought to myself, hardly daring to dream.

The next day Stuart and I managed to fit in an extra practice session on the Monday night after *Loose Women*. If we made it through to the final we'd need to perform a flying routine where I'd be suspended by wires. I'd spent the evening strapped up to the harness flying about and practicing summersaults. It was quite strange, and scary, attempting to flip myself around in the air like a circus performer, but also really exhilarating. Suddenly I felt a twinge. 'I think I've hurt my back,' I told Jayne.

'Do you want to stop?' she asked.

'No, I'm sure it's fine,' I replied. 'I'll carry on for now.'

So I did five more summersaults and suddenly I felt a gripping spasm. The team quickly lowered me down but the minute they took the harness off the pain really kicked in. I couldn't straighten up and Sharon and Fred, the paramedic, had to help me to the treatment room. I was in excruciating pain. As they attempted to manoeuvre me on to the examination bed I screamed the room down and cried my eyes out. I was in there for two and a half hours as Sharon attempted to control the pain but the agony carried on.

'Coleen,' Sharon told me gently. 'I'm worried your rib might be broken so I'm going to have to get you to hospital.'

So they called an ambulance and I was strapped to a spinal board and taken to Barnet hospital. In A&E I was given a morphine injection in one thigh and an anti-sickness one in the other. Then they wheeled me off to X-ray.

Afterwards as I lay on my back in a side ward, high on gas and air and morphine, I found myself in the surreal situation of being asked for my autograph by a member of staff. I tried to look enthusiastic as she gushed on about loving *Loose Women* and how much she wanted me to win *Dancing on Ice*. Bless her.

To my relief the X-ray showed I hadn't actually broken anything, although it seemed I'd sprained my rib and lower back, so still high on painkillers I was allowed back to my hotel. Accompanying me was my own little Mother Theresa in the form of Jake. Apparently Stuart had called Ray (who was up in Cheshire) and Jake, who immediately came over to be my little carer – which was just as well as I couldn't even get my shoes on! He spent the next 48 hours with me, waiting on me hand and foot like a complete angel.

The following day Sharon gave me five and a half hours of intense physio in a desperate attempt to get me mobile again. 'Am I going to be able to skate?' I asked, anxiously.

'I don't know Coleen,' she replied. 'I think we've got about fifty per cent of your movement back today so we can only do our best.'

On Wednesday I awoke to more spasms but could feel a definite improvement. I had more physio with Sharon and she strapped my back up to protect it. 'What do you think?' I asked her, trying to keep the desperation out my voice.

'Well I'm prepared to let you have a go at training tomorrow,' she said slowly. 'But we'll really have to take it one step at a time and if it's too much you're going to have to stop.'

In some ways I can't believe that after hurting myself so badly I wanted to keep on skating. No one would have blamed me for walking away and Jake even asked me to give it up. 'I hate you being hurt, Mum,' he told me. 'I want you to stop.' And if it had happened three or four weeks previously I would have agreed in an instant. But not at the semi-finals. *I don't want to give up!* I thought. *I've done six months of skating to get to this point.*

The fact was I didn't want to bow out of the competition at a point where I couldn't even walk. I wanted to end it where it all began – facing my demons on the ice. On the Thursday, the day of my forty-fourth birthday, I went for more physio with Sharon then tentatively headed for the rink in the afternoon. As I stepped on to the ice and started to move slowly, I knew my face was contorted with pain no matter how hard I tried to hide it.

'Are you sure you want to do this?' Stuart asked me, looking worried.

'Yes,' I yelped, rubbing my back. 'It's just a spasm, it'll pass.' So for an hour I tried to stifle cries of pain as we quickly worked on a very simple routine for Sunday.

'Right, that's it,' Sharon instructed after our sixty minutes were up. 'Coleen needs to get back in physio now.' She wouldn't let me do any skating the following day either. 'If you want to skate on Sunday you have to give your back a break,' she told me firmly. It was frustrating not to be able to practice but I knew I wasn't in a position to argue. You don't mess with backs, do you?

When, on Friday evening, Ray arrived at the hotel with Ciara, I shuffled to greet them at the door, gingerly opening it. 'Are you serious?' Ray asked me, looking horrified. That night neither of us got a wink thanks to my constantly turning, slowly and carefully, to try and find a more comfortable position. I even got up in the night to be sick from the pain. 'This is ridiculous,' Ray told me as I crept back to bed. But still on Saturday morning I was determined to carry on. I dosed up on painkillers so Stuart and I could do a quick camera rehearsal for the next day's show and hoped for the best.

With my back still spasming on Sunday morning I crammed in yet more physio and Sharon strapped up my back for the live show. The required element that week was a twenty second solo performance. When my turn came I skated out alone to perform the first bit of the routine Stuart and I had thrown together in just one hour. As I began my solo spot, skating backwards and moving my arms gently, the opening chords of 'You're Still The One' by Shania Twain filled the studio. I glanced over to where Ray was sitting in the crowd to clock his reaction to the special song that I'd sung to him at our wedding. All week Ray had been saying to me in an increasingly irritated fashion, 'You're hurt, why are you so insistent that you want to do it?' But I kept replying, 'You'll find out on Sunday…' Now as he watched, his face streaming with tears, he instantly understood that I was dedicating my last performance to him.

The fact was I knew I wasn't going to make it into the final and I didn't want to. The three finalists would have to put together three routines each for the last show, two of which I couldn't even do – the flying one which could cause long term damage to my back and The Bolero which I just didn't have the skill for. *I'm happy to go out now, on a high*, I thought.

When Stuart and I had finished the rest of the routine I was pleasantly surprised to see we'd scored 16.5. Not bad for an hour's work. Next we watched as Jessica performed a stunning routine. Then it was the usual hour wait before the results show. For once I didn't feel nervous. *I'm going home tonight*, I thought. *And I can't wait!*

So, later, as the four of us lined up on the ice to await our fate, it was no surprise to hear that I was in the skate-off along-side Donal. Donal performed first and then it was Stuart and my turn. 'I'm so out of the competition – we shouldn't even waste time,' I joked to Phillip afterwards. 'Just bring on the flowers.'

Without a moment to lose Donal and I took our places in front of the five judges. As I'd predicted Karen, half crying, half laughing, was the first to vote me off, telling me earnestly, 'It is not going to be the same without you.' Next came Nicky's vote, then Jason's – rather gleefully I thought! Then Ruthie sounded the death knell saying, 'You have been funny, coura-geous and inspiring...' Robin finally sealed my fate. It was a landslide vote to save Donal. Relief just rushed through me. *I can't bear another week of hour-upon-hour physio*, I thought. *It's worked out just how I wanted it to.*

After the show I gave my flowers to Sharon to thank her for everything she'd done to make me better. Then I chatted to some of the crew. All the people off-camera get forgotten but they work so hard and are so supportive. 'I've done this show since it first started and I've never voted for anyone,' one crew member told me. 'But I voted 10 times for you tonight!' I was so touched. It was nice to hear I was walking away with people actually liking me. I know there are obviously some people out there who will detest me, but I don't want to think about them! I couldn't bear to be hated like Jason (although he loves it!).

It meant so much to me that week in, week out, people actually voted for me. And that night, lying in bed, my mind raced with a heady mix of memories and emotions from the last six months. I felt so euphoric that I only got three hours sleep!

Despite my lack of sleep, the next morning I jumped out of bed to head for the *Loose Women* studio full of the joys of spring. I felt on such a high! *I got to the semi-final!* I kept thinking. *That's incredible. What a great way to end it.*

Of course poor old Ray was mortified about being caught blubbing on telly. Ciara had cried too but arguably not as much as her dad! 'Don't worry,' I told him. 'Women will love you for it!'

At the final a week later it was an amazing feeling to be reunited with all the other contestants. I was particularly glad to see Melinda, who raced over to me grinning from ear-to-ear but thankfully not trying to kiss my boobs again.

About halfway through the live show we all skated on one by one in the order we'd been voted off. As I came out of the tunnel with Stuart – who I adore and now count as one of my best friends – I was delighted to hear a big cheer. Best of all, I felt completely relaxed, without a single leg wobble.

When Ray Quinn finally won with a breathtaking flying routine and a mind-blowing Bolero I was over-the-moon. He'd been brilliant from day one and absolutely deserved to lift the trophy. People make the mistake of thinking he's a bit smug because his skating looks effortless but he's not – he's just super-enthusiastic and loving every moment.

With my *Dancing on Ice* experience over I couldn't wait to

step very happily back into my comfort zone. 'I think I've challenged myself enough don't you?' I laughed to Ray as we snuggled up on the sofa with Ciara, a few nights after the final.

Doing *Dancing on Ice* really changed my whole attitude to life. It made me realize that no matter what anyone says you're never too old and it's never too late to try something new. I'm proud of myself and my kids and husband are too. I've practiced what I've preached – it's not about being the best, more importantly it's about trying your best.

You can't do more than that…

A Final Word

Writing this book has been one of strangest experiences of my life.

It's amazing how much you go through which you put so far in the back of your mind that you think you've forgotten about it all. Writing it down is like someone suddenly opening all the windows and doors in a softly lit room. Somehow the extra air and light release those stored up feelings that you've never fully acknowledged or realized were still there. Whilst at times it was painful to relive those moments and see how unhappy I was, there was genuine joy and laughter remembering many great experiences that I'd also lost by the wayside.

At times I was shocked at the person I was and the person I've become. It's a bit like looking at photographs of yourself during a really dodgy fashion decade (and I've seen a few) and thinking, *did I really believe I looked good in that*? Only when you look back can you see all the mistakes you made and the way you corrected them.

I've learned that I am a very loyal person and will do anything for those I love.

I've learned that despite my big personality I'm actually quite shy.

I've learned that as much as I would like to, I can never fully trust anyone one hundred per cent. But I won't give up trying to change that.

I've learned that I'll always have a weight problem but it's OK to have one biscuit with my cup of tea – just not the whole packet – and if I put all my weight back on again then it's nobody's fault but mine.

I've learned that excuses don't work.

I've learned to forgive those who hurt me because, as the old saying goes, life really is too short to hold grudges. Although I can now forgive I don't forget, but I'm happy with that balance.

I've learned that I am most content when I am with my husband and family and that I would always put them first.

But most of all I've learned that I'm finally happy being 'me'.

I want to thank you for reading my story. I hope you enjoyed it as much as I've enjoyed living it! So now it's time to close this chapter on my life and get out there and start living it again. Let's make every moment count and never give up on finding happiness within ourselves. It's something we all deserve, whoever we are.

Love Coleen x